The Ekven Settlement

Eskimo beginnings on the Asian shore of Bering Strait

Edited by

Yvon Csonka

BAR International Series 2624
2014

Published in 2016 by
BAR Publishing, Oxford

BAR International Series 2624

The Ekven Settlement

ISBN 978 1 4073 1259 0

BAR Publishing is the trading name of British Archaeological Reports (Oxford) Ltd.
British Archaeological Reports was first incorporated in 1974 to publish the BAR
Series, International and British. In 1992 Hadrian Books Ltd became part of the BAR
group. This volume was originally published by Archaeopress in conjunction with
British Archaeological Reports (Oxford) Ltd / Hadrian Books Ltd, the Series principal
publisher, in 2014. This present volume is published by BAR Publishing, 2016.

Printed in England

BAR
PUBLISHING

BAR titles are available from:

BAR Publishing
122 Banbury Rd, Oxford, OX2 7BP, UK
EMAIL   info@barpublishing.com
PHONE   +44 (0)1865 310431
FAX   +44 (0)1865 316916
www.barpublishing.com

TABLE OF CONTENTS

PREFACE

I

Whoever knows the book version of Yvon Csonka's dissertation "Les Ahiarmiut : à l'écart des Inuit Caribous" can foresee what is to be expected from this new work: a publication which combines high scientific standards with easy readability. This is true also from the other contributions in this volume, by Bernard Moulin, Owen K. Mason, and Agnès Gelbert.

This report presents the results of the Swiss-sponsored contributions to an international research project at Ekven, a prehistoric settlement situated on the Siberian coast of the Bering Strait (Chukchi Peninsula, Russian Federation), in 1995-98. After Reto Blumer reported on the preliminary results of the first two seasons, the purpose here is to present an overview of the excavations conducted in the ensuing two years. An overall evaluation of the entire international research project at Ekven will only be possible once the Russian, German and Danish researchers involved will have presented their own results. The fact that this international archaeological collaboration was possible can be traced to the fall of the Berlin wall in 1989, and the end of the Soviet regime two years later.

In this richly illustrated volume, Csonka begins by presenting the state of knowledge about Western Arctic Eskimo prehistory and about Ekven in particular, discussing the cultural terminology and chronology, and exposing the goals of the project. The author then describes the location and topography of Ekven, the vegetation, fauna, climate, and recent settlement history by Yupik (called Eskimosi in Russian) and Chukchi. Bernard Moulin presents a detailed description and analysis of the cut through the settlement created by marine erosion, erosion which grinds away at the site and will make it eventually disappear. In his contribution, Owen K. Mason compares paleoclimatic data from the Ekven area with those just across the Bering Strait in Alaska. Agnès Gelbert's contribution analyses the pottery recovered during the excavation and preparation of the erosion cut for documentation.

The entire publication is an important contribution regarding the infiltration, in the still poorly known prehistoric past, of the ancestors of present-day Yupik in the peninsula settled by, and named after, Chukchi people. This process had great significance for the Eskimo migrations from the Arctic regions of the Old, to those of the New World.

Prof. emer. Dr. Dr. h.c. Hans-Georg Bandi, Bern

II

After a long hiatus, Yvon Csonka and his colleagues present the results of their 1997-1998 excavation of the prehistoric settlement, Ekven. Unfortunately, such discontinuities between the collection and the presentation of data are common, due to the lack of institutional and financial support for large-scale excavations. This is especially true for archaeological research carried out by non-governmental organisations, but has become an increasing problem for the entire discipline. Under these circumstances, it is even more notable that the author pursued this work, in parallel with other research and despite the absence of direct funding. The present publication is the first monograph detailing the international expedition directed by K. A. Dneprovsky and M. M. Bronshtein under the auspices of the State Museum of Oriental Arts in Moscow (SMOA), formerly directed by A. M. Leskov.

The main goal of the fieldwork was to explore the coastal settlement area associated with the burial ground at Ekven. After its discovery in 1961, the latter has been the subject of archaeological investigation for several decades.

In the years after 1993, various exhibitions of the finds were held in Germany, Russia and Denmark by SMOA, in collaboration with the University of Tübingen and the Department of Culture, Tübingen.

The first stage of the project was funded by SMOA, various Canadian, Danish and German research bodies, as well as INTAS (International Association for the promotion of cooperation with scientists from the independent states of the former Soviet Union). In addition to SMOA, financial support for the second campaign derived from the German Research Foundation (DFG), the Swiss National Science Foundation and the Swiss-Liechtenstein Foundation for Archaeological Research Abroad.

In his introduction, Yvon Csonka modestly discusses the considerable problems he encountered during his work in the Far East of Russia (the Chukotka Peninsula is even more remote than Siberia!). After the collapse of the Soviet Union and the decline of its centralised power, a political and administrative vacuum prevailed, that was only very slowly compensated for by local developments. Fortunately, the collaboration initiated by A. Leskov between the State Museum of Oriental Arts and the Museum of Chukotka in Anadyr (which became our base camp) allowed the fieldwork to continue. Additionally, the regional administration of Lavrentiya (the final stop for air traffic) and the local museum contributed to the successful completion of our expedition.

Thanks to the contacts of M. M. Bronshtein we were supported by the ferryman of Pinakul – a village situated just across the bay from Lavrentiya – and his son, who gave us several rides with their small 'dora', and its indestructible diesel engine (once we even made a trip to Uelen). Finally, we owe a lot to the walrus hunters in Uelen, who transported our equipment with their vezdekhod (tracked all-terrain vehicle) and allowed us to relax in their banya (Russian-style sauna).

Due to the increasing risks for the team members, it was not possible to complete the work at Ekven in 1999. Nevertheless, the data collected form an important starting point for future research. Amongst other things, it is necessary to extend the excavation within the domestic zone of the site. This is, however, only possible if the financial means for the subsequent evaluation can be secured...

Prof. emer. Dr. Hansjürgen Müller-Beck, Tübingen

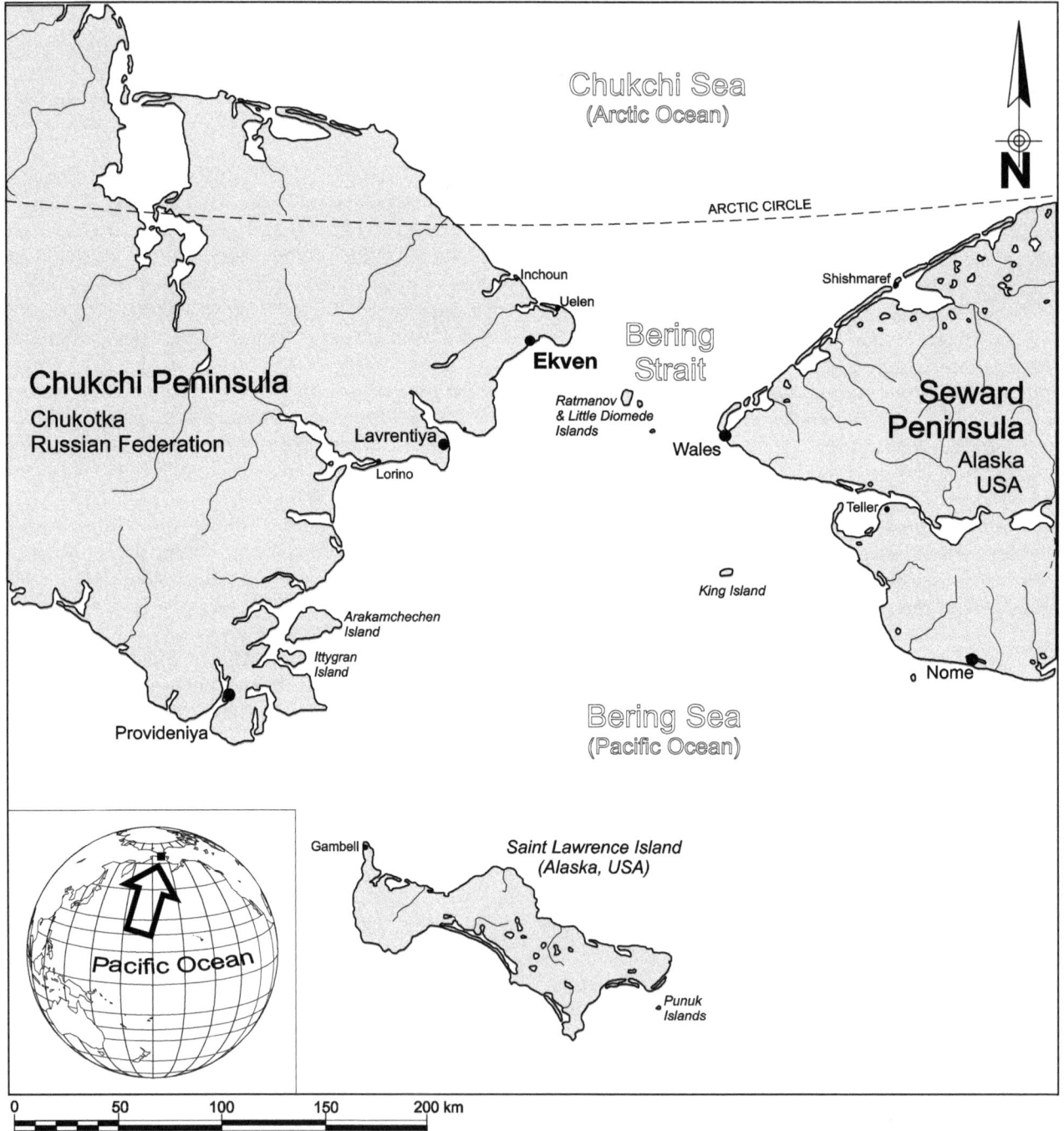

Figure 1. Map of the Bering Strait region. Illustration by Reto Blumer.

1.
INTRODUCTION

YVON CSONKA

1.1
PURPOSE OF THE PRESENT PUBLICATION

This publication presents some of the results of archaeological fieldwork carried out in 1997 and 1998 as a subproject within the Ekven Settlement International Archaeological Project. It is not a final report on the Ekven settlement excavations conducted by an international team between 1995 and 1998 (see Fig. 1). Synthesis of the results of these excavations will only be possible after the full publication of the results of the other subproject, consisting in the detailed excavation of a single house mound (code-named EH-18), by crews from Denmark, Switzerland (Blumer 1996, 1997a), but predominantly from Germany and Russia; after 1998, our Russian colleagues continued the excavation of EH-18 for another two seasons. Likewise, a thorough comparison with the adjoining Ekven cemetery, which was one of the outcomes we had foreseen at the beginning of the project, will have to await the full publication of the results of the excavations conducted there by the team from the State Museum of Oriental Arts in Moscow between 1987 and 1995 (partially presented in Leskov and Müller-Beck 1993); for earlier Ekven cemetery publications, see Arutiunov and Sergeev 1975 and 1983).

1.2
THE PROJECT, ITS BACKGROUND AND ITS CONTEXT

The Ekven Settlement International Archaeological Project reported upon here is truly an outcome of the opening of the former Soviet Union – confirmed by the subsequent Russian Federation –, to international collaboration and to visits by foreigners in formerly "closed" parts of the country. The first breach in the "Ice Curtain" which since 1948 had sealed the USSR-USA border between Chukotka and Alaska occurred in 1988 (Krauss 1994). In 1991, I was invited to participate in an international and interdisciplinary expedition to Kamchatka, the Commander Islands, and Chukotka (Chichlo, ed. 1993). Several archaeological sites were visited during the season. Archaeologist Patrick Plumet spent a few days at Ekven, a site situated a few kilometers southwest of East Cape (Cape Dezhnev), where a Russian team from the State Museum of Oriental Arts (Moscow; thereafter abbreviated SMOA) was excavating a prehistoric cemetery (Plumet 1993). That summer, Plumet and I visited the sites of Avan and Kivak near Provideniya, and I was able to spend two weeks in Enmelen, where important unexcavated sites are situated.

In the summer of 1992, I was back in Russia to investigate the possibilities of archaeological collaboration in Chukotka[1]. In Moscow, I had positive responses from Professor Sergei Arutiunov, as well as from Dr. Mikhail Bronshtein, head of the Siberian division of the SMOA. In Anadyr, capital of the Chukotka Autonomous Region, and in the Provideniya district, neither the representatives of the regional and local authorities, nor those of the Native organizations, voiced any objection to the project of archaeological fieldwork on their territory, which I presented.

Chukotka was then in the first stages of the process of emancipation from the central authority of Moscow, via that of Magadan[2]. It was unclear where this course would lead to. The implication for archaeology was that the representatives of several institutions in Chukotka attempted to regulate the licensing of fieldwork. In Moscow, of course, the prevailing point of view was that the licensing remained the sole prerogative of the Institute of Archaeology of the Russian Academy of Sciences. This ambiguity was not the only problem to reckon with. The country was by then in dire economic straits. Transportation within Chukotka was already

---

[1] With seed funding provided by the Swiss-Liechtenstein Foundation for Archaeological Research Abroad (SLSA). Professor Hans-Georg Bandi, who had conducted important excavations in the Asian Eskimo zone on St. Lawrence Island (belonging to Alaska), founding member and then Secretary General of the SLSA, was of course supporting this project which represents an extension of his own interests in Beringian archaeology.

[2] In 1992, the Chukotka Region (okrug) managed to severe its ties to the Magadan Province (oblast) and became a direct subject of the Russian Federation.

severely reduced. Any party operating in the region would need the support of local air transport officials and state farm administrations, in addition to the blessing of the regional and local authorities.

In subsequent years, the course of the project went along the recommendations I had made following this exploratory trip: desirability of associating with Russian archaeologists, while keeping sufficient autonomy in the setting of scientific goals and ways to reach them, in the direct relationships we would have with the local authorities and population, and promotion of deontological codes for the conduct of archaeological research, which were becoming common in the North American and Greenlandic Arctic (Csonka 1993, 1998b).[3]

In the meantime, Professor Hansjürgen Müller-Beck had also made contact with the SMOA in Moscow, and was organizing the exhibition in German museums of the finds collected at the Ekven cemetery by the Museum crew (Leskov and Müller-Beck 1993). At the end of 1992, a "Committee for Archaeology in Chukokta" was created at the issue of a meeting convened by Prof. Plumet in Meudon, near Paris[4]. There was no fieldwork in Ekven in 1992. In September of 1993, I met the leaders of the SMAO team, Kirill Dneprovskyi and Mikhail Bronshtein, in Anadyr: their excavations in the Ekven cemetery had been stopped by the authorities of Chukotka. They had been arrested when they reached Anadyr, and had been assigned to residence while charges of plundering the regional heritage were being investigated.

After several months of negociations, the Chukotka Regional Department of Culture and the Museum of Chukotka signed a five-year agreement with the State Museum of Oriental Arts in Moscow, with the explicit approval of the Minister of Culture of the Russian Federation, and of the Governor of Chukotka. We can only guess what influence the letters of support from our Committee for archaeology in Chukotka had on that process. What the Chukotka stakeholders were asking for, and had inscribed in the agreement as condition for their approval of further excavations, was local participation in archaeological training and research, participation in and sharing of the financial profit of exhibits of Chukotka artifacts outside Russia, information about the research by archaeologists to the public in Chukotka, and the return of half of the archaeological collections to Anadyr. Their grievances were later bitterly expressed in an article which appeared in the Chukotka newspaper (Zheleznov, Otke and Riga 1996). Notwithstanding the resentful tone of this article, the grievances must be understood in the context of a colonial relationship where over the years too little attention had been paid to local interests and feelings.

Chukotka Native representatives[5] participating in the 1994 session of the United Nations Working Group on Indigenous Peoples in Geneva protested to the German government against the display of Siberian Native grave finds (those from Ekven) in German Museums. They were requesting the discontinuation of German support to the excavations, the return of the grave goods, and some financial compensation to the local Native organizations. Thus, the rapid evolution of the relations between Natives and archaeologists in Chukotka was the outcome not only of the changes which were taking place in post-Soviet Russia, but also of a growing awareness of current Native issues, especially those in nearby Alaska. One of them, of course, was the implementation in the USA, since 1990, of the Native Grave Protection and Repatriation Act (NAGPRA). Under such circumstances, and especially in light of the legal exploitation of archaeological resources on St. Lawrence Island – which belongs to Alaska but lies closer to Chukotka –, supported by a strong legal commercial market (Hollowell 2004), it is remarkable that Natives in Chukotka, who are suffering dire economic hardship, have not yet massively resorted to "pot hunting". Such a market is not legal under Russian law, but it is not inexistent, and the temptations are strong.

The first field season of the Ekven International Archaeological Project took place in 1995. An INTAS[6] subsidy allowed the participation, beside that of a small crew from the Museum of Oriental Arts led by Kirill Dneprovskyi, of two representatives of the Department of Culture and of the Museum of Chukotka in Anadyr, one of them Native, and of two natural scientists from the Group for Historical Ecology of the Severtsov Institute for Ecology and Evolution in Moscow. The Canadian team was composed of Robert McGhee, curator at the Canadian Museum of Civilizations, and Nicole Bondreau. Participants from the National Museum of Denmark in Copenhagen were Hans-Christian Gulløv and Hans-Christian Kapel (Gulløv 1996, 2005). Hansjürgen Müller-Beck, from the University of Tübingen, was accompanied by his student Leif Steguweit (more details see Blumer 1996). Reto Blumer, then graduate student at the University of Geneva, participated with the support of the SLSA.

In conformity with their objectives, the non-Russian participants concentrated their investigations exclusively on the settlement of Ekven, while the Russians continued their cemetery excavations. Shortly after the end of the 1995 field season, the local population finally managed to have their longstanding unease about grave disturbance turned into an official decision prohibiting further cemetery excavations. The Russian crew thereafter participated in the settlement

---

[3] Not to mention all the deontological codes for the conduct of social sciences research in the Arctic, and of archaeological research in general, which we were aware of and agreed with, we strived specifically to uphold the "Principles for Partnership in Cross-Cultural Human Sciences Research with a Particular View to Archaeology" elaborated at the initiative of the SLSA (SLSA 1997).

[4] The initiators, Hans-Georg Bandi, Yvon Csonka, Hansjürgen Müller-Beck, and Patrick Plumet, were soon joined, at their invitation, by Jørgen Meldgaard, Robert McGhee, and Jean-Loup Rousselot.

[5] One of them, in fact, grew up in a Chukchi village as son of the (Russian) director of the local State farm. Still young, he emigrated to the United States, whence he later returned to Moscow where he coordinated a Native Rights NGO.

[6] International Association for the Promotion of Co-operation with Scientists from the Independent States of the Former Soviet Union, established by the European Commission in 1993. The principal investigator was Müller-Beck, with the backing of the Committee for Archaeology in Chukotka.

Photo 1. The camp for the excavation of Ekven was situated 2 km away at Cape Verbliuzhi (Camel Point or Sphinx Point). It consisted of a "balog" (prefabricated wooden house), a former coast guard shelter which served as mess and lab, and tents. Big Diomede (Ratmanova) Island is clearly visible in the background. Photograph by Yvon Csonka.

Photo 2. Breakfast and discussion at the camp. From left to right Reto Blumer, Marina Makarova, Oliver Rück, Galina Diachkova, Hansjürgen Müller-Beck, Kirill Dneprovsky, Konstantin Dneprovsky, Mikhail Bronshtein. Photograph by Yvon Csonka.

excavations. During the subsequent three field seasons, in 1996, 1997 and 1998, fieldwork was conducted by a stable core group from Switzerland, France, Germany, the State Museum of Oriental Arts in Moscow, and the Chukotka region.

Financial contributions from the Swiss National Science Foundation, in 1997 and 1998, replaced INTAS in its support to Russian participation and, in conjunction with continued SLSA subsidies, allowed a small crew from Switzerland and France to take part in the excavations, while supporting the participation of several Russian members of the crew as well. Fieldwork was conducted under the umbrella authorization delivered nominally to the head of the Russian crew, Kirill Dneprovskyi, by the Archaeological Institute of the Russian Academy of Sciences. The names of the participants and the schedules of the field seasons can be found in the annual progress reports (Blumer 1996, 1997a; Blumer and Csonka 1998; Csonka, Blumer and Moulin 1999).

Meanwhile, in Chukotka, both trends evoked above, that of the emancipation of regional and local authorities from the central State, and that of a severe deterioration of the socio-economic situation, continued throughout the decade. Although, as agreed, our Russian colleagues had written well in advance to request from the Chukotskii District Council of Elders the authorization to conduct fieldwork, it was not until our arrival in Anadyr in June 1997, that we were notified of a "moratorium on all scientific and touristic activities" issued by the said Council. The district authorities would not grant permission against the wishes of the leaders of the Council. After having thus missed the weekly flight, we took the risk to fly to Lavrentiya with all participants and gear, to try to negotiate an agreement. How representative was the council of local Natives, we wondered, as only two persons met with us in presence of the chief of the District administration, and expelled another elder who had wished to attend the talks. The problem which had occurred between Anadyr and Moscow in 1993 now repeated itself in another center-periphery context, that between Lavrentiya and Anadyr. Apparently, the Anadyr Museum was not making good on its promise to redistribute to Lavrentiya some of the artifacts from Ekven it was getting back from Moscow. Now Lavrentiya was trying to obtain artifacts directly from the archaeologists, and did receive such a promise from the head of the Russian team. We were thereafter authorized to proceed to Ekven.[7]

Logistics had by then deteriorated to the point that one could not count on any kind of scheduled transport, aerial or otherwise, beyond the district centers. All our travelling between Lavrentiya and Ekven, and between Ekven and Uelen,

took place by hunters' boats and by tracked land vehicles – sometimes simply on foot. Combined with administrative hurdles, the time spent in transit to and from fieldwork location averaged more than three weeks each season. It must be mentioned here that our difficulties were only a sample of the hardship experienced by the population of Chukotka, particularly in the peripheral villages inhabited by a majority of Natives (Csonka 1998a; 2006; 2007). As a telling example among many indicators of hard times, the domesticated reindeer population of Chukotka, which together with sea mammal hunting in coastal villages, is the mainstay of the Native economy, has decreased from about 500'000 at the end of the 1980s, to no more than about 100'000 at the end of the 1990s (Vladimir Ettylen, 1999: written communication; Gray 2000).

We had scheduled an additional field season in 1999. However, after four seasons, foreign participants had to admit that the conditions under which fieldwork was conducted were not improving, and the lack of control over basic issues such as personal safety in an isolated spot of the tundra (no weapons, no radio transmitter, no vehicle, no provision in case of emergency), led us to give up on the opportunity. In July 1999, the present author spent a few weeks excavating in Wales, just across Bering Strait from Ekven, at the kind invitation of Roger Harritt from the University of Anchorage, head of this important project (Csonka 2000).

I have been hesitant whether to go into more or less details of the socio-economic and political contexts which surrounded the Ekven international project. On the one hand, anecdotal difficulties are part and parcel of every research of this kind, and their narration does not add anything to the archaeological results proper. On the other hand, they contribute to explain the extra-scientific constraints on aspects of the research design. The Ekven International project was also a special enterprise in different contexts: the evolution of the relations between Anadyr and Moscow as well as that of the center-periphery relations within Chukotka itself, the evolution of the relations between Natives and non-Natives within Russia, the evolution of relations between Natives and archaeologists, and the development of collaboration between foreign and Russian scientists in the field, among others. I have thus strived to strike a balance between these antagonistic rationales to either not mention the story surrounding the project, or to treat it as a subject worthwhile of a thorough presentation and comment, especially in light of the partial treatment by Holzlehner (1999). The reader will bear in mind that I have been an actor, and a self-consciously active actor at that, in the story I have summed up above.

---

[7] Notwithstanding this fixation on artifacts, one should not construe it into a leading strand, as Holzlehner (1999) has done in order to enhance intended literary effect. In fact, it is mostly the social relationship between archaeologists, symbolizing the power imposed from outside – but a conveniently weak power in this case – and the local population, that was at stake. Here as elsewhere, archaeology may represent a convenient scapegoat, which allows the venting of frustrations while the exploitation of natural resources goes on unchallenged (Plumet 1993: 305; 1999: 117).

1.3
ACKNOWLEDGMENTS

The project reported upon in this volume was funded by the Swiss National Science Foundation, and by the Swiss-Liechtenstein Foundation for Archaeological Research Abroad (SLSA), whose support is gratefully acknowledged. Many of the persons and institutions who contributed to making this project possible are mentioned earlier in this chapter; to each and all of them, I express my heartfelt gratitude. Hans-Georg Bandi, mentor and friend, indefectibly accompanied and facilitated our research from the very beginning. Hansjürgen Müller-Beck kept the international collaboration centering on Ekven going, during the years when life circumstances prevented others from outside Russia from joining in, and inspired us all in the field. Our colleagues Mikhail Bronshtein and Kirill Dneprovsky made us welcome in Moscow as well as at the site of Ekven in Chukotka, with which they were already very familiar, having spent several field seasons there previously. May Mikhail Bronshtein and his family be deeply thanked for having accommodated us colleagues from abroad so many times in their home in Moscow.

Reto Blumer, Bernard Moulin and I collected most of the data reported upon in this publication. I am grateful to them for their highly competent collaboration and for their inspiring companionship. My thanks extend to all our other comrades in the field, coming from Moscow, from Anadyr, from other parts of Chukotka, and from Germany. Special thanks go to Arkady Savinetsky, of the Severtsov Institute of Ecology and Evolution in Moscow, from whose expertise we all greatly benefited.

We received great support from the local population and authorities in Chukotka. The Museum of Autonomous Region of Chukotka provided staff and authorizations and the Museum of Lavrentiya offred accommodation in its premises. Vladimir Eineucheivun and his family accommodated us in their hunting camp at Pinakul, provided us with country food, and arranged water transport of personnel and gear to and from the field site. For local transport, we could count on the services of Yuri Klimakov and his sons, driving their carefully maintained, yet aging vesdekhod (tracked all-terrain vehicle). I thank the population of the village of Uelen, and of nearby reindeer herder camps, who are the true keepers of the land of their ancestors, including those from the prehistoric settlement of Ekven, for their help, which took too many forms to be mentioned here.

In Moscow, we received support from the State Museum of Oriental Arts (SMOA), where the greatest part of the material we collected at Ekven is kept. Agnès Gelbert, author of the last chapter of this volume, studied the pottery we collected at Ekven, with a grant from the SLSA, in the premises of the SMOA. The line drawings of artifacts published in this volume were all realized at the SMOA by Nina Survillo. In the early 2000s, Owen Mason graciously accepted to write a chapter of paleoclimatic comparisons between nearby Alaska and the Ekven area for this volume; due to delays in producing it, it first appeared in another collection, just as Agnès Gelbert's did. Our thanks go to Don Dumond for having authorized the reprinting of these two papers.

I am also pleased to acknowledge the professional counsel and constant friendly encouragements from Professor Sergei Arutiunov, and from my colleagues and friends, the late Patrick Plumet, and Igor Krupnik. Michel Egloff graciously accepted me as research associate at the Prehistory Institute of the University of Neuchâtel, which he was then directing, thus providing institutional anchoring to the project. In more recent years, Denis Ramseyer diligently fulfilled the task of facilitating the final stages of preparation of this manuscript, on behalf of the SLSA. Finally, I also wish to thank Bastien Ramseyer for the very professional and pleasing layout of this volume.

2.
STATE OF KNOWLEDGE, RESEARCH QUESTIONS, AND GOALS

YVON CSONKA

2.1
A PRELIMINARY NOTE ABOUT CULTURAL TERMINOLOGY AND CHRONOLOGY

All the archaeological data collected in Ekven are situated within the context of the Neoeskimo period. This period extends from approximately the beginning of the Christian era, or perhaps a few centuries earlier, until late prehistoric times. I use the term Neoeskimo in the sense defined by Bronshtein and Plumet (1995: 41-42), which follows a tradition established by European researchers. It is widely recognized in the prehistory of Arctic Canada and of Greenland, and it is also accepted in the prehistory of the Bering Strait area (e.g. Ackerman 1988: 52). Some American archaeologists working in Alaska have criticized the notion of Neoeskimo (e.g. Collins 1960), and have preferred, to designate the same entity, various names such as "Northern Maritime Tradition" (Collins 1964), "Thule Tradition" (Dumond 1984: 77; 1987: 101-139; 2000a: 16-17), and "Arctic Whale Hunting Culture" (Larsen and Rainey 1948: 39).

Having spent some effort refuting the "suffix-eskimo" interpretations of Arctic prehistory by Kaj Birket-Smith (Csonka 1986, 1995), I am well aware of their shortcomings. I use the term Neoeskimo in a well-defined sense which overlaps neatly with the other current designations mentioned above (see Giddings and Anderson 1986: 107). "The best known and most sharply defined Arctic tradition is the Okvik-Old Bering Sea-Birnirk-Punuk-Thule-Inugsuk sequence, a cultural continuum which originated in Northeast Asia" wrote Collins (1960: 135). The names of these subdivisions of the Neoeskimo sequence, except the last one which applies only to Greenland, are the ones which will appear time and again in this report. As seen from an American perspective, the onset of this tradition "is marked by the even stronger shift toward maritime subsistence [compared to the Norton tradition] and a concurrent, near-revolutionary change toward an almost exclusive reliance on polished slate for stone implements" (Dumond 2000a: 16).

Okvik, Old Bering Sea (OBS), and Punuk, are closely associated with the Asian side of Bering Strait. In order to facilitate comparison with material from Okvik and the three OBS stages collected in other sites near East Cape, readers may wish to use the stylistic definitions elaborated by Arutiunov and by Bronshtein (Arutiunov and Bronshtein 1985; Bronshtein and Plumet 1995), rather than those of Collins; correspondences between the two are commented by Dumond (2002a). Birnirk was first recognized at the eponymous site near Point Barrow, on the northern shore of Alaska, but it is also present on the Chukchi Peninsula. According to a widely shared view, its roots lie mostly in the Old Bering Sea Culture, with perhaps some Ipiutak admixture in northwest Alaska (Mason 1998: 288, quoting the appropriate sources)[1]. As to Thule, it is its "Western" variety first defined by Larsen and Rainey (1948: 39) that may apply in extreme northeastern Asia. I do not intend to distract the reader from the main objective of this publication, which is to report the results of empirical research and not to contribute to the refinement of terminology: if I refer to the Neoeskimo as a tradition, and its above mentioned subdivisions as cultures, it is for the sake of convenience, without intention to condone whatever connotations these terms may carry.

As to Russian archaeologists, they have also immediately recognized the relationship of the archaeological remains they were finding on the Asian shore of Bering Strait with the North American "Eskimo" (in an archaeological sense). However, viewing the Chukchi Peninsula as an appendage of the huge expanses of their country, they have also classified them within the regional taxonomy, naturally keyed to that of Old World prehistory, as "remnant Neolithic" (e.g. Dikov 1977: 157), or "hunting Neolithic" (Bronshtein et al., 2000;

---

[1] An alternative view is presented by Arutiunov and Fitzhugh: "Birnirk culture developed on the shores of the Chukchi sea. [...] Birnirk culture seems to have developed with influence from Okvik and Ipiutak but with few ties to Old Bering Sea." (1988: 128); earlier, Arutiunov and Sergeev had claimed the opposite (1990 [1975]: 63, repeated in Arutiunov 1979: 28).

2007). Dikov (1977) has introduced a distinction between "Ancient Bering Sea Dwellers" (OBS, Okvik, Punuk, as he was meaning the Asian side of the Bering Sea), and "Ancient Eskimo" (Birnirk and Thule), on the basis of a perceived geographical difference in origin and orientation, the second being more American than Asian.

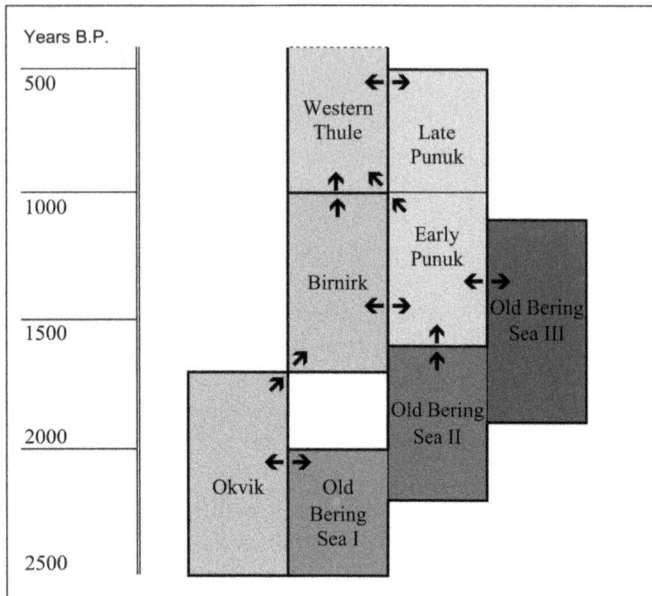

Figure 2. Chronological framework of the Neoeskimo cultures present on the Asian coast of Bering Strait (redrawn after Bronsthein 1993: 80, Tab. 1: C). Mostly based on uncalibrated radiocarbon dates. After Blumer 1997b: 55, Figure 6.

2.2
PREVIOUS RESEARCH IN EKVEN AND IN THE REST OF THE ASIAN ESKIMO ZONE[2]

The early manifestations of Neoeskimo cultures were first identified and studied on islands belonging to the United States but lying close to the Asian continent: on Little Diomede (Jenness 1928), but especially on St. Lawrence Island and on the neighboring Punuk Islets (Collins 1937, Geist and Rainey 1936, Rainey 1941). They were baptized Okvik, Old Bering Sea (subdivided in three phases), and Punuk, and thought to follow each other in that order. On the Soviet side, research started in 1945 with the surveys of Rudenko on the eastern and southern coasts of the Chukchi Peninsula, between Uelen and Enmelen (Rudenko 1961). On the northern coast of the

Peninsula, houses containing artifacts attributed to Birnirk and Thule, but a few also to Old Bering Sea, were excavated in 1946 at Cape Baranov, near the mouth of the Kolyma and more than a thousand kilometers from Bering Strait (Okladnikov and Beregovaya 1971). Other finds attributed to the same cultures were reported even further west on the Four Columns Island in the Bear Islands off the mouth of the Kolyma (Beregovaya 1954, Raushenbakh 1969).

The prehistoric cemetery of Uelen was excavated between 1957 and 1960 by Levin, Sergeev and Arutiunov (Arutiunov and Sergeev 1969). Dikov also conducted limited excavations there between 1956 and 1963 (Dikov 1967). In 1961, Arutiunov and Sergeev moved to the newly discovered cemetery at Ekven (Ivanov 1967), about 25 km southwest of Uelen, and in seven seasons, until 1974, excavated 210 graves (Arutiunov and Sergeev 1975, 1983). Debets (1975) and Levin (1963: chapter 4) published the prehistoric anthropological material. Alekseev conducted physical anthropological research also among the modern inhabitants of the Chukchi Peninsula (e.g. Alekseev 1972, 1979; Alekseeva et al. 1983). Not far to the south of Ekven, in 1963-65, other excavations took place at the cemetery of Chini, which was attributed to OBS (Dikov 1974). Dikov and his collaborators later surveyed, discovered and tested many other sites in different parts of the Chukchi Peninsula, on Wrangell Island, and in Kamchatka (e.g. Dikov 1977, 1979, 1997; Tein 1990). The islands Ittygran and Arakamchechen, including the so-called Whale Alley, were surveyed in 1976-79 (Arutiunov, Krupnik and Chlenov 1982); in 1981, the survey was extended north to Mechigmen Bay (Krupnik 1984). On St. Lawrence Island, within the Asian Eskimo zone but on the American side of the border, cemeteries of comparable age and cultural affiliation were also discovered and excavated at the beginning of the 1970s (Bandi 1993; Bandi ed. 1984; Hoffmann-Wyss 1987; Staley, 1994).

Excavations of the Ekven cemetery were resumed in 1987 by a team from the State Museum of Oriental Arts in Moscow, led by Mikhail Bronshtein and Kirill Dneprovskyi. The material collected until 1991 has been partially published in exhibition catalogues (Bronshtein and Dneprovsky 2008; Fitzhugh et al. 2009; Leskov and Müller-Beck 1993). In 1995, grave disturbance was banned by the local authorities at the request of Native organizations; the project was thus halted (Bronshtein and Plumet 1995: 43-4; Csonka 1998b: 68-9; 2006). By that time, 120 graves had been excavated (see Photo 3) – in addition to the 210 graves from the previous expedition, see above –, and it was estimated that at least as many as the total figure (330 excavated graves) remained untouched.

---

[2] This subject has already been thoroughly treated in a number of publications (e.g. Ackerman 1984; Alexeeva et al. 1983; Arutiunov 1993; Arutiunov and Sergeev 1975: chap. 1; Bronshtein and Plumet 1995; Krupnik 1998).

Photo 3. Part of the Ekven cemetery hill which has been excavated. In the background, the Ekven settlement and Bering Sea. Photograph by Yvon Csonka.

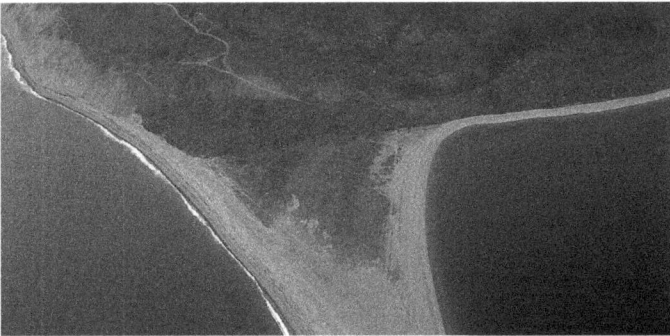

Photos 4. Aerial view of Avan, near Provideniya. The site, which was abandoned in the middle of the twentieth century, is situated at the western end of a spit of pebbles and sand, which separates a lake (bottom right) from the sea (left). There are lookouts on the nearby hills (top left). Photograph by Yvon Csonka, summer 1991.

Photo 5. The site of Puuten (see Figure 3) is characterized by a string of mounds which probably correspond to the ruins of houses from the Punuk period, located on the picture between the pond (still frozen, lower left) and the bay. Photo Yvon Csonka, juin 2008.

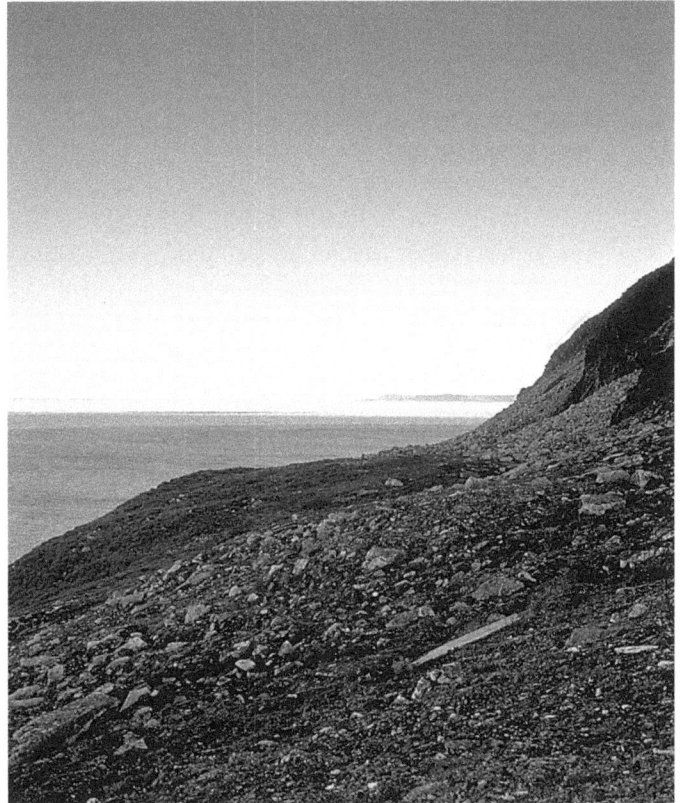

Photo 6. Near the foot of Mount Tunitlen are the ruins of a settlement situated on a ledge about 30 meters above the sea (number 1 on Figure 4). By land, this site can only be approached through a pass east of it. Photograph by Yvon Csonka.

In recent years, sites along the coast of the Chukchi Peninsula were surveyed and inventoried by a team from the Russian Research Institute for Cultural and National Heritage, but detailed results have neither been published nor been made available to us (there are some allusions in Gusev et al. 1999). The same team also summarily excavated several houses at the site of Dezhnevo, six kilometers northwest of Ekven (1995). Lists of sites have been published by Ackerman (1984: 107-108, compiling Russian sources), Bogoslovskaya (1993), Dikov (1977: 9, 33, 252 sq.; 1997), and Krupnik (1983a).

Studies of prehistoric and contemporary whaling were conducted along the coast of the Chukchi Peninsula in the 1980s by L. Bogoslovskaia with I. Krupnik, T. Semenova and L. Votgorov (Bogoslovskaya et al. 1981, 1982; Krupnik 1983c, 1987, 1988, 1993a; Krupnik et al. 1983). Krupnik (1983b) also summarized data bearing on house construction, settlement size, and demographic evolution for the southeastern corner of the Chukchi Peninsula, and drew some conclusions on prehistoric processes among maritime hunters, based on ethnographic data (1993b). The question of prehistoric whaling was the object of new field studies in archaeological sites between the Chegitun River north of Bering Strait and Mechigmen Bay south of it (Knyazev and Savinetsky 1995; Dinesman et al. 1999; Dinesman and Savinetsky 2003; Krupnik and Bogoslovskaya 1999). Dinesman et al. (op. cit.) also contributed an important study of the palaeoenvironmental history of the northeastern part of the Chukchi Peninsula, which contains a wealth of data, including radiocarbon dates, about Ekven.

2.3
STRENGTHS AND WEAKNESSES OF THE CURRENT STATE OF KNOWLEDGE

Cemeteries yielded large quantities of well preserved artifacts of high aesthetic value, without the difficulty of having to excavate through permafrost. They also provided material for physical anthropological studies. Interesting conclusions were reached on the basis of the study of grave materials (e.g. Arutiunov and Sergeev 1975; Bronshtein 1993; Bronshtein and Plumet 1995). Arutiunov and Bronshtein (1985) refined, but also modified (Dumond 1998: 98-103; 2002a: 19-22), the stylistic distinctions in the ornamentation of Okvik and the different aspects of Old Bering Sea Culture (OBS) which had originally been proposed by Collins (1937) and Rainey (1941) on the basis of St. Lawrence Island material. In the cemeteries near East Cape, at Uelen and Ekven, they identified patterns in the combinations of artifacts of different styles which were recovered in graves (Bronshtein and Plumet 1995: 33-38). In both cemeteries, the chronocultural affiliation of artifacts ranged from Okvik and the three subdivisions of OBS (as redefined by Arutiunov and Bronshtein), to Birnirk and to Punuk. The main higher level conclusions of these publications consisted in establishing that those cultures chronologically partly overlapped each other, and that their distinct ornamental traditions corresponded to the need for cultural differentiation among ethnic groups occupying the same territory simultaneously. It was also hypothesized that social differentiation was present from the beginning, ranging from slaves to shamans and secular leaders (further elaborations see Mason 1998: 255-9).

Except for cemeteries, almost no detailed excavations were conducted on the coasts of the Chukchi Peninsula. Even survey data remain scanty. It is agreed that Rudenko, in 1945, realized a very important survey under difficult conditions (Arutiunov 1993: 53; Krupnik 1998: 209, 212). Rudenko was thoroughly conversant with the relevant literature about St. Lawrence Island and the rest of Alaska, and immediately placed his findings within the taxonomic context created by his American colleagues – in Stalin's time, this was an act of courageous defiance to do so (Krupnik 1998: 209). No doubt, practical difficulties prevented him from investigating long stretches of the coast in between the sites he discovered. Path breaking and important as it was, this survey was literally only skimming the surface of the archaeological record. Likewise, Dikov's numerous publications bear testimony to his remarkable perseverance and perspicacity in unveiling Chukotka's archaeological heritage. Significant as they are as regional syntheses, his books (1977, 1979) leave many questions unanswered concerning the nature of the occupation of the numerous coastal sites he cursorily describes. Many of these sites are designated as single component on the basis of surface finds or summary test excavations. Under such conditions, one must adopt Mason's (1998: 308) cautiousness towards Rudenko's and Krupnik's attempts at characterizing house and population sizes by epochs on the basis of rather impressionistic data. The geographically important Ratmanova (Big Diomede) Island barely appears in Russian publications (e.g. Tein 1985).

Traces of the passage of early humans from the Old to the New World are so far almost nonexistent near Bering Strait. The links between inland cultures and coastal ones cannot yet be established. The early ethnogenesis of the Chukchi, and the relationships of their ancestors with the Neoeskimo people, are highly hypothetical. In the same publication, Arutiunov, and Dikov (1972), presented contrasted views on that subject. There is agreement however that intensive herding developed among the Chukchi only in the fifteenth or sixteenth century, and did not become prevalent until well into the eighteenth century. Their economic and demographic expansion, and perhaps also the Russian encroachments on their lands, pushed them towards the coasts of the Chukchi Peninsula, where they chased or assimilated many of the late prehistoric Eskimo, while adopting their maritime culture (idem; Arutiunov and Fitzhugh 1988: 128; Dikov 1997: 104-5; Krupnik 1984: 15; 1993b: 195). The latest studies of linguistic interactions (De Reuse 1994; Fortescue 1998), in the absence of firm archaeological evidence, do not shed much light on the time depth of the interactions between Chukchi and Eskimo.

Direct predecessors to the first fully developed Neoeskimo cultures – Okvik and Old Bering Sea – have not been found. At the site of the Devil's Gorge (Chertov Ovrag) on Wrangell Island (Dikov 1977, 1979; Tein 1979), evidence was found of a maritime adaptation, with material compared by Ackerman (1984: 107) to that of the Old Whaling culture of Alaska, and five dates ranging between 3360±155 and 2850±50 14C years B.P. (comments in Mason and Gerlach 1995b: 20). Notwithstanding Dikov's (1988: 85) suggestion that the Devil's Gorge only harpoon head might be ancestral to the

OBS types, there is a wide temporal and cultural gap between these assemblages. And despite the presence of ceramics in some sites, neither the data obtained so far from Chukotkan inland sites, nor those from nearby Alaska, provide any close link. Searching for the origins of the Norton "phase" (Alaskan Bering Sea coast, ca. 2500-1000 BP), Ackerman wrote: "the two areas, Chukotka and Alaska, are roughly contemporaneous in age and comparable in many aspects of material inventory. It would perhaps be best at this point to consider Chukotka and Western Alaska a single cultural area" (1982: 21). He later added that the developments "during Norton times formed the basis of a cultural complex which ultimately led to further cultural elaboration as expressed in the Okvik/Old Bering Sea and Ipiutak cultures" (1998: 258). Dumond (1987: 127) agrees with Ackerman's first statement, but nevertheless cautiously concludes that "it remains evident that there is no acceptable progenitor of any sort for the St.Lawrence-Chukchi Peninsula cultures, let alone one that would relate them directly to cultures of the Alaskan mainland" (1998: 110)[3].

The fact that the second Ekven standing expedition was conducted out of an art museum prolonged the "long-standing Russian bias towards cemetery remains and the more elaborate Old Bering Sea styles" (Mason 1998: 286) which had already been pointed out by Larsen (1968: 88). Thus, even for these cultures, data about dwellings, activity areas, daily life, settlement patterns, are very limited. The relationships between the early Neoeskimo cultures of the Chukchi Peninsula, and such partly contemporary Alaskan manifestations as Norton and Ipiutak, are still mostly hypothetical. Up until the recent work of Roger Harritt on the Seward Peninsula (1994; fieldwork in progress in Wales and Tin City), and his interest in the spread of whaling technology from Asia to America (1995), comparisons between both sides of Bering Strait at the most likely point of passage were restricted by the lack of data from Alaska. As to the late prehistoric period, it remains poorly known (Schweitzer and Golovko 1995: 140). Closer to our end of the time scale, a few recent studies have shed light on the history of the Yupiget and their relationships with their close neighbours, Chukchi and American Eskimo (Chichlo 1981; Krupnik and Chlenov in prep.; Schweitzer 1990; Schweitzer and Golovko 1995).

Specialists working on each side of Bering Strait have strived to take data from the other country into account in their interpretations. During the Cold War, it may well be that Eskimo studies were the area of the most intense cooperation between American and Soviet archaeologists (Krupnik 1998: 210). Nevertheless, this cooperation was not very intense in absolute terms, opportunities to meet were few, and common fieldwork was out of the question. Research focuses and taxonomies also diverged during the Cold War (see Bronshtein and Plumet 1995: 18-20). There is ample room for research that will address today's most pressing questions.

2.4
GOALS OF THE PROJECT

The above summary assessment of the current state of knowledge about Neoeskimo prehistory in the Asian zone puts our goals into perspective. Grave excavations were facing diminishing scientific returns; furthermore, they were going against the will of the local Native population. It was thus clear that such activities could and should be suspended, at least for the time being (Bronshtein and Plumet 1995: 43-4). On the other hand, everything pointed to the need for detailed data from the settlement.

As appears from the previous chapter, Ekven was already one of the best known sites on the Chukchi Peninsula – at least its cemetery was. The portion of the settlement remaining today is extremely well preserved in permafrost. At the same time, erosion destroys it at a pace which justifies a salvage enterprise. Inferences based on results from the cemetery and from palaeo-environmental research, indicate that Ekven must have been a large settlement, occupied perhaps continuously during a great part of the Neoeskimo period; most dates cluster in the 2100-500 14C years BP interval (Dinesman et al. 1999: 127-9). The conclusions of Arutiunov and Bronshtein also indicate a considerable blending of different cultural traditions. Residents must have been attracted and kept there by the abundance of marine resources. The settlement is situated at the intersection of two contrasted environments, the northern, Chukchi Sea coast, and the southern, Bering Sea coast of the Chukchi Peninsula. Furthermore, its situation at the crossroads of the continents let us expect other potentially interesting findings. All these elements encouraged us to begin excavations there.[4]

We aimed at investigating the duration of occupation, the number and nature of phases of residence and their chronology, and at gathering detailed data about architecture, subsistence, economic pursuits and daily life.

---

[3] The question of the origin of the Asian Neoeskimo cultures, within the context of North Pacific maritime adaptations, has been adequately summed up by Ackerman (1984; 116-118). The Russians tend to favor an Asian origin for Okvik and OBS, but the analogues there are not more convincing than the American ones. Likewise, Dumond and Bland see the origins of Arctic maritime adaptations on the Alaska Peninsula (1995; 444-5), whereas Vasil'evski (1987) would have them on the Asian continent. A recent summary on these questions can be found in Workman and McCartney (1998, in an important volume about "North Pacific and Bering Sea Maritime Societies").

[4] We must mention that this choice was also influenced by practical reasons. A number of sites in the vicinity of East Cape look potentially as interesting as Ekven in terms of size and/or probable age, e.g. Tusilen, Puuten, Nuniamo, etc. And, without leaving the Neoeskimo problematic, excavations on the north coast of Chukotka, or on the south coast in and about Enmelen, for instance, would also help solve crucial unanswered questions.

In the field, the research has been subdivided into several subprojects. The first season, in 1995, was dedicated to a reconnaissance of the site: mapping, test pits, assessment of the erosion front stratigraphy, choice of a mound and beginning of its detailed excavation. By choosing a mound of relatively small size, at the periphery of the settlement, it was hoped that the remains it contained would be those of a single occupation episode, which fortunately proved to be the case: the well preserved and complex material assemblage recovered from the ruin are attributed to Birnirk and Punuk. In 1996, the Russian team joined the Germans and the Swiss in the excavation of this single house mound, code named Ekven House 18 (EH-18; Photo 8); work continued in the next two seasons (Blumer 1996, 1997a). After the termination of international field seasons in Ekven, our colleagues from the State Museum of Oriental Arts completed the excavation of Ekven House 18 (EH-18) in 2000 and 2001 (partial results until the 2000 season in Dneprovsky 2002). In 2001, Dneprovsky started excavating a well-preserved Birnirk house in the settlement of Paipelghak, on the northern shore of the Chukchi Peninsula (Dneprovsky 2006). This systematic excavation of EH-18, a well preserved semi-subterranean dwelling ruin should yield precise data about architectural characteristics and past activity patterns. Comparatively much more work time has been invested in the excavation of this house ruin, than in any other activity in the settlement.

As the detailed excavation of house EH-18 was well under way and sufficiently staffed, the Swiss team resumed and expanded, in 1997 and 1998, the reconnaissance work started during the first season. We undertook three types of activities:

1. Documentation of the erosion front

The neat natural stratigraphic section of the erosion front was a tempting and logical way to approach the stratigraphy of the site, and to gain easy access to its lowermost deposits. We were well aware, from other researchers' experiences in comparable Neoeskimo sites (e.g. Mason 1998: 267-8 about the Kukulik mound, Hall 1990: 403-4) that it would be a daunting task to try to make even partial sense of it. The appearance of the stratigraphy clearly confirmed these warnings. The French geo-archaeologist Bernard Moulin accepted the challenge. In addition to stratigraphic documentation, several hundred artifacts were collected in situ while cleaning the stratigraphy in preparation for documentation, and over a thousand more were collected in the sediments collapsed at the foot of the erosion front. The present report covers only the results of this activity, and this, to the exception of the artifacts collected. Some of the artifacts figure in an exhibition catalogue (Bronshtein et al. 2007), where they are designated as "surface material from the Ekven settlement". The pottery is described in chapter 6.

2. Test excavations

Three test excavations were conducted. One, 3 m x 1 m, was situated within a ring of whale skulls, where we were hoping to find traces of activities related with that ring; excavation was stopped as soon as it proved not to be the case. The other two test pits, each with a surface of 1.5 m x 1.5 m, were located near the center of two large mounds situated between the erosion front and EH-18. As permafrost was slowing the excavation, and as we had to cancel the 1999 season, we could not reach sterile ground in either of them. These two tests and their locations were meant to evaluate the complexity of the mounds and their chronocultural affiliation, with a view to facilitating the choice of a location for further large scale excavations.

3. Survey of neighbouring sites

To broaden our perspective on the settlement of the region, we also visited, and in two cases summarily mapped, many of the sites surrounding Ekven (Photos 4-6). This activity was restricted by the fact that the authorization for surveying was refused by the Institute of Archaeology of the Russian Academy of Sciences.

The above activities were carried out in two field seasons (1997-1998) by 2.5 personnel. Summary field reports on these activities can be found in Blumer and Csonka (1998) and Csonka, Blumer and Moulin (1999).

Photo 7. Geoarcheologist Bernard Moulin documenting the erosion front, summer 1998. Photograph by Yvon Csonka.

Photo 8. The excavation of Ekven House 18 (EH-18) in 1997. Here three archaeology students from the University of Tübingen. In the background the Ekven cemetery hills. Photograph by Yvon Csonka.

Photo 9. The Ekven region looking northeast from Mount Tunitlen. Photograph by Yvon Csonka.

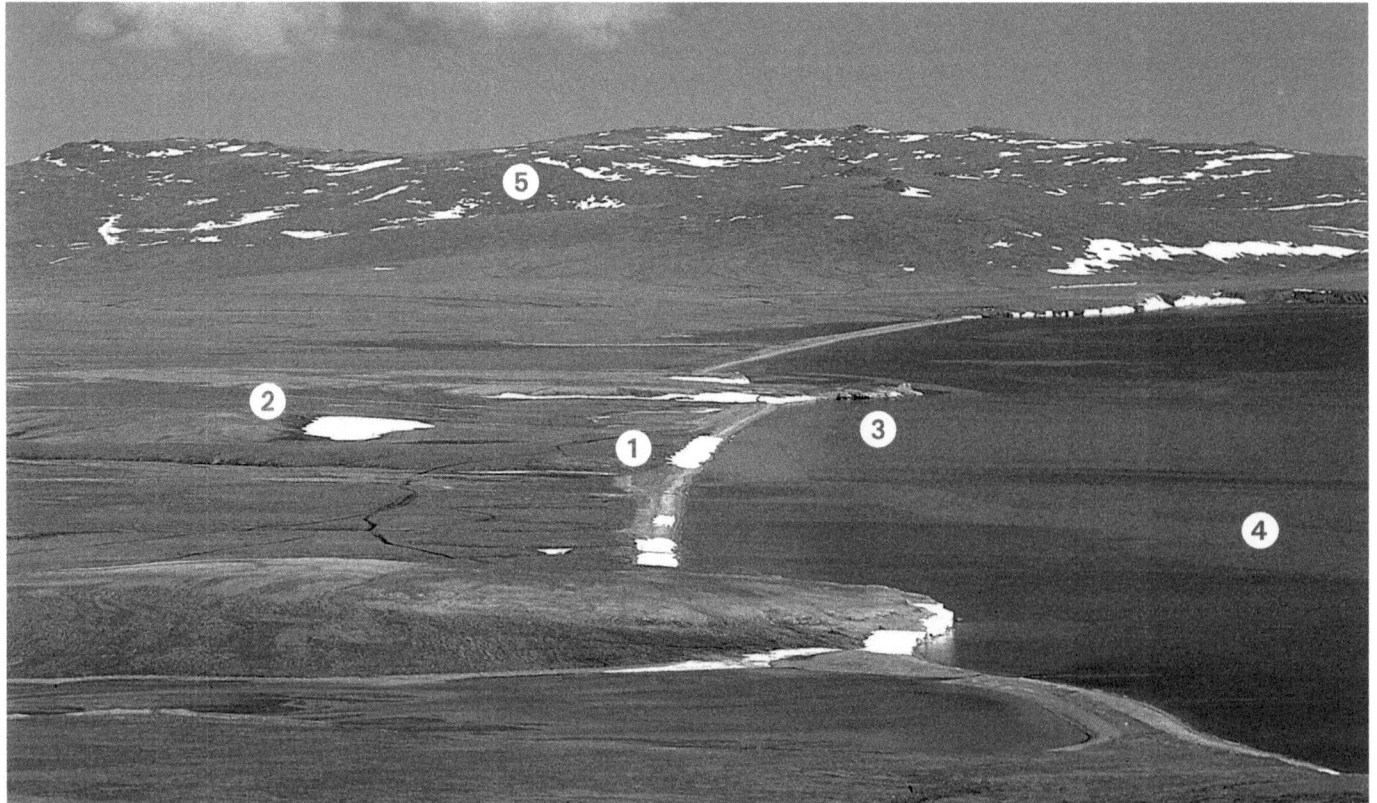

Photo 10. The Ekven region and the East Cape mountain massif looking northeast from Mount Tunitlen. Photograph by Yvon Csonka.

3.
EKVEN: LOCATION, TOPOGRAPHY, AND ENVIRONMENT

YVON CSONKA

3.1
LOCATION AND TOPOGRAPHY

The toponym Ekven applies to the ruins of a settlement and of a nearby cemetery. In the Chukchi language, it is pronounced Ik'ven, the Yupiget equivalent being Ikpawaq; its etymology is not known (Leont'ev and Novikova 1989: 425; Jacobson 2004: 388), but according to Bronshtein (1993: 73) it would mean Cape of the Big Sod House. The settlement is situated on the coast of the Chukchi Peninsula, at 170 06' 05 E and 66 01' 10 N; this is about eighteen kilometers, as the crow flies, west of East Cape (Cape Dezhnev), the easternmost point of land of the Old World, which demarcates the Asian shore of Bering Strait. West of the Dezhnev mountain massif which rises abruptly from the strait, the Chukchi Sea is separated from the Bering Sea by a rolling plain. On the southern shore of that plain, sand and gravel bars demarcate several lagoons, interspersed with a few rocky scarps. The Ekven cemetery hill, culminating at about 40 m above sea level some 500 m from the shore, is one of the highest points near that shore. It is located midway along the ca. 12 km stretch of low coast between the foothills of the Dezhnev mountain massif and Mount Tunitlen (Figures 3, 4, Photos 9, 10, 11). Big Diomede (Ratmanova) Island, in the middle of Bering Strait, is clearly visible from the site and so are, on the clearest days, the mountains near the tip of the Seward Peninsula (Photos 12, 13).

❶ Ekven erosion front and settlement
❷ Ekven necropol
❸ Cape Verbliuzhi (Camel or Sphinx Point)
❹ Bering Sea
❺ Cape Dezhnev mountains
❻ Village of Uelen
❼ Arctic Ocean
❽ Ekven Lagoon

Photo 11. Ekven and its lagoon, looking southwest from Cape Verbliuzhi (Camel Point). Photograph by Yvon Csonka.

Photo 12. Big Diomede (Ratmanova) Island seen from Mount Tunitlen near Ekven. Mountains on the Alaskan shore are clearly visible to the left. Photograph by Yvon Csonka.

Photo 13. Little Diomede Island profiling itself against Big Diomede, as seen from Wales, Alaska. The mountains on the north shore of the Chukchi Peninsula are visible to the right, appearing as a mirage. Photograph by Yvon Csonka.

Little Diomede, on the United States side of the border, is hidden behind it, and so is the mountain just south of Wales, so that the American continent, although only 80 km away, is only visible on the clearest days.

The ruins of the settlement stretch ca. 250 m along the shore, at the foot of the hill where the cemetery is situated. The presence of ruins is indicated by a series of fourteen mounds, eight of which are aligned parallel to the beach, and in the process of being arased by coastal erosion. Some of the mounds are oval, others are coalescent and truncated by erosion. The maximum diameters of the mounds range between ca. 15 and 30 m. In all, twenty six depressions in the mounds were interpreted as collapsed house interiors[1]. Over the course of time, probably more dwellings existed, but their remains are now buried at the base of the larger mounds where the thickness of anthropic sediments reaches up to three meters, and they cannot be identified on the basis of surface topography. The northeasternmost mounds are situated near a lagoon, and also in proximity of a small stream, which provides fresh water during the melting season. The mound furthest inland is about 120 m from the seashore. The summits of the mounds culminate between five and twelve meters above the present mean sea level.

The beach of pebbles and sand allows the smooth landing of small watercrafts in good weather, but is exposed to storms from the south and east. Ekven has not been affected by uncontrolled excavations. However, the seaward face of the settlement is being washed away by the encroaching sea (Photos 14-16). South storms have been frequent in the summer during our seasons of fieldwork there. Waves sometimes reach one meter higher than the top of the beach, situated 2.5 - 3 m above mean sea level, and remove sediments from the bluff. The height of the bluff gently decreases along the beach from about 10 m a.s.l. at the southwestern corner of the settlement, to 4 m at the northeast one. This gentle slope is interrupted approximately in its middle, between mounds VII and VIII, by a shallow gully. The anthropic layers are perched on top of a sandy substrate, which sinks under the present beach around mound XIV in the northeast, exposing the ruins to a direct attack by the waves. It is certain that the village originally extended further out to sea, but we can only speculate how much larger it might have been.

More informations about the geological substrate and its recent evolution follow below in the chapter by Moulin (4.2 below). That changes in the coastline took place at Ekven from the time when it was first settled is evident from the fact that house interiors have been exposed by swash action. Dinesman et al. (1999: chapter 2) suggest that the underwater coastal slope, and the line of the coast, must have changed considerably over the last few millennia. According to them, the lagoon itself may have been a shallow bay until the sand and pebble bar was formed some two millennia ago (uncalibrated B.P.), and its connection with the sea remained more widely open than it is now until only a few centuries ago. One may imagine that it was possible to land kayaks and umiaks near the houses in the northern corner of the settlement. Ruins bordering the northwestern shore of the nearby Dezhnevo lagoon may in a like fashion have been situated in a bay when it was in existence (extreme dates 1886±88 and 1035±98 14C years B.P.)[2]; later on, the bay would have become a lagoon separated from the sea (ibid.: 42, 46). This hypothesis is based on the relatively safe assumption that sea mammal hunters almost always position their dwellings near open sea.

---

[1] The Russian team had drafted a rough map of the settlement and cemetery (Leskov and Müller-Beck 1993: 74). The sketch mapping and numbering of mounds and depressions was realized by Gulløv and Kapel in 1995, with the aid of a GPS receptor. This map was updated in 1999 by Reto Blumer, on the basis of our most recent observations. We completed it by a precise topographic map of the northeastern part of the settlement (Fig. 6).

[2] Concerning the reporting and calibration of these dates, see below, footnote 1, p. 70.

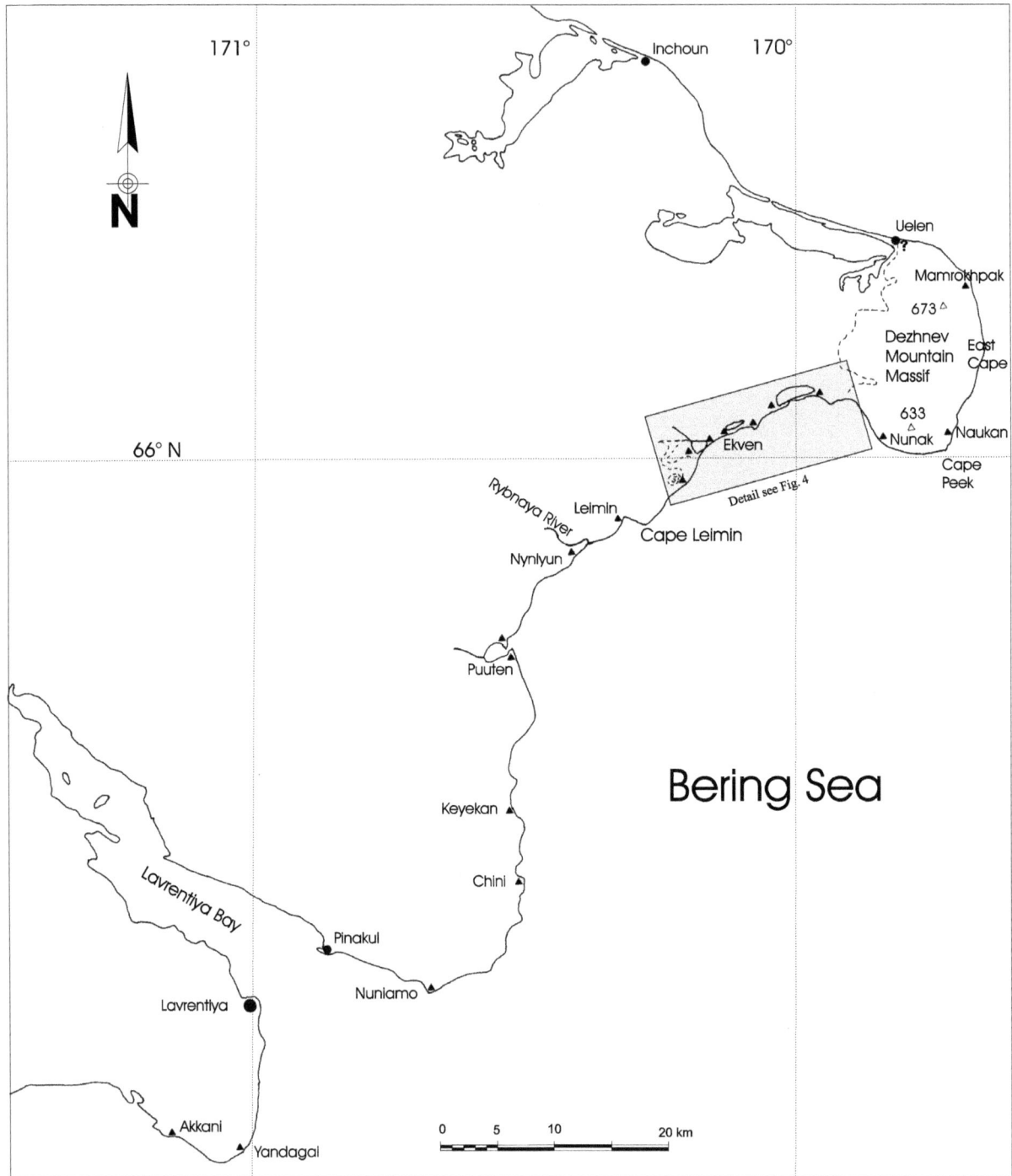

Figure 3. The eastern extremity of the Chukchi Peninsula. Solid triangles represent known archaeological sites, solid dots are localities still occupied today. Illustration by Yvon Csonka.

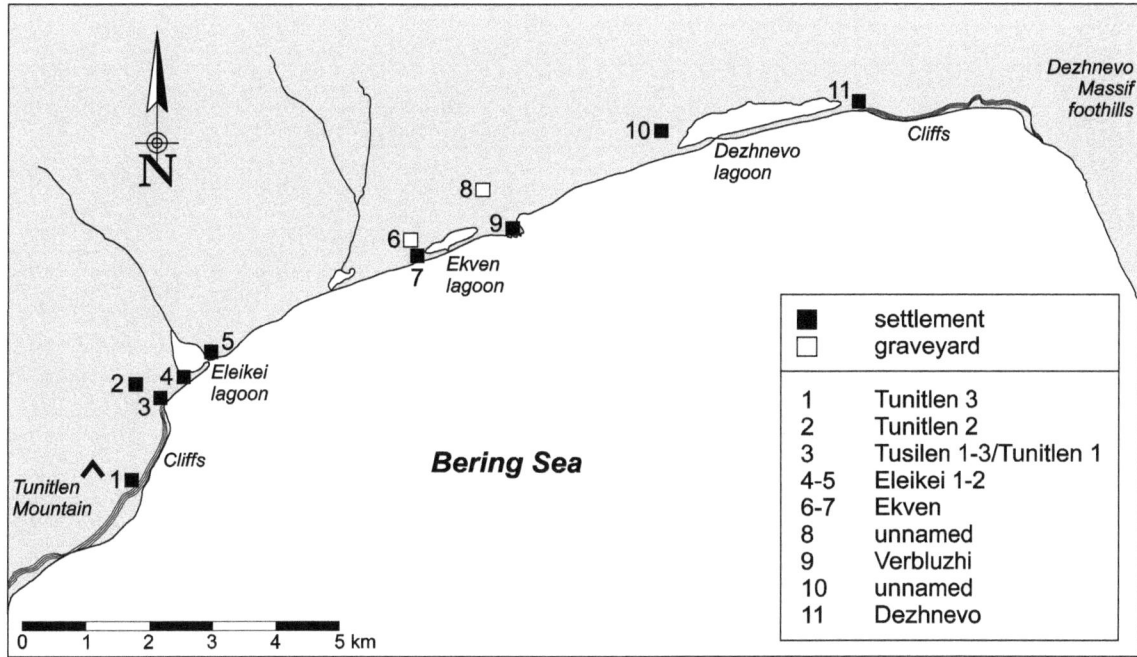

Figure 4. Locations of Ekven and other sites between Mount Tunitlen on the west and the foot of the Dezhnevo massif on the east. Illustration by Reto Blumer.

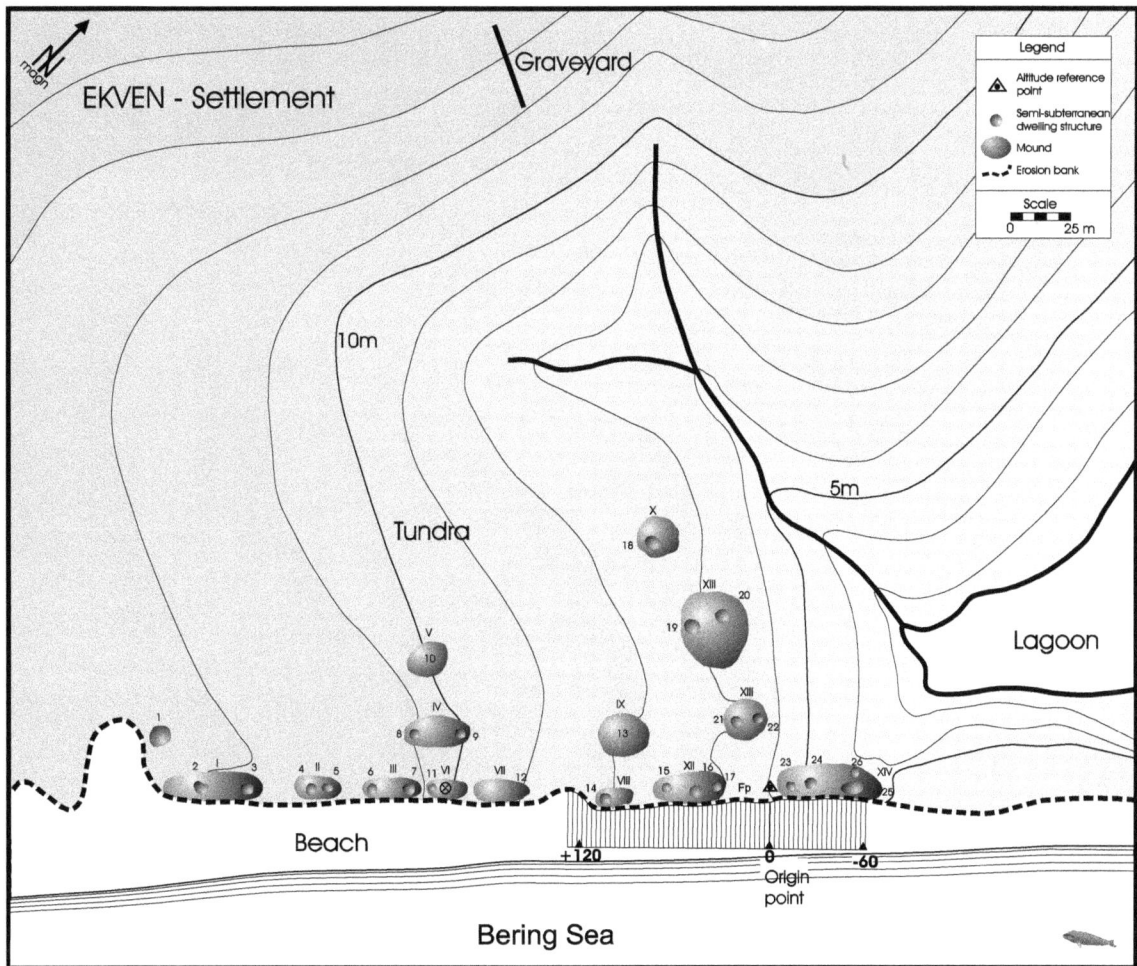

Figure 5. Rough sketch of the Ekven settlement. For a more exact and detailed view of the western half of the settlement, see figure 6. The cross on mound 6 shows the location of the ring of whale skulls on photo 19. Illustration by Reto Blumer.

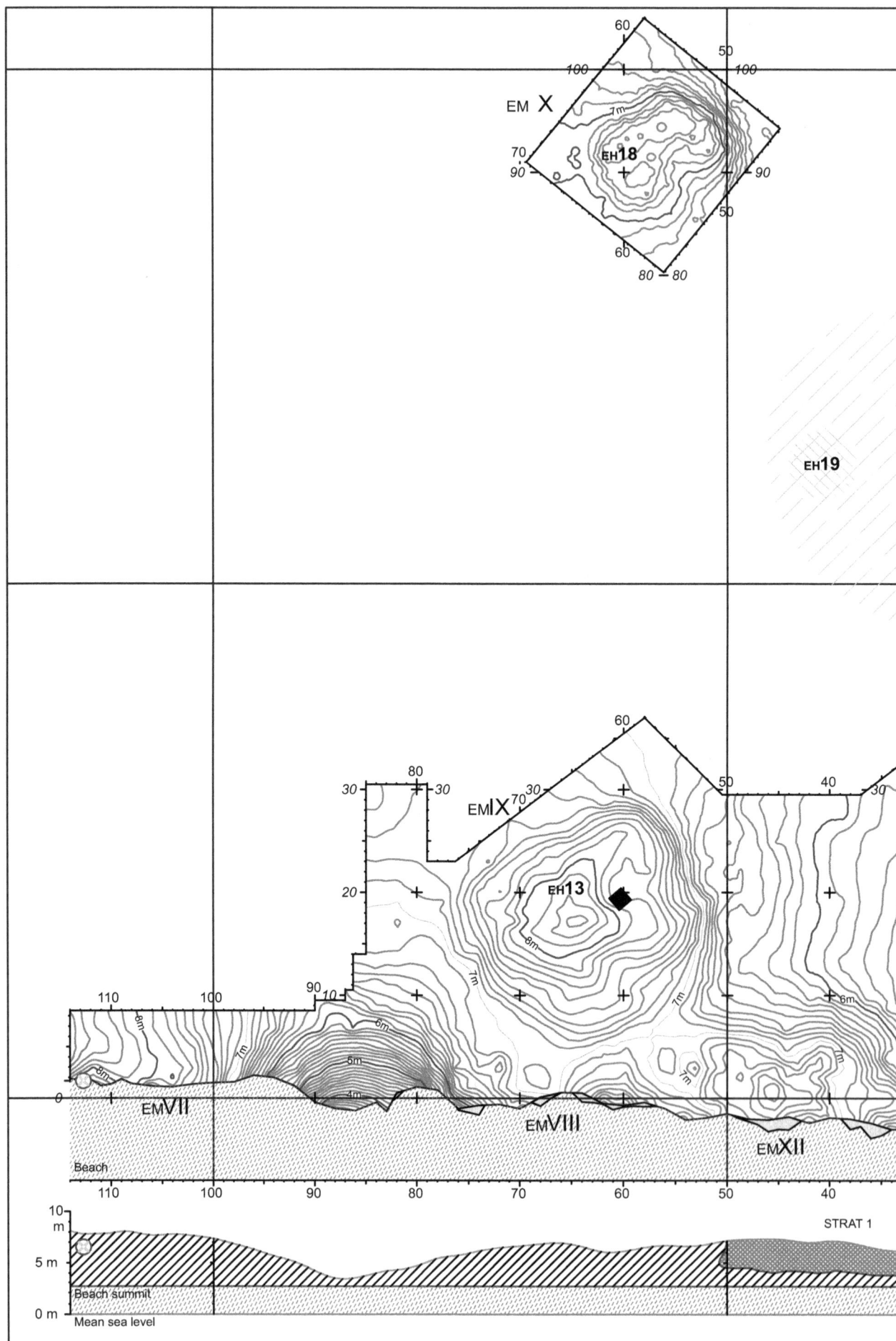

Figure 6. Topography of the Ekven site near the erosion front study area, with location of the two main cuts, Strat 1 and Strat 2. Two complete mounds are clearly recognizable behind the erosion front; four others at the edge of the embankment have been largely destroyed by marine erosion. Illustration by Reto Blumer.

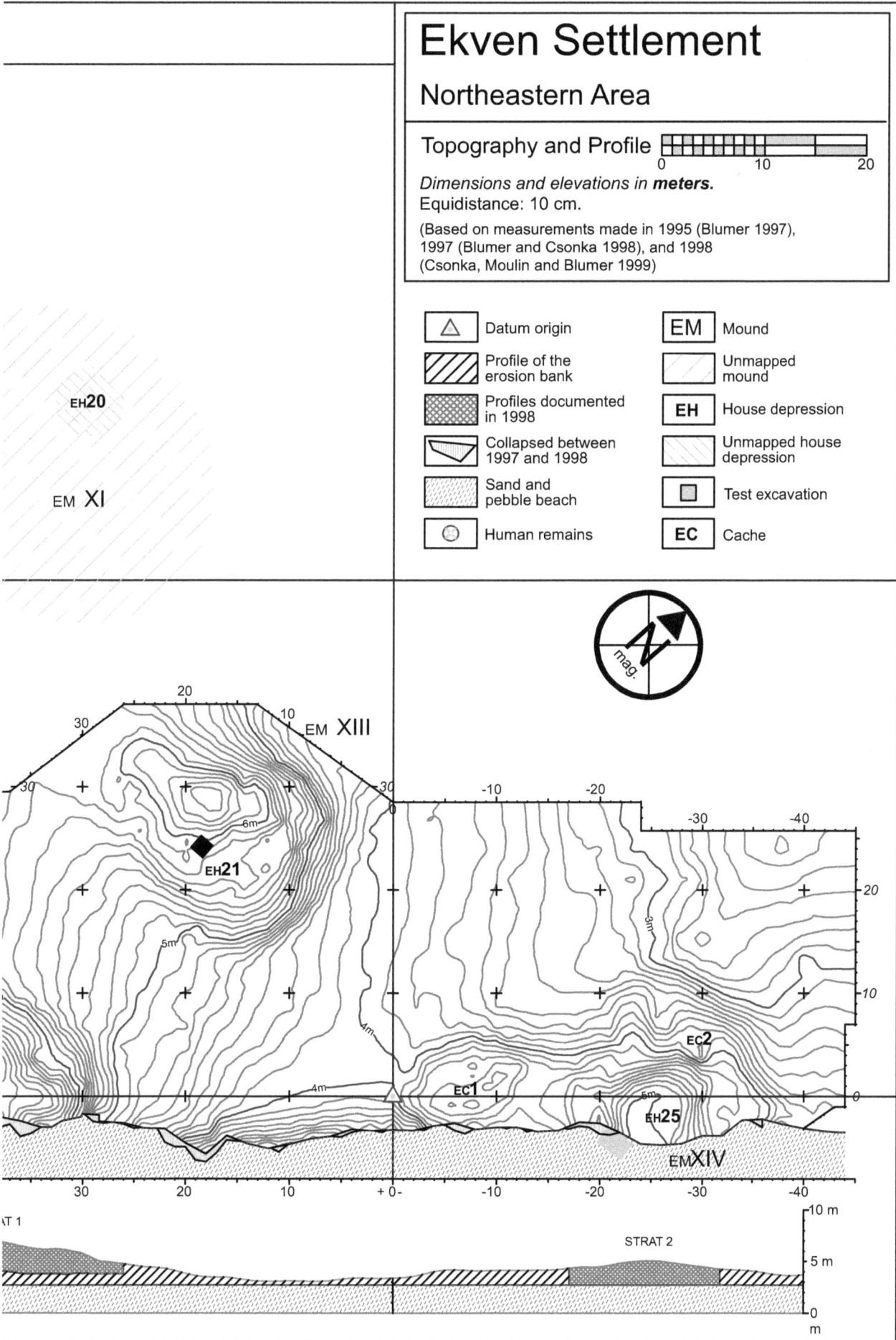

Ekven Settlement

Northeastern Area

Topography and Profile

0   10   20

*Dimensions and elevations in **meters.***
Equidistance: 10 cm.

(Based on measurements made in 1995 (Blumer 1997),
1997 (Blumer and Csonka 1998), and 1998
(Csonka, Moulin and Blumer 1999)

△ Datum origin	EM Mound
▨ Profile of the erosion bank	Unmapped mound
▦ Profiles documented in 1998	EH House depression
▽ Collapsed between 1997 and 1998	Unmapped house depression
Sand and pebble beach	☐ Test excavation
⊙ Human remains	EC Cache

EH20

EM XI

EM XIII

EH21

EC2

EC1

EH25

EMXIV

STRAT 1

STRAT 2

10 m

5 m

0
m

Photo 14. The Erosion front as it appeared in June 1998, still protected by snow from the previous winter. Dezhnev mountains in the background. Photograph by Yvon Csonka.

Photo 15. The erosion front in July 1997. Large amounts of sod and sediments have recently crumbled. Photograph by Yvon Csonka.

3.2
VEGETATION

The vegetation in and about the Ekven settlement is of the wet tundra kind, with Poa and Artemisia dominant on the enriched humus of the anthropic mounds (Dinesman et al. 1999: 6-7). The Ekven hill itself consists of the same sands and gravels on which the settlement was constructed (pp. 40-41). Its top drains early in the season, and therefore has little vegetation. In the Uelen-Ekven region, "2400 years BP it was already an impoverished variant of hypoarctic tundra and did not differ from the present-day plant cover", although "about 2100 years BP the northern variant of hypoarctic tundras was changed for a short time by the southern variant of hypoarctic tundras" (ibid.: 91, 88, see also pp. 54-5). There are no trees in this part of the Chukchi Peninsula. Dwarf Salix and Betula grow barely above a foot high. Driftwood is currently abundant on the beaches, including quite large trunks of coniferous trees.

3.3
FAUNA

Today's fauna and the historic variations of the populations of mammals and birds are described in the same publication (Dinesman et al. 1999: 8-14 and chapter 4; see also Savinetsky 2002); it is the basis for the following summary listing.

Sea mammal species seasonally found near Ekven are the bowhead whale (Balaena mysticetus), gray whale (Eschrichtius robustus), Minke whale (Balaenoptera acutirostrata), beluga (Delphinapterus leucas), common porpoise (Phocoena phocoena), Dall's porpoise (Phocoenoides dalli), killer whale (Orcinus orca), walrus (Odobenus rosmarus), bearded seal (Erignathus barbatus), ringed seal (Pusa hispida), spotted seal (Phoca largha), and ribbon seal (Phoca fasciata). The polar bear (Thalarctos maritimus) also belongs to the marine animals.

Photo 16. Same location as Photo 15, the day after the storm of Aug. 20, 1998. Crumbled sediments have been washed away and the sterile substrate is exposed. Photograph by Yvon Csonka.

Among the land mammals are two species of shrews (Sorex sp.), two species of lemmings (Lemus sibiricus and Dicrostonyx torquatus), the large eared vole (Alticola macrotis), the hare (Lepus arcticus), the northern pika (Ochotona hyperborealis) the ground squirrel (Citellus parryi), the ermine (Mustela erminea), the weasel (Mustela rixosa), the wolverine (Gulo gulo), the arctic fox (Alopes lagopus), the red fox (Vulpes vulpes), the wolf (Canis lupus), and the brown bear (Ursus arctos). The wild reindeer was recently replaced by the domestic variety (Rangifer tarandus). The Ekven villagers apparently always kept dogs (Canis familiaris).

At least 108 bird species can be seasonally found in the general area of Ekven, 17 of which are marine, 47 are shore based, and 44 tundra dwellers. The snowy owl (Nyctea scandiaca) and the raven (Corvus corax) are among the few birds which remain year round.

Salmonidae (Onchorynchus sp.) are the most common fish near Ekven in summer. Among molluscs, most common are the Pacific mussel (Mytilus trossulus), the cockle (Serripes groenlandicus), and the soft shell clam (Mya truncata).

Dinesman et al. also document which species were hunted by the prehistoric inhabitants of Ekven and nearby Dezhnevo, and how some of the catches evolved through the centuries (1999: 72, 76, 95, table 5.3 p. 117). Although the Bighorn sheep disappeared from the region 2280-1940 years BP, and the willow ptarmigan, 1730-1450 years BP (ibid.: 95), "the gross species composition of the mammalian and avian fauna of the region has changed only insignificantly over the last 3000 years. However, the relationships of species and their numbers have varied in relation to environing condition" (Savinetsky 2002: 301).

3.4
CLIMATE

Due to its location on the coast of an isthmus, the climate, vegetation and fauna in and about Ekven are strongly influenced by the sea. Figures 7 and 8 present the monthly average temperature and precipitation, during the twentieth century, at the meteorological station of nearby Uelen.

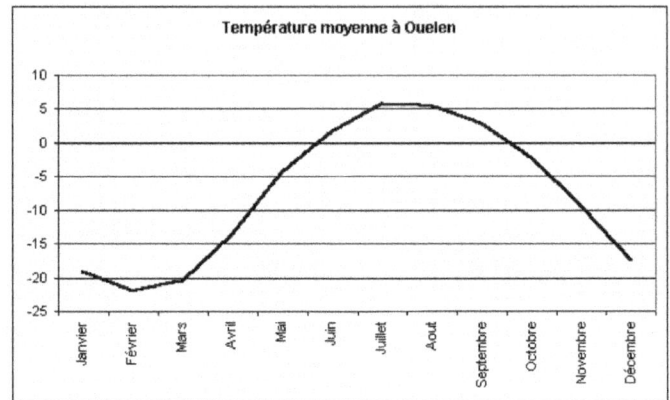

Figure 7. Average temperatures in Uelen, in degrees centigrade. Observations during 736 months between 1918 and 1990. Source: www.worldclimate.com

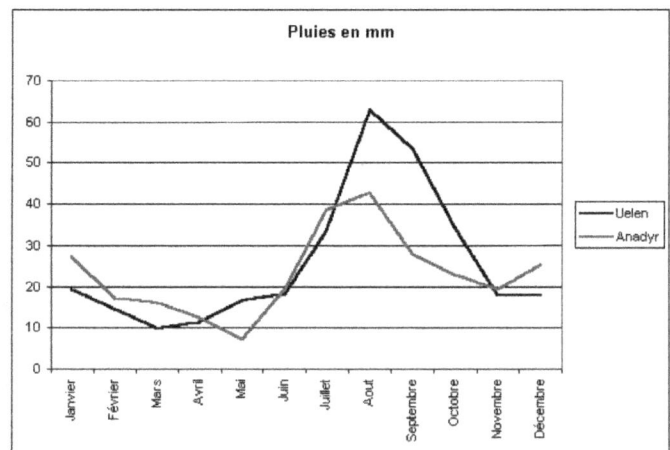

Figure 8. Average rainfall in Uelen and in Anadyr, in millimeters. Observations in Anadyr during 922 months between 1898 and 1988. Observations in Uelen during 518 months between 1928 and 1988. Source: www.worldclimate.com

A fine reconstruction of the local history of climate is not yet available. The waters near the Asian side of the Bering Sea have relatively high nutrient concentrations (Mason and Gerlach 1995a: 123), which attract sea mammals. These concentrations are probably related to the existence of perennial polynyas, but, to say the least, "reconstructing the extent of 'paleo-polynyas' remains a considerable problem" (ibid.: 114). Bering Strait itself acts as a bottleneck through which must pass all sea mammals migrating between the Bering Sea and the Chukchi Sea.

According to Dinesman et al. (1999: 48), there was a short but intense increase in precipitation 2100-2000 BP. They add that "over the last two millennia the winter air temperatures gradually decreased" (p. 47). Furthermore, "it is obvious that 1730 years BP the secular depression of abundance concerned all animals of the Dezhnevo hunting ground. It reached its culmination 1450-1270 years BP. It was not possible to ascertain its actual reasons. However, it is clear that such a large-scale unidirectional change in abundance of animals could be caused only by a very intensive process, general for this region" (p. 88). Later, an apparent increase in the number of walrus about 1200 BP could be correlated with increased sea ice in summer (p. 86). Increased sea ice remaining in the summer protected the coast from waves during storms; such conditions are inferred from episodes of humus accumulation in areas just above sea level. Correlations with summer storminess and wind directions derived from beach ridge evolution on the shores of nearby Alaska (Mason and Jordan 1993, etc. quoted by Mason 1998: 247) have not yet been attempted.

One must remember at this point how highly variable the subarctic climate can be from year to year, and especially how important the consequences of such phenomena as wind and extent of ice may be for people depending essentially on sea hunting. Diachronic variability was paralleled by geographic variations, even on a small scale. Thus, for instance, favorable ice and wind conditions are generally opposite in southeast facing Ekven and in nearby but north facing Uelen (Krupnik and Bogoslovskaya 1999).

3.5
RECENT SETTLEMENT

Ekven was abandoned several centuries ago. Until they were closed in the 1950s, the site was surrounded by two Chukchi settlements, Kaniskun (Dezhnevo) 6 km to the northeast, and Eleikei the same distance to the southwest. Nowadays, the entire surrounding coastal plain is considered Chukchi land. During the twentieth century until it was closed in the late 1950s, Naukan was the only Eskimo (Yupiget) settlement in the district. Since then, Uelen, whose sovkhoze (State farm) controls the surrounding land, including Ekven, is the closest inhabited settlement, 25 km across land following the foot of the Dezhnov mountain massif.

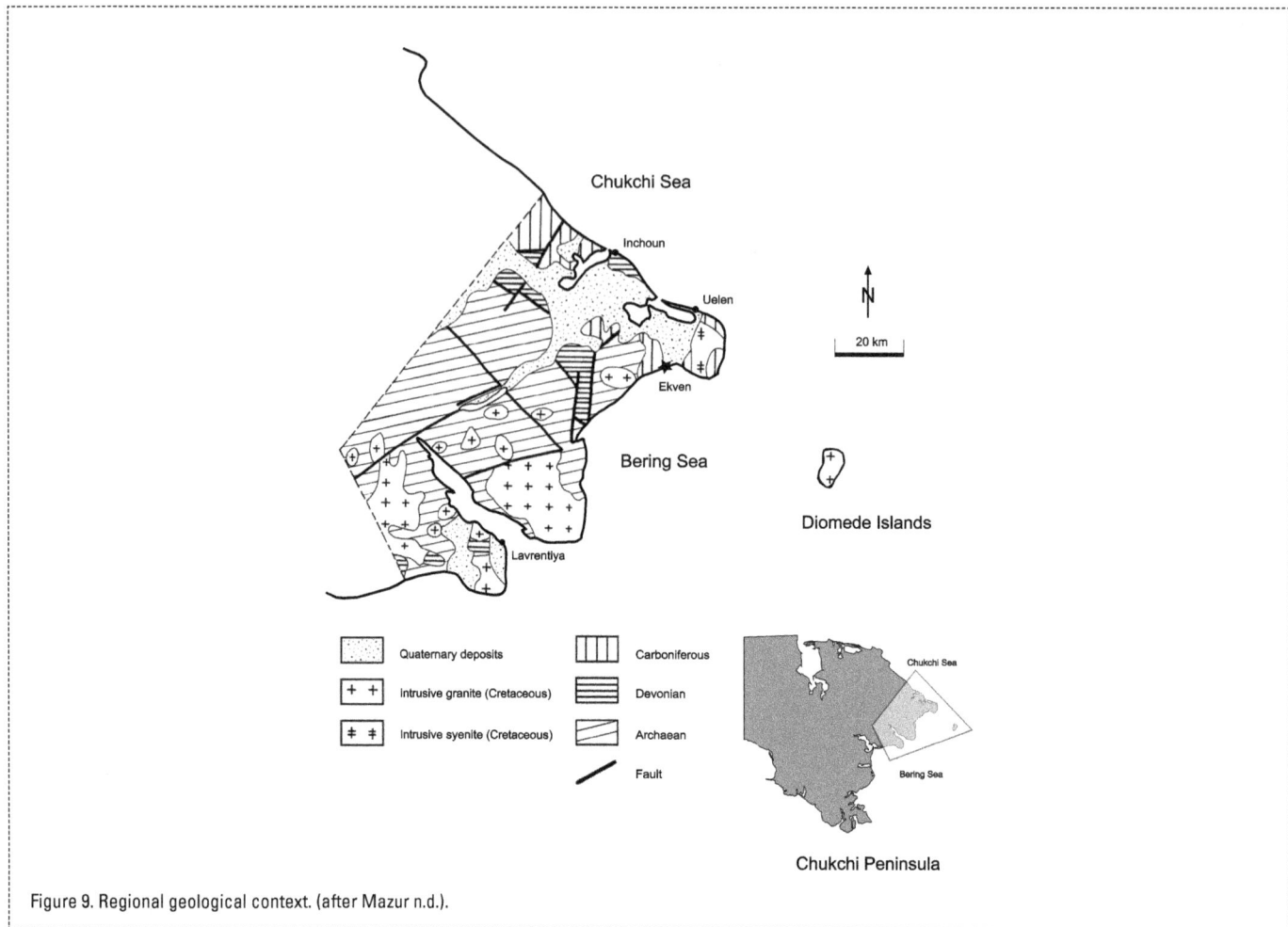

Figure 9. Regional geological context. (after Mazur n.d.).

Photo 17. View of the western extremity of Stratigraphy 1 at the beginning of the project (beginning of July, 1998); the accumulation of snow permits easy access to the summit of the erosion front. Photograph by Bernard Moulin.

4.
EKVEN, THE EROSION FRONT[1]
GEOARCHAEOLOGICAL ANALYSIS OF THE STRATIGRAPHY
THE SEDIMENTS: PALEOETHNOGRAPHIC AND
PALEOENVIRONMENTAL ARCHIVES

BERNARD MOULIN (WITH CONTRIBUTIONS BY YVON CSONKA)

4.1
CONTEXT OF THE STUDY

4.1.1
PROBLEMATICS AND METHODOLOGY

The contribution of geology and geomorphology helps understand the paleoenvironmental context in which the archaeological sites occur in the Arctic domain (Crowell and Mann 1998; Dinesman et al. 1999; Mason 2002), but a link in the chain concerning understanding in detail the complex interactions that are a part of the stratigraphic sequences of the dwelling sites is often lacking. It is this last that we will try to approach in this study. This approach could provide a significant contribution to the problematics developed on those sites, namely, a precise analysis of the chronostratigraphy, a better understanding of the paleo-environmental context (paleotopography), or even more for paleo-ethnographic questions (occupation of space, structure of the dwelling, utilization of primary materials). In the following chapter, Mason integrates and discusses the results from the present study in a wider paleoenvironmental and paleogeographic context encompassing Alaska.

The work presented here takes a geoarchaeological approach to a stratigraphic sequence of sediments, most of which contain an organic component of anthropogenous origin. Dwelling sites such as Ekven are present in the form of coalescent mounds of different sizes, almost entirely the results of human activity: they are "tells" of the Arctic. The sediments of these mounds are characterized by their relatively dark color (brown to gray-beige) and their abundance of organic remains well preserved by permafrost, in which mingle elements of architecture, artifacts, and various accumulations resulting from domestic activities and the decay and dismantling of house feature. Understanding the construction of the large features that are these mounds is of profound interest, as much for the person interested in Arctic archaeology as for anyone who, by the application of comparative logic to the various contexts of fossilization, tries to understand the various taphonomic processes acting on the results of past human activity.

When a planimetric excavation was carried out by a part of the crew after several ventures in the field (Blumer 1996, 1997a), it seemed opportune, on the basis of the preliminary work conducted in 1997 (Blumer and Csonka 1998), to undertake, during the 1998 field season stratigraphic work on the erosional front, work that would reconcile two objectives, on the one hand, a certain degree of precision with regard to the collected documentation, and on the other, a certain extension regarding the documented surface. The marine erosional front (Fig. 6) gave us direct access to the topic we wanted to study, i.e., the complete sequence of the stratigraphy of an anthropogenic sedimentary accumulation, here developed at a thickness of 2.5–3 m, and this over a lateral extension of several tens of meters (Moulin and Csonka 2002; Csonka 2003).

We will not enter here into the details of certain aspects of the problematics and methodology, in particular those concerning the field work, those points having been amply explored previously (Csonka & al. 1999). We do remind, however, that it is on the basis of work carried out in contexts other than here (Butzer 1982; Hassan 1978; Stein & Farrand 1985; Water 1992) that we have outlined a methodology that can be applied and adapted here, considering, of course, the inherent characteristics and constraints of this environment. There are, among others, the works undertaken on lacustrine sites, but also on terrestrial habitats (Beeching & Brochier 2003; Brochier 1984, 1986, 1994, 1999), which have clearly shown that we need to consider the sedimentary strata other than as a mere material enclosing archaeological remains: these sediments can be considered as veritable archives (Brochier 1988), just as the artifacts they enclose, and we need to take advantage of the wealth of information stored in these archives by attempting to decipher them (Courty 1982, Courty & Miskovsky 1987). As J. L. Brochier (1994) emphasizes, "The archaeological restoration of history should not dispense with using the vast bed of information that is the sediment."

---

[1] This chapter is an expanded version of a report that was originally published as Moulin and Csonka (2002) in a volume edited by Don Dumond and Richard Bland.

The course of work that we have adopted consisted first of a detailed analysis of the stratigraphy. It is the basis of the documentary and interpretive work, because it allows us to place the sedimentary facies, elements of architecture, artifacts, etc., in stratigraphic, chronological, and geometric correlation, and that structure will support the entire project.

While rectifying the profile of stratigraphy 1, one sector revealed itself particularly dense in archaeological material, more than 200 artifacts were recorded in tri-dimensional coordinates: They include 70 walrus ivories, 54 pieces of worked wood, 34 lithic objects, 13 ceramics, 13 cervidae antlers, 8 worked bone, 7 artifacts of baleen, and 4 reindeer antlers (Pl. 2a). The stratigraphies were worked out in detail at 1:10 by successive modules of 4 m (Photos 17, 22), in which the maximum of information concerning the texture and structure of the sediment, as well as the nature of the microscopically visible compositional elements, have been reported. On the other hand, each of the characteristic sedimentary facies has been elaborated in detail at 1:5 (Fig. 13).

It is only upon completion of the study that sample analysis was undertaken. This provided, on the one hand, a necessary characterization on the basis of the quantified data and, on the other, an affirmation (or a negation) of the working hypotheses proposed on the terrain. These analyses were conducted on thirty samples, most coming from stratigraphic cuts (Photo 23); some samples, coming from exterior referentials (recent sediments, ancient substrate), were attached to this body of data. The detailed analysis of the elements of the sediment included between 8 mm and 2 cm was carried out on the spot after water screening; the laboratory analyses (granulometry of sand fractions and breakdown of the composition of the 0.6–2 mm fraction, granulometry of silt-clay fractions, and chemistry of the smaller fractions to 0.5 mm) were done later. These last two series of analyses were carried out in the Laboratory of Sedimentology in the College of Prehistory at the University of Basel, Switzerland. We will not go into detail here either on the procedures of analysis or on the keys of interpretation, rather the reader should refer to the appropriate preceding works (Joos 1980; Moulin 1991). We will give here only the main outlines: The screening of the sand fractions was carried out dry through a series of 17 screens from 2 mm to 50 μm, after weighing the dry sediment from a bath and washing in a screen of 50 microns; the granulometry of the fine fractions (smaller than 50 μm) was done by the Malvern process. The weight percentages are represented in the form of cumulative curves in a logarithmic scale on the abscissa axis (size of the particles) (Fig. 12). These curves allow us to calculate the following granulometric parameters: P10, Q1 (first quarter), Md (Median), Q3 (third quarter), and P90, particle sizes respectively at the Y-axis at 10%, 25%, 50%, 75%, and 90%, and to establish a sorting index (So1) = log (Q3/Q1), an index in which the values get lowered as the sediment gets well sorted (Miskovski & Debard 2002). The presentation of the data as a binary graph median/sorting index (Fig. 14) permits differentiating the sediments according to the conditions of their deposition (Selmer-Olsen 1954). The composition of the fraction 0.6–2 mm was determined by a detailed analysis of 150–200 grains with a binocular microscope; the data of the chemical analyses are presented in percentages (content of organic matter, carbonate content) and in units of color (u.c.) for the values in phosphates and in "humus" (fine organic matter).

4.1.2
NOMENCLATURE AND TERMINOLOGY

The terminology of the anthropogenic strata, rich in organic matter, was created on littoral lacustrine dwelling sites (Joos 1976, 1980). In these particular contexts, in an anaerobic environment, the slow degradation of organic matter permitted good preservation of plant remains associated with human activity. That is how the "dwelling middens", archaeological strata particularly rich in organic matter, have been defined (Brochier 1984). We will use this term to designate certain archaeological strata particularly rich in organic matter from dwelling sites in an Arctic context such as we were able to define in stratigraphic cuts of the Ekven erosional front. There is indeed a certain similarity of sedimentary facies between the organic strata of the littoral sites and the Arctic sites, where the conditions of preservation are exceptional because of the presence of the permafrost. We will also use in this work the term "sedimentary ethnofacies" as it has been defined by Brochier (1994): "we designate as sedimentary ethnofacies all sediment that is found to be in one way or another an ethnographic reflection of the life of people and their society."

4.2
GEOGRAPHIC AND GEOMORPHIC CONTEXT

4.2.1
GEOGRAPHIC CONTEXT

The geographic context of the Ekven site has been expounded upon above in this volume. We will identify here some more specific points concerning the strictly geomorphological aspects, and we will refer to previous investigations of the evolution of the coastal dynamic. The northeast end of the Chukchi Peninsula, between Lavrentiya Bay, Kolyuchinskaya Bay, and Cape Dezhnevo is made up essentially, with the exception of more recent and acidic intrusions, of sedimentary and metamorphic terrains going from the Precambrian to the Carboniferous (Lamblin 1993: 238; Mazur n.d.) (Fig. 9).

The Ekven site (Photo 1) is in a zone of the Bering Sea coast that is topographically rather low, halfway between the relief of the Dezhnevo massif on the northeast and the north-south oriented crest of Mount Eulyun (310 m, which extends from Mount Tunitlen to Cape Leimin) on the southwest, made up of metamorphic terrains of Archaean age, in the midst of which granite massifs of Cretaceous age were later formed (Mazur n.d.). Shallow quaternary deposits mask the rocky substrate in the largest part of this low zone, which appears at the surface only on small denuded promontories, like that of the cemetery, as well as in rare sections of rocky coast – for example at Capes Dezhnevo and Verblyzhi. A large part of the actual coast consists of gravel bars that delimit small lagoons at the mouth of each small water course – the consequence of fluvial terrigenous deposits concentrated by the sea during storms (Fig. 4: local context from Dezhnevo to Tunitlen).

Photo 18. View to the east from the shore at the level of the Ekven site. At the beginning of the summer season, the beach extending the erosion front is still covered by heavy snow. In the second plan, Ekven Lagoon, then Dezhnevo massif, and East Cape. Photograph by Bernard Moulin.

Photo 19. View to the northeast, from the above the edge of the Ekven site erosion bluff. In the middle ground, the Ekven lagoon, and in the background the Dezhnev mountain range. The location of the ring of whale skulls can be seen on figure 5. Photograph by Bernard Moulin.

The works of the multi-disciplinary crew of the Severstov Institute of Ecology and Evolution in Moscow, under the direction of L. G. Dinesman et al. (1999), have made it possible to retrace the significant traits of geomorphic evolution of the shore in the area dealt with by our work, and the fluctuations of sea level during the last millennia. We now believe, on the basis of previous work (Kaplin 1982; Kaplin & al. 1991, cited in Dinesman et al. 1999), that sea level 7,000 years ago was 10 m lower than it is today. This brings the coastline, because of the very weak declivity of the sea bottom, about 2 km out from the present one. We also believe that the stabilization of the sea level at close to the one we know today dates to between the third and second millennium B.C. After that date the fluctuations had weak amplitudes. Around 2400–2200 B.C., the sea level must have been 1.5–2 m lower than it is today, and an increase of the same amplitude in water level took place around 1450–1280 B.P., leading to the transformation of small sheltered bays that existed then into lagoons such as we know them today (Dinesman & al. 1999).

4.2.2
THE QUATERNARY SUBSTRATE

4.2.2.1
The sedimentary and environmental context before the first occupations

The constituent anthropogenous sediments of the occupation strata at Ekven lie on a series of detrital deposits that outcrop in the lower part of the embankment of the erosion front. This outcrop series is increasingly developed from east to west, extending continuously as far as the small lagoon at the mouth of the Kytylynveem River, between the lagoons of Ekven and Eleikei. Several sedimentary facies can be recognized in this sequence, from bottom to top:
- lacustrine facies: They are characterized by rather fine stratified deposits (sands and silts) in which deformation structures of slump type and diapir or dome type can be observed several times.
- deltaic facies: These are relatively coarse deposits (gravels and pebbles) in foreset beds.
- solifluction and colluvium deposits: These are heterometric sediments, poorly sorted, in an olive-hued sand-silt matrix, enclosing gravels and some pebbles. This sequence is always beneath the lacustrine and deltaic deposits, and generally makes up the substrate of the occupation strata.

4.2.2.2
The STRAT 3 cut

It is an exemplar type of this Quaternary sequence. This is presented in Figure 10. The profile shows at the base a well developed sequence composed of an alternation of silty, silty-sandy, and sandy strata of gray, gray-beige to olive-green tint (sedimentological samples: Sample S28, Sample S29, and Sample S30). Following this sequence, deformed after its deposition, is a lenticular stratum of sorted gravels (deltaic deposits), very likely contemporaneous with the phase of deformation. Deformations are of two types: the main structure is an anticlinal diapiric structure; laterally, a structure of weaker amplitude is characterized by a bending of the strata (lying folded) (Photos 20, 21). These deformations, which could be too prematurely interpreted as periglacial structures (Butrym & al. 1964; Dzulynski 1963, 1966), are to be classified among supporting figures (Anketell & Dzulynski 1968; Anketell & al. 1970), and result in hydroplastic behavior of the sediment saturated in water in a subaquatic context at the moment of destabilization by the aggressive arrival at the top of the sequence of the coarse deposits (deltaic gravels). This type of figure has been repeatedly studied in different sedimentary contexts, in particular lacustrine (Aartolati 1987; Moulin 1991; Vesajoki 1982) and glacio-lacustrine and deltaic (Tissières 1990). Later, this sequence is truncated horizontally and the heterometric deposits are set in place by solifluction before the occupation of the site.

4.2.2.3
Paleo-environmental context

The deltaic and lacustrine facies probably correspond to the environmental context of a zone close to a lake or lagoon: arrival of coarse detrital material during periods of snow melt from the side of the basin by small water courses, deposits of foreset beds on deltas, deposits of fine sediments in more distal zones, with localized phenomena of plastic deformation in a badly stabilized sequence and at an elevated rate of sedimentation. These non-dated deposits, located 4–6 m above present sea level, could correspond to an ancient lake or older lagunar systems that were later raised by isostatic readjustments.

4.3
GENERAL CHARACTERISTICS OF THE SEDIMENTS AT EKVEN

The sediments studied relate to three distinct contexts: 1) the context forming the substrate of the anthropogenic formations (paleo-environmental context), 2) recent deposits analyzed as a referential, and finally, 3) the anthropogenic formations themselves.

4.3.1
THE FACIES OF PALEO-ENVIRONMENTAL CONTEXT

These contain:
- fine lacustrine/lagoonal sands: Sample S28, Sample S29, Sample S30 (Stratigraphy 3);
- heterometric sediments of flow of solifluction and colluviation: Sample S8 (Stratigraphy 1);
- gravel-filled sands of fossil beaches: Sample S22, Sample S23, Sample S24, Sample S25 (Stratigraphy 2).

From the granulometric point of view, these are extensive dominant sandy sediments, rather well sorted for the lacustrine/lagoonal sands (Samples S28-S29-S30, Fig. 12a) and the beach deposits (Samples S22-S23-S24-S25, Fig. 12b), more rarely sandy-silt and poorly classified (solifluction deposits, Sample S8, Fig. 12h). In these facies, the detrital mineral component constitutes the almost-totality of the sediment (Fig. 11). The amounts in carbonates are low (2–8%, Fig. 15), which reflect the weak part played by the calcareous

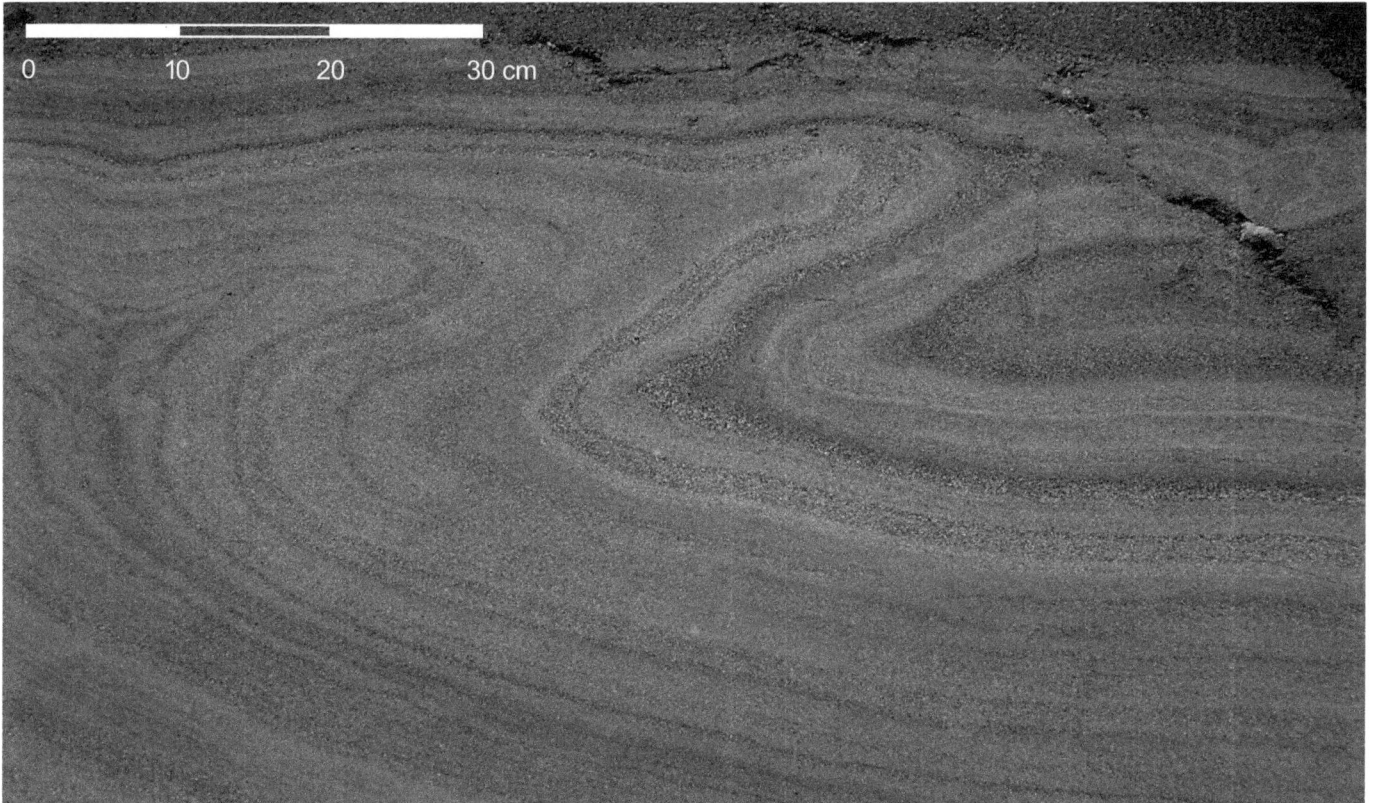

Photo 20. Stratigraphy 3; sequence of the Quaternary substrate: these lacustrine sands and silts with diapiric structures and structures of slump precede solifluction deposits that make up the substrate of Mounds EM VII, EM VIII, and EM XII. Photograph by Bernard Moulin.

Photo 21. Stratigraphy 3; sequence of the Quaternary substrate: these lacustrine sands and silts with diapiric structures and structures of slump precede solifluction deposits that make up the substrate of Mounds EM VII, EM VIII, and EM XII. Photograph by Bernard Moulin.

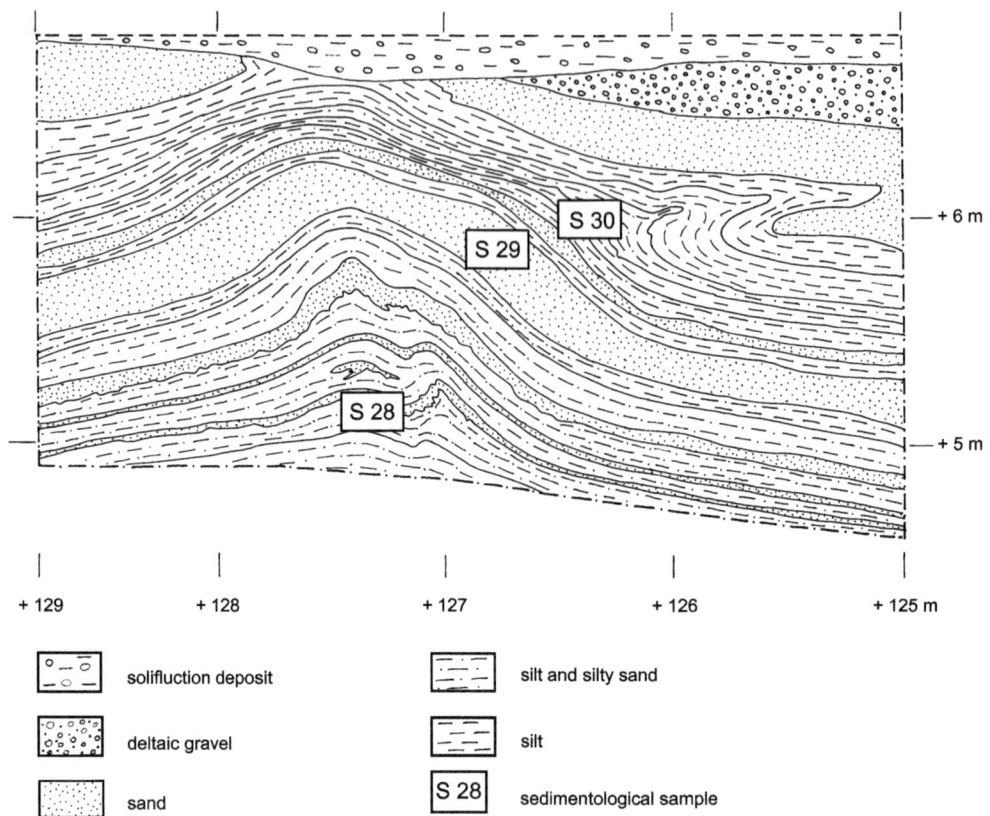

Figure 10. STRAT 3 cut: sedimentation of the Quaternary substrate: sandy and silty lacustrine/lagoonal deposits with diapiric structures, topped by deltaic gravels.

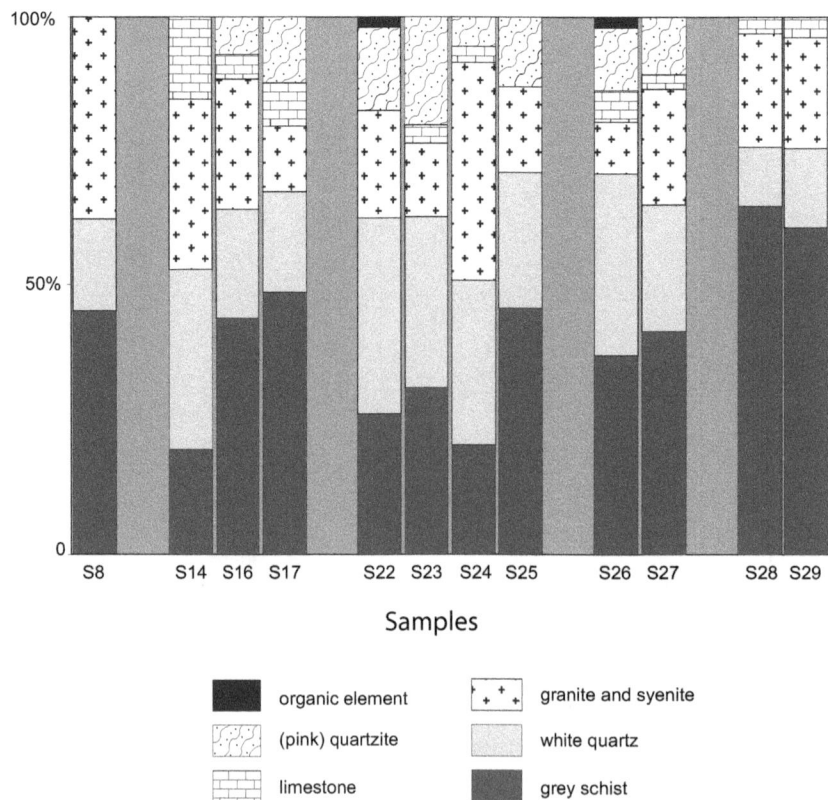

Figure 11. Composition of the coarse sand fraction (0,6 mm-2 mm) of detrital deposits: solifluction deposit (S8); modern sand from aeolian sorting (S14, S16, S17); coarse sand from fossile beaches (S22, S23, S24, S25); coarse sands from modern beach (S26, S27); Quaternary substrate: lagoonal/lacustrine sands (S28, S30).

Photo 22. View of the western part of Stratigraphy 1 during the course of elaborating it with successive 4-meter panels. Photograph by Bernard Moulin.

Photo 23. Detail of a fragment of stratigraphy rectified by elaborating the terrain at 1:10. To the left (behind the vertical measure), a column has been allotted (Samples S0 to S8) for screening sediments (8-20 mm fraction) and analyses in the laboratory. Photograph by Bernard Moulin.

elements in the detritus (Fig. 12): the calcareous component always remains lower than 4% in the coarse sand fractions. The gray schist, preponderant (60–65% of the coarse sand fraction) in the deposits of the ancient substrate (lacustrine sands with angular grains or only slightly rolled), do not constitute more than 45% of the coarse sand fraction of the solifluction deposits. They become clearly more abundant (20–45%) in the sands of the marine beach (sands with rolled grains), which show a distinct enrichment in quartz grains (30–35%), more resistant (Fig. 11).

4.3.2
MODERN FACIES OF REFERENCE

These facies contain:
- recent beach sand (Sample S26, Sample S27);
- aeolian sands coming from the vicinity of the beach (Sample S14, Sample S16, Sample S17).

The facies of the marine beach can present a large range of granulometric facies: fine to coarse sands, gravels and pebbles in a sandy matrix, the consequence of rapid change in hydrodynamic conditions linked to storms. Two facies have been analyzed: Sample S26 is a medium sand (averaging 300 μm), Sample S27 is a coarse sand (averaging 1 mm); the granulometric curves, strongly righted, indicate a good sorting of the particles (Fig. 12d).

During storms, the winds, principally those from the south and southeast, can displace the fine littoral sediments over short distances; the particles thus displaced can then take a non-negligible part in the mineral detrital component of the sediments recovered episodically by those fine layers of aeolian deposits: the humiferous soils of the present tundra located in the vicinity of the marine beach, like the fossil anthropogenic accumulations, can, by this process, incorporate sandy detrital fractions. Certain fine sandy intercalations observed in Stratigraphy 2 (STRAT 2, stratigraphic sequence VII) seem to result from this process. We have acquired three samples from littoral sands displaced by the wind during storms. Sample S14 was accumulated, in one day, in a low-lipped container placed on the ground at the foot of the erosion front; Sample S17 comes from an aeolian selection uphill from the present beach and was carried out after the seasonal snow melt; Sample S16 was collected on a rise of the erosion front, 2.5 m above the level of upper edge of the beach.

From the granulometric point of view, these sediments are of well sorted sands, with cumulative adjusted curve: medium sand for Sample S14 and Sample S16 (averaging 300 μm), coarse sand for Sample S17 (averaging 1 mm) (Fig. 12c).

The petrography of the coarse sand fractions of the mineral detrital sediments (Fig. 11) shows that it is possible to differentiate several assortments according to their provenance. The sediments of terrigenous detrital contribution from the substrate (solifluction deposits: Sample S8; lacustrine deposits: Sample S28 and Sample S29) are characterized by the absence of pink quartzite, in general always present and easily identifiable in the deposits of marine origin (beach sand or altering aeolian from the latter). These terrigenous deposits are characterized by the large predominance of schists.

4.3.3
ANTHROPOGENIC FACIES

The anthropogenic strata clearly differ from most of the natural strata by their abundance of organic matter, whatever the granulometric fraction taken into consideration (Figures 15bis and 16). This high content of fine organic matter, comparable to that encountered in the occupation strata of littoral lacustrine sites, gives them their characteristic dark (brown to gray) color. The contents in organic matter of the lower fractions to 0.5 mm make up between 12 and 34%, with a mode around 18–20% (Fig. 17b), while these contents remain low (0 to 4%) in the natural sediments analyzed. The values in "humus" are higher than those of anthropogenic organic sediments of littoral lacustrine sites (Fig. 16). The pH values are particularly low in the organic sediments of anthropic origin (Fig. 17c). These anthropogenic sediments are characterized, besides, by a poor sorting of the particles: the cumulative granulometric curves (Figures 12e, 12f, and 12g) are less adjusted than those of the natural facies with a mineral dominant, with the exception of colluvial/solifluction facies. The median of the different samples analyzed falls between 200 and 400 μm. The different facies are studied in more detail in the following chapter.

4.3.4
DISCRIMINATION OF SEDIMENTS
FROM DIFFERENT CONTEXTS

The median/sorting index diagram (Fig. 14) permits distinguishing three groups of sediments: 1) the well screened facies (sorting index below 0.5), in which the median is divided over a large spectrum (100 μm to 1 mm), corresponding to deposits of hydrodynamic and aeolian sorting over a short distance; 2) facies rather poorly sorted (sorting index falling between 0.5 and 1) and at median rather homogeneous, corresponding to the anthropogenic facies, and 3) the solifluction deposits of the substrate, which are characterized by their very poor sorting (sorting index above 1) and a rather low value for the median (100 μm).

The content in carbonates/content in organic matter diagram (Fig. 15) permits distinguishing two groups of sediments: 1) the natural detrital mineral facies, with a content in organic matter lower than 5% and whose content in carbonates varies from 2% to 12%, and 2) the anthropogenic facies, with a content in organic matter falling between 12% and 35% and, with exceptions, a content in carbonates less than 5%; we note that two samples of anthropogenic sediments present exceptional contents of 10% carbonates, which has to be correlated with the presence of carbonate concretions whose genesis cannot be defined in the scope of this work.

The content in organic matter/sorting index diagram (Fig. 15bis) allow to distinguish easily the natural facies from the anthropogenic facies. In the anthropogenic facies, the strata with fine dominant matrix are distinguished from middens with coarse elements by a more elevated sorting index, indicating a poorer sorting of the particles; among the natural strata, the solifluction deposits are clearly individualized.

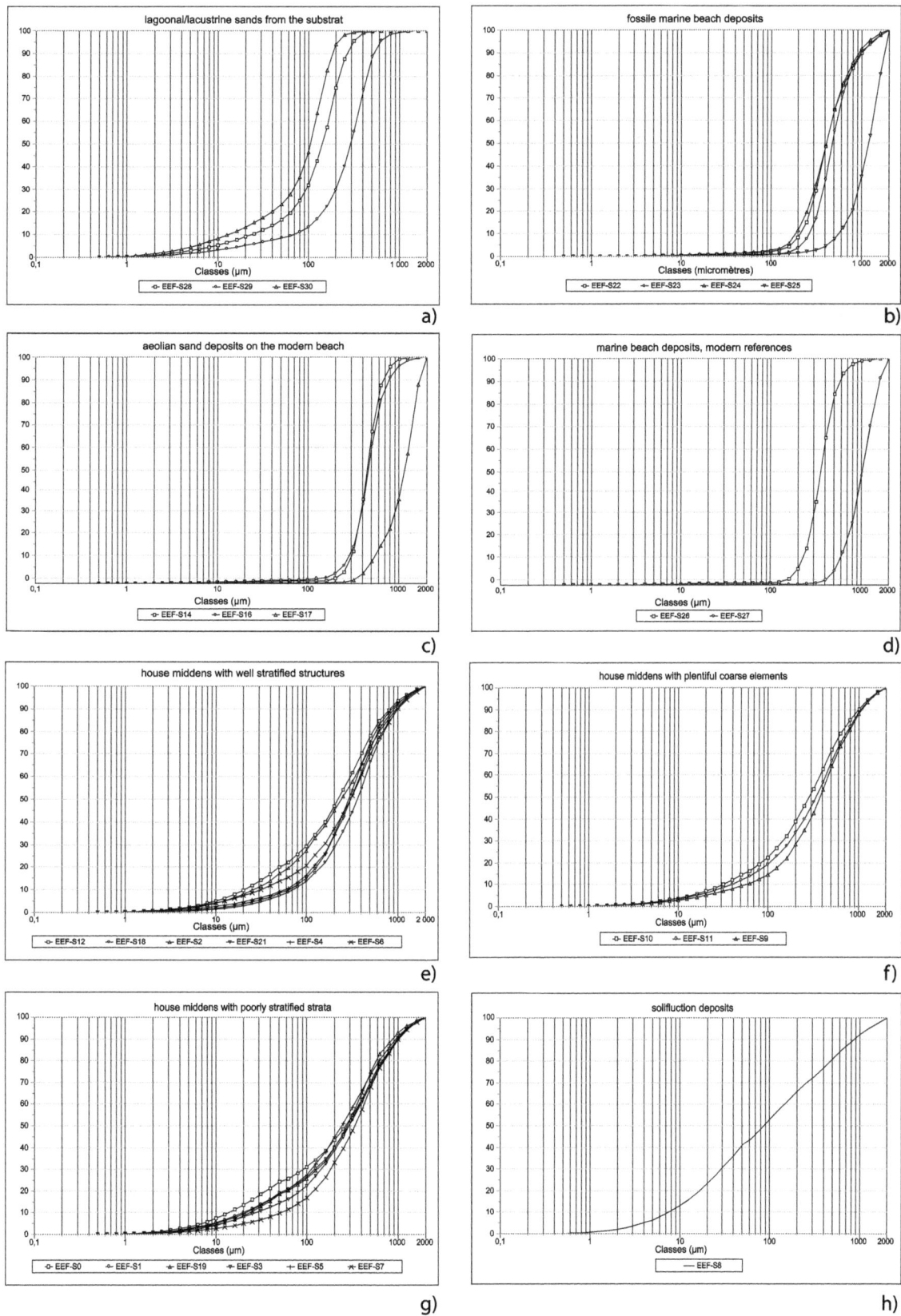

Ekven, erosion front. Cumulative granulometric curves from sediment < 2 mm

Figure 12. Cumulative granulometric curves of sediments lower than 2 mm; a) Quaternary substrate, lagoonal/lacustrine sands of the STRAT 3 profile presented in Figure 10; b) coarse sands from fossil beaches; c) modern sands from aeolian sorting; d) coarse sands from modern beaches; e) middens with a well stratified internal structure; f) middens with abundant coarse elements; g) middens with a poorly stratified internal structure; h) solifluction deposits.

4.4
ANTHROPOGENIC SEDIMENTATION: CHARACTERIZATION OF THE DIFFERENT SEDIMENTARY ETHNOFACIES

The sediments, such as we observe today, present characters that reflect their conditions of sedimentation (primary or secondary deposits, partial or total changing at the time of collapse of the architectural structures), but also their conditions of post sedimentary evolution and transformation (alterations, pedological evolutions, various washings and impregnations, etc.). It is not possible in this study, based on a single field trip, to answer all the questions that are posed on these different points. We will try rather to establish a first "typology" of facies encountered on the basis of observations and descriptions of terrain with different focuses, and of analyses that have been carried out on a restricted selection of samples.

4.4.1
SEDIMENTS: COMPOSITIONAL ELEMENTS

On the scale of fine observation of the sediment, it is possible to distinguish the matrix (characterized by its texture, its color, its cohesion, its relative abundance in relation to the more coarse constituents) from the compositional elements of the sediment. Certain characteristics also concern the type of organization existing between the elements and the matrix, the degree of homogeneity of the sediment, the localized presence of certain impregnations, as for example those of vivianite, a phosphate of hydrated iron, which give a characteristic tint (sky blue to more vivid blue) at the surface of certain bones or in the anfractuosities of the sediment.

4.4.2
COMPONENTS OF THE COARSE FRACTIONS

At the time of detailed analysis of the 8 mm–2 cm fraction, carried out on an initial volume of 3 dm^3 of sediment, we recognized the following types of compositional elements:
- rock fragments;
- shavings of driftwood;
- fragments of local wood (dwarf willow and ericaceae);
- mollusk shells (whole or fragmented);
- whole or fragmented bones;
- walrus ivory;
- ceramic fragments;
- strips of baleen;
- feathers.

The results of detailed analyses carried out on 16 samples of anthropogenic sediments are presented in two diagrams: a histogram showing the number of compositional elements in the 8–20 mm fraction by unit of volume (1 dm^3) (Fig. 19a) and a histogram presenting the respective percentages of the constituents themselves (Fig. 19b). These two diagrams show the great variability of composition of one sample from another, regarding the absolute numbers of elements per unit of volume as well as their respective percentages; the number of wood chips varies from very weak values (4 to 7 in Samples S0 and S20) to 153 to 170 in Samples S6 and S12. The mollusk shells are represented by 46 fragments in Sample S10 (which represents, besides, the maximum of osseous remains–87 units) while these elements do not exceed 5 units in the other samples.

These data show that the composition of the sediment is the manifest reflection of a localized activity or of a function of the spatial area considered: the area of craft activity (working of driftwood, for example) for Samples S6 and S12, the area of food refuse for Sample S10. The osseous remains and the mollusk shells coming from the screening have were identified by A. Savinetsky.

4.4.3
COMPOSITION OF SAND FRACTIONS

Observations with the binocular microscope and the detailed analysis of the 0.6–2 mm fraction permitted specifying the composition of those coarse sandy fractions and deducting from them certain characteristics of the sediments. A component detrital mineral (which can include angular elements and rolled elements), made up of rock grains of diverse nature (calcareous, gray schist, quartz, quartzite, various crystalline rocks), contrasts with an organic component, in general largely preponderant in the anthropogenic sediments, and within which the following classes have been differentiated: various plant debris (herbaceous, Sphagnum, Lycopodium remains), fibrous elements (hair, debris from feathers, strips of baleen), bone fragments (burned and not burned), charcoal, organic agglomerates (organic agglomerates are aggregates of plant remains cemented by a fine organic matrix; cohesion can then be assisted by the presence of phosphates), carbonized agglomerates (carbonized agglomerates are carbonized particles of a generally bubbly texture; these can correspond to the residue from the combustion of fat or other organic materials), more rarely fly pupae and fish scales. Whitish concretions are attached to these elements; these, very likely of carbonated nature since the two samples from the organic strata that enclose them are characterized by a content more elevated in carbonates than the other organic strata, are probably of post-sedimentary origin (recarbonation of ashes?).

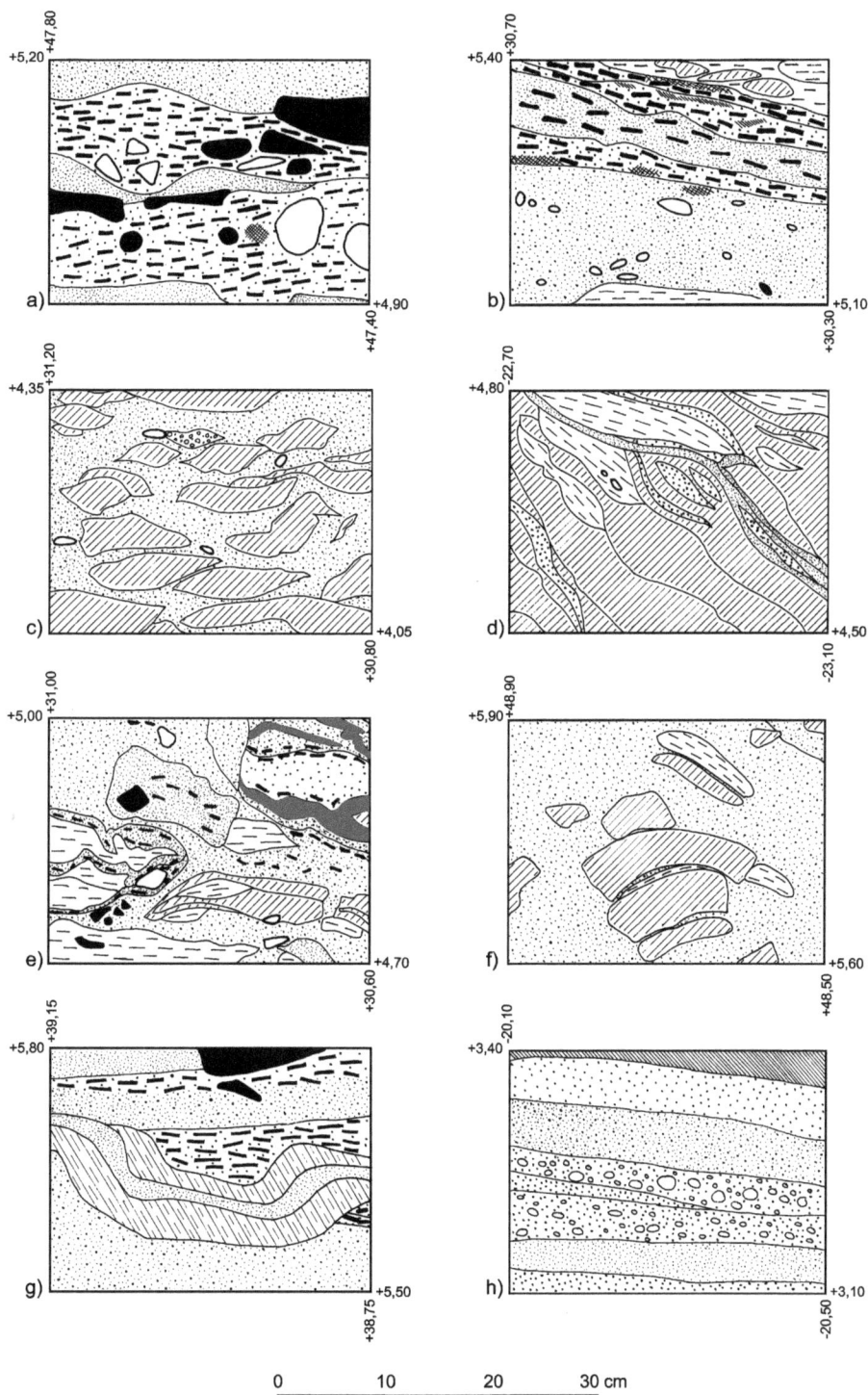

0   10   20   30 cm

house midden with well stratified coarse elements	gravels	silt and silty sand	baleen
house midden with silty brown matrix	roof and wall accumulation of sod and peat clumps	carboniceous strata	hair
organic strata with sandy matrix	strata indurated by impregnation of greases	stone, wood, ceramic	
sand	humic natural strata	bone	

Figure 13. Details of cultural sediments. Horizontally aligned marginal figures indicate metric distance above sea level; vertically aligned figures indicate distance nominally east or west of the zero grid axis (see Figure 6 "datum origin") : a) alternation of house midden with stratified elements and house midden with fine matrix (+ 47.40 to + 47.80) ; b) superposition of four house midden strata with stratified elements above a midden stratum with fine matrix (+ 30.30 to + 30.70); c) facing of sod chunks overlapping with a fine interstitial matrix (+ 30.80 to + 31.20); d) roofing of joined sod and peat clumps in oblique accumulation, with silty passages from the natural substrate that were pulled up with the clumps (- 23.10 to – 22.70); e) bed of old building material with heterogeneous elements (+ 30.60 to + 31.00); f) bed of old building elements with homogeneous elements likely from the collapse and restoration of roofing with peat (+ 45.50 to + 48.90); g) accumulation in depression of two sediment strata with beige-orange tint, indurated by greases (base of a food cache, + 38.75 to + 39.15); h) alternation of sandy-gravely strata and sandy humic strata, from sequences in which natural deposits predominate (Strat 2, stratigraphic sequences III and V, - 20.50 to - 20,10).

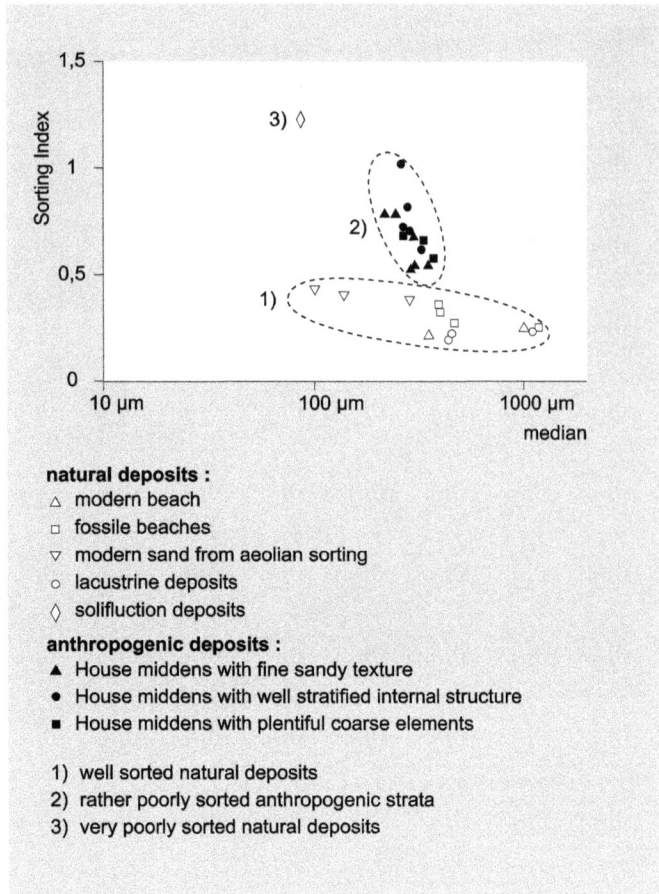

natural deposits :
△ modern beach
□ fossile beaches
▽ modern sand from aeolian sorting
○ lacustrine deposits
◇ solifluction deposits

anthropogenic deposits :
▲ House middens with fine sandy texture
● House middens with well stratified internal structure
■ House middens with plentiful coarse elements

1) well sorted natural deposits
2) rather poorly sorted anthropogenic strata
3) very poorly sorted natural deposits

Figure 14. Granulometry of sediments : median / sorting index diagram.

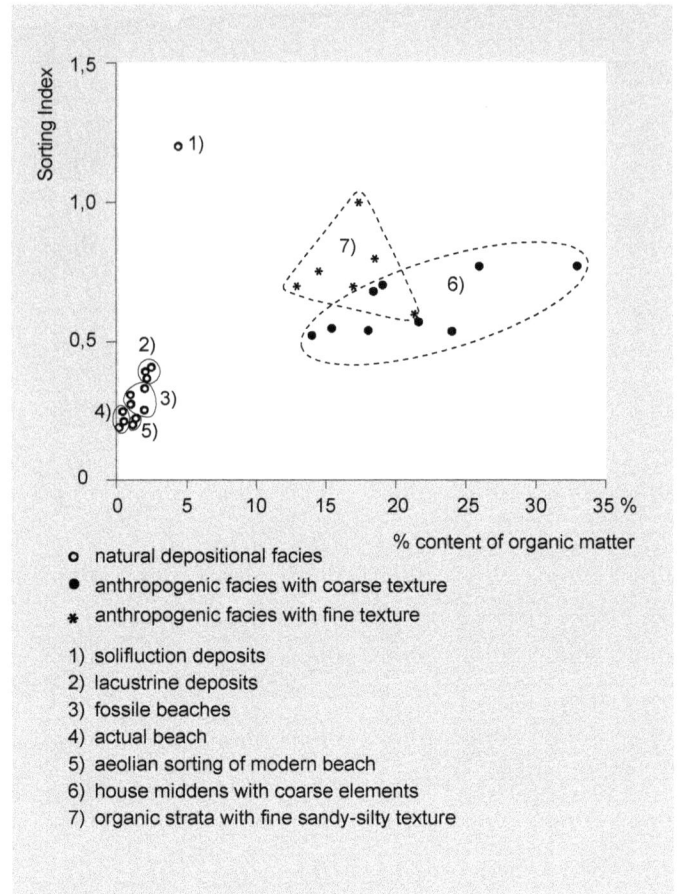

○ natural depositional facies
● anthropogenic facies with coarse texture
∗ anthropogenic facies with fine texture

1) solifluction deposits
2) lacustrine deposits
3) fossile beaches
4) actual beach
5) aeolian sorting of modern beach
6) house middens with coarse elements
7) organic strata with fine sandy-silty texture

Figure 15bis. Diagram of content of organic matter / sorting index.

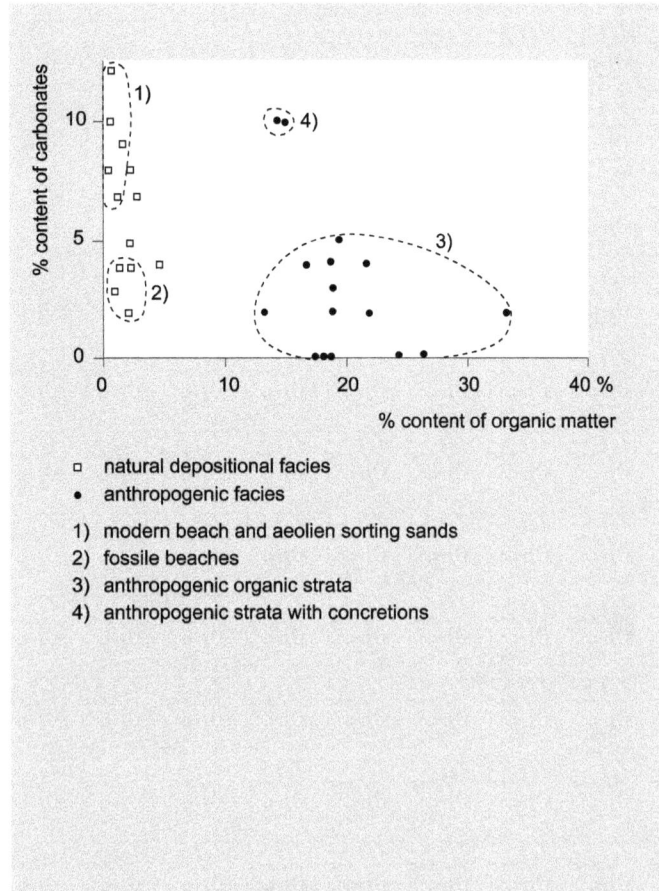

□ natural depositional facies
● anthropogenic facies

1) modern beach and aeolien sorting sands
2) fossile beaches
3) anthropogenic organic strata
4) anthropogenic strata with concretions

Figure 15. Diagram of content of organic matter / content of carbonates ; comparison between the anthropogenic strata and the natural strata.

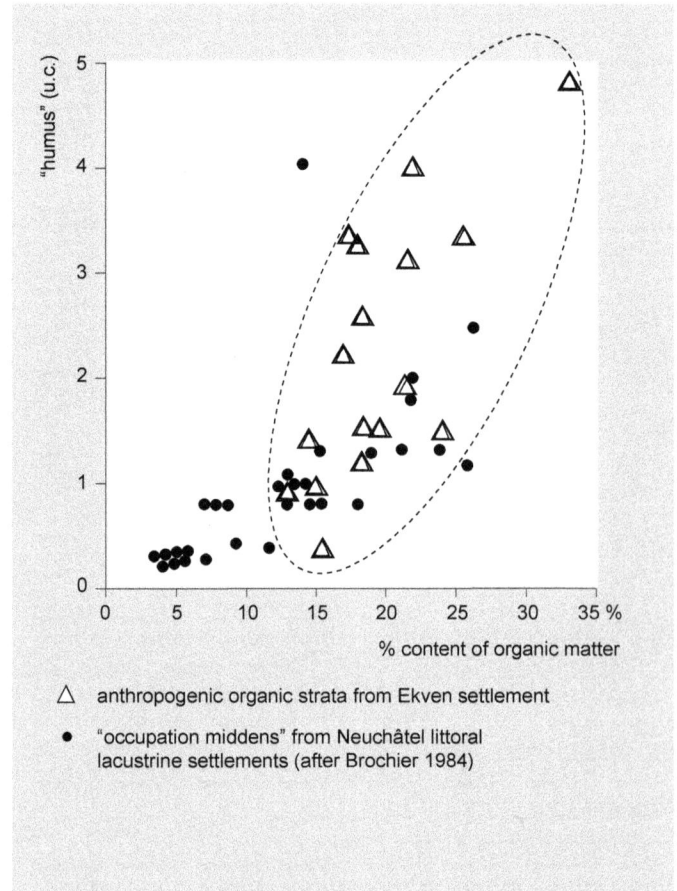

△ anthropogenic organic strata from Ekven settlement

● "occupation middens" from Neuchâtel littoral lacustrine settlements (after Brochier 1984)

Figure 16. Diagram of content of organic matter / "humus" ; comparison between the anthropogenic strata of the Ekven erosional front and the organic strata (house middens) of the littoral lacustrine sites of Lake Neuchâtel.

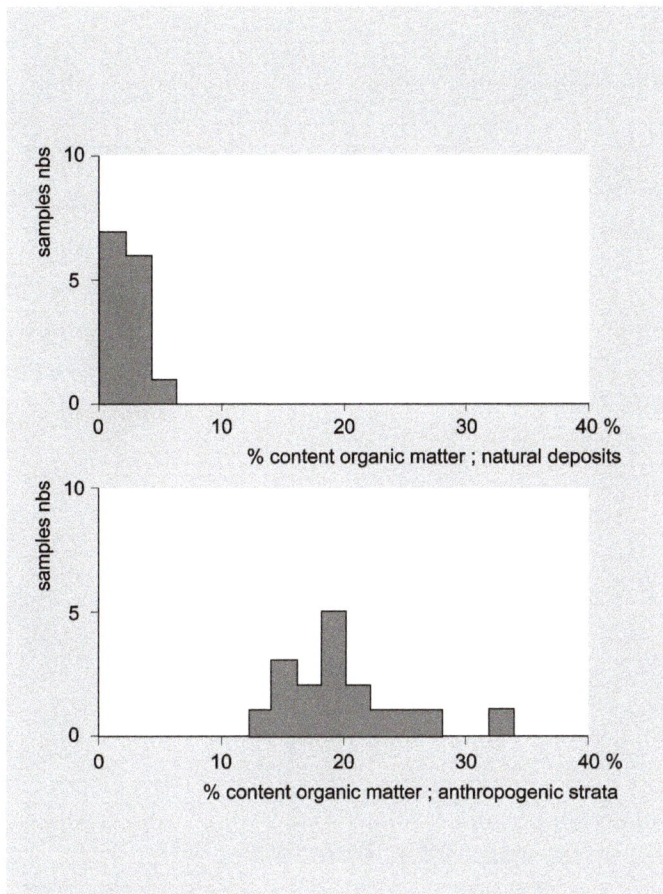

Figure 17a. Comparison between the natural strata and the anthropogenic strata: values of "humus" (scale based on color units).

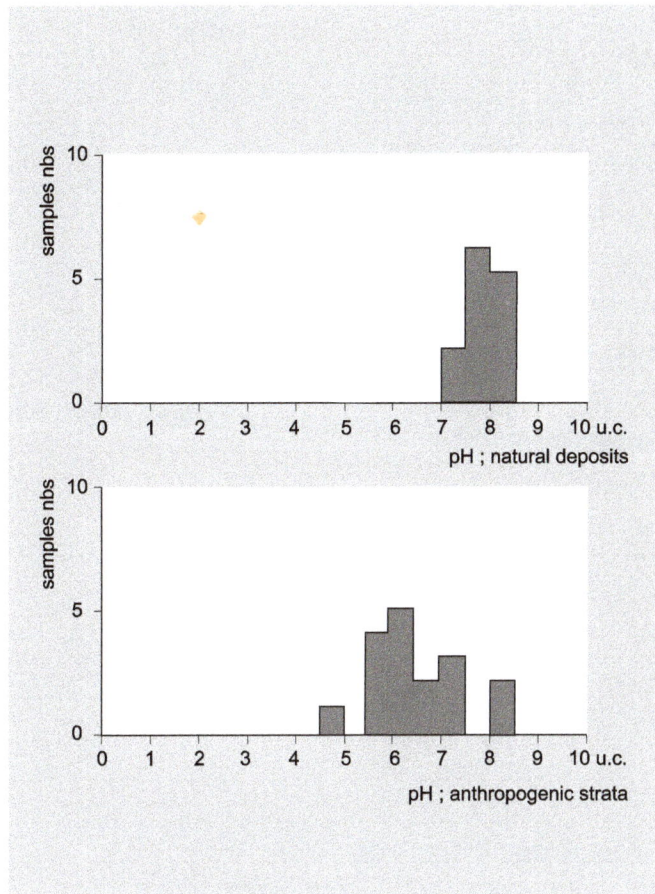

Figure 17c. Comparison between the natural strata and the anthropogenic strata: pH values.

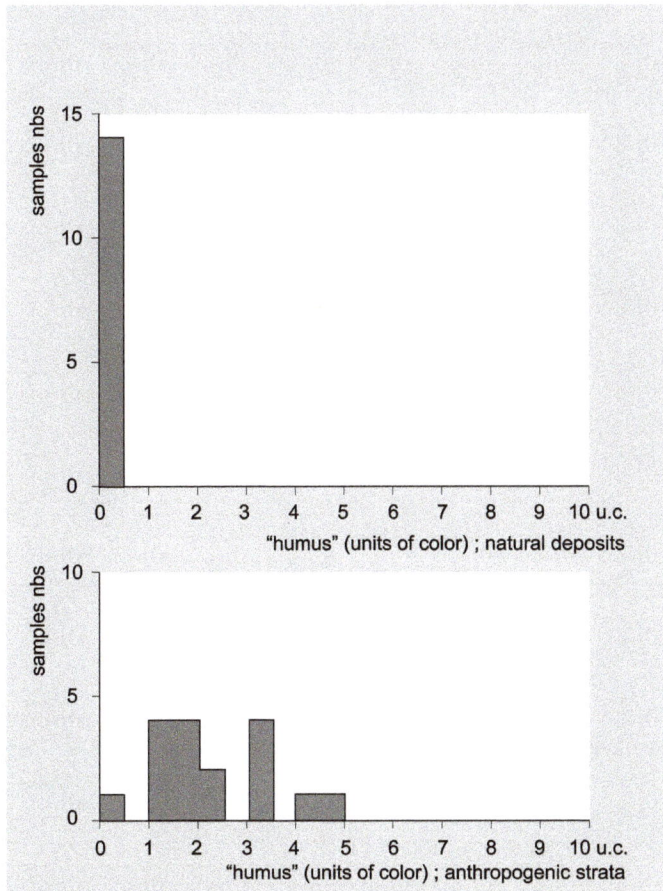

Figure 17b. Comparison between the natural strata and the anthropogenic strata: content of organic matters.

	Middens with stratified elements						Middens with fine texture						Middens with coarse texture		
	S2	S4	S6	S12	S18	S21	S0	S1	S3	S5	S7	S19	S9	S10	S11
WOOD SHAVINGS	40	25	153	175	50	15	4	23	40	43	27	18	47	70	51
WOOD FRAGMENTS	3	5	0	1	3	0	1	1	4	1	0	0	2	1	2
ERICACEOUS PLANTS	0	0	5	0	0	0	0	0	0	0	0	0	0	3	0
BALEEN	12	18	1	12	4	3	0	0	2	11	0	0	5	3	6
FEATHERS	0	25	0	2	8	0	0	0	0	2	0	0	1	0	0
BONES	12	12	11	8	21	10	2	0	14	16	5	32	30	87	13
WALRUS IVORY	0	1	0	1	1	0	0	0	0	0	0	0	1	1	0
MOLLUSK SHELLS	0	1	5	2	3	0	0	3	1	5	0	1	0	46	4
CERAMICS	0	0	0	0	0	0	0	0	3	6	1	8	1	0	3
ROCK FRAGMENTS	36	13	36	24	58	39	50	29	32	39	125	110	30	57	30

Figure 18. Component of the coarse fraction (8 mm – 2 cm) of anthropogenic strata by unit of volume (1 dm³).

4.4.4.
ANTHROPOGENIC SEDIMENTS, CHARACTER AND FIRST INTERPRETATION CONCERNING THE "SEDIMENTARY ETHNOFACIES"

In this chapter we will take into account the descriptive data of the terrain (in particular the elaborated detail at 1: 5), as well as the data of analysis, those concerning detailed analysis of the elements of the 8–20 mm class and those resulting from analyses in the laboratory. We immediately note the heterogeneity of the number of analyses by type of facies, certain sediments being in effect inappropriate for analyses of this type because of their too great heterogeneity (facies of dismantling) or their impossibility to go through a screen (facies indurated by fat), while others, like the house middens, are much better adapted to these analyses. We will try to discern the principal criteria that permit differentiating these types, the structural context in which they are found, and their macroscopic and physico-chemical characteristics (organization of the elements among themselves, structure, texture, composition).

4.4.4.1
House middens with well stratified internal structure

Context:

Occupation base; subhorizontal strata of several meters extension; upper and lower limits distinct; in association with stone slabs.

Example:

(+ 47.40 to + 47.80) (Fig. 13a)
(+ 30.30 to + 30.70) (Fig. 13b)

Macroscopic facies:

Brown organic deposits, generally of little thickness (5 to 10 cm), rather compact, with plentiful debris (wood shavings, baleen fragments, hair, feathers) lying flat, often tangled, more abundant than the matrix.

Samples:

S2, S4, S6, S12, S18, S21.

Results of analysis:

The contents in organic matter are elevated in the fine fractions (14.5 to 33%); The component of the fractions 8–20 mm varies strongly from one sample to another: Sample S4 is characterized by a great quantity of baleen, feathers (25), and fibrous elements (hair) while Samples S6 and S12 show a large predominance of wood chips (153 and 170) (Fig. 19a).

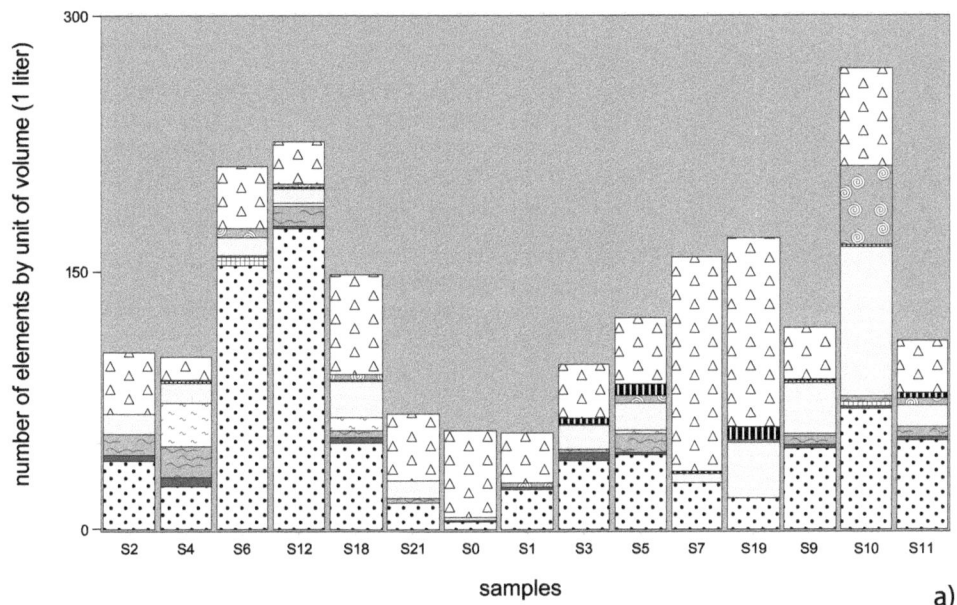

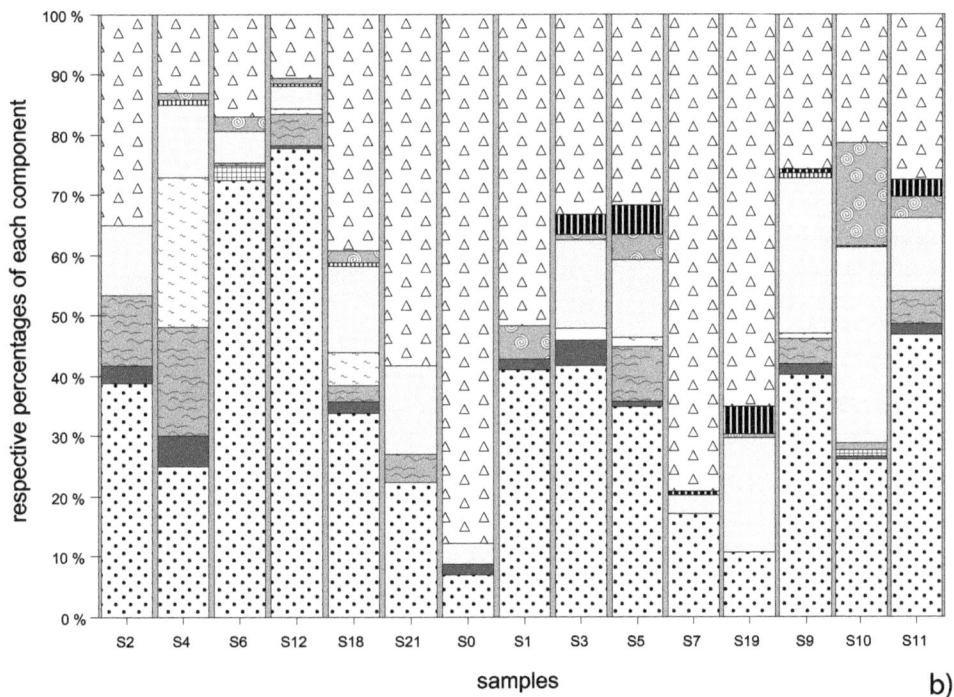

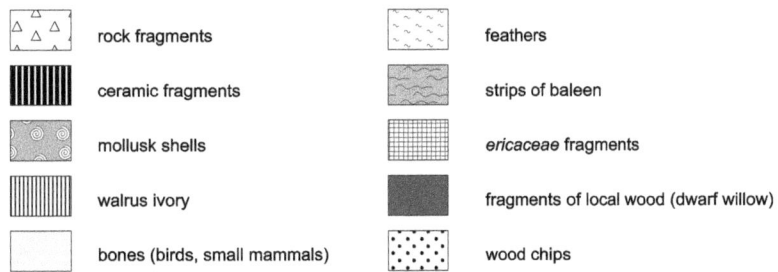

Figure 19. Components of the coarse fractions (8 mm – 2 cm) of anthropogenic strata: a) number of compositional elements by unit of volume (1 dm³); b) respective percentage of each constituent.

Zoarchaeological remains of faunal (identified by A. Savinetsky, bones/minimum number of individuals):

Sample S2
Pusa hispida (ringed seal)–3/1
Mammals indet.–5

Sample S4
Alopex lagopus (Arctic fox)–1
Aethia cristatella (crested auklet)–1
Aves indet.–feathers

Sample S6
Ursidae–1
Philacte canagica (emperor goose)–1

Sample S12
Canis familiaris (dog)–1
Rissa tridactyla (black-legged kittiwake)–1
Larus sp. (gull sp.)–1

Sample S18
Mammals indet.–17
Aves indet.–2

Sample S21
Calidris alpina (variable sandpiper)–1

Interpretation:

These are occupation middens; they can correspond on the one hand to beds (sleeping areas with a large concentration of fur remains) and on the other to areas of activities such as wood working (e.g., middens with great density of wood shavings).

4.4.2.2
House middens with fine sandy texture and poorly stratified internal structure

Context:

Sometimes in relation to middens with internally well stratified structure between which they are interbedded, but also in thicker and badly differentiated strata. The example of the well stratified sequence at + 47 to + 48 meters shows a succession of four strata of sandy midden, between which are bedded three middens with well stratified structure. These are subhorizontal strata of several meters' extension, with well defined upper and lower limits.

Example:

(+ 47.40 to + 47.80) (Fig. 13a)
(+ 30.30 to + 30.70) (Fig. 13b)

Macroscopic facies:

Organic-rich deposits, with a fine sandy to sandy-silty texture, brown to grayish, where the matrix largely predominates among the components.

Samples:

S0, S1, S3, S5, S7, S19.

Results of analysis:

The contents in organic matter of the fine fractions fall between 13 and 21%; The 8–20mm fractions are sometimes relatively poor in organic elements (7 in 57 for Sample S0, 59 in 170 for Sample S19) within this case a predominance of rock fragments (Fig. 19a);

Zoarchaeological remains of faunal (identified by A. Savinetsky, bones/minimum number of individuals):

Sample S1
Odobenus rosmarus (walrus)–1
Pusa hispida (ringed seal)–3/1
Canis familiaris (dog)–1
Mammal indet.–1

Sample S5
Pisces–2 scales
Odobenus rosmarus (walrus)–1
Pusa hispida (ringed seal)–5/1
Canis familiaris (dog)–1
Mammals indet.–3
Somateria sp. (eider)–2
Uria sp. (guillemot)–2/1
Aves indet.–1

Sample S7
Pusa hispida (ringed)–3/1
Mammals indet.–2

Sample S19
Pusa hispida (ringed seal)–1
Canis familiaris (dog)–2/1
Lepus timidus (hare sp.)–1
Mammals indet.–28
Somateria spectabilis (royal eider)–1

Interpretation:

When they are interbedded between the middens with well stratified internal structure, these facies may reflect activities such as trampling which have resulted in accumulation of particles of sandy texture. One can also see mineral sediments deposited during intentional cleaning of semisubterranean dwellings as permafrost thaws slightly in summer.

4.4.4.3
Poorly stratified house middens with plentiful coarse elements

Context:

Strata of rather weak lateral extension (50 cm), sometimes rather thick (25 cm).

Example:

(+ 46.20, + 46.90)

Macroscopic facies:

Organic sediments where cultural debris (shavings of wood, bone) predominates over the matrix; structure of deposits sometimes lenticular, localized areas of weak lateral extension, upper and lower boundaries rather diffuse.

Samples:

S9, S10, S11.

Results of analysis:

The detailed analysis of the 8–20 mm fraction of Sample S10 is characterized by a great quantity of bone (87 fragments), and fragments of mollusk shells (46 fragments) in the 8 mm to 2 cm fraction (Fig. 19a). Analysis by A. Savinetsky shows the important part played by the bird remains in the fauna of Sample S10 (62 remains in 87 bones, 6 species identified, 13 individuals minimum). Sample S9 is characterized also by the importance of the bird bones in the faunal remains (18 remains in a total of 30).

Zoarchaeological remains of faunal (identified by A. Savinetsky, bones/minimum number of individuals):

Sample S9
Odobenus rosmarus (walrus)–1
Pusa hispida (ringed seal)–3/1
Mammals indet.–3
Clangula hyemalis (oldsquaw)–3/1
Somateria fischeri (spectacled eider)–2/1
Phalaropus fulicarius (red phalarope)–1
Aves indet.–12
Pisces–1

Sample S10
Odobenus rosmarus (walrus)–1
Pusa hispida (ringed seal)–4/1
Mammals indet.–23
Phalacrocorax pelagicus (pelagic cormorant)–1
Calidris ptilocnemis (rock sandpiper)–1
Stercorarius parasiticus (parasitic jaeger)–1
Rissa tridactyla (black-legged kittiwake)–1
Aethia cristatella (crested auklet)–21/6
Aethia pusilla (least auklet)–16/3
Aves indet.–21
Mytilus–1
Serripes–2
Mya–1
Brachyopoda–1

Sample S11
Pusa hispida (ringed seal)–1
Alopex lagopus (Arctic fox)–1
Mammals indet.–11

Interpretation:

This facies may correspond to areas of refuse (e.g., from cooking).

4.4.4.4
Accumulations of sod and peat clumps

Context:

Sides of houses (example a), roofing of the horizontal architectural superstructure (example b), sometimes isolated clumps without direct relation to any architectural elements.

Example:

example a (+ 30.80 / + 31.20) (Fig. 13c)
example b (- 22.70 / - 23.10) (Fig. 13d)

Macroscopic facies:

Deposits characterized by the accumulation of sod or peat chunks, and of a more or less abundant interstitial sediment. The chunks can be accumulated flat, alternately or not, or diagonally. They can be of rather irregular form, sometimes diamond-shaped or lenticular, sometimes clearly rectangular. They can have regular or irregular edges. They vary from clumps of sod to brown peat sediment with fine texture, in some cases still showing in cross-section the original aerial part of the vegetation, the roots, and the top of the mineral substrate (olive-greenish silty sand from the solifluction deposit). The matrix is generally sandy, rather organic, and grayish. These strata can have a great lateral extension (12 m recognized for the roofing of feature EM XIV) (Strat. 2) and constitute important vertical accumulations (up to a meter in thickness).

Interpretation:

These facies correspond to materials of walls and roof, the insulating elements that sometimes act as supports, the latter commonly being whale bones (mandibles and ribs) or beams of driftwood. Small isolated accumulations may be remains of initial stages of house dismantlement.

4.4.4.5
Strata with a Heterogeneous Component

Context:

Poorly defined strata, diffuse lateral limits, often rather thick (up to 50 to 60 cm).

Example:

example a (+ 48.50 / + 48.90) (Fig. 13f)
example b (+ 30.60 / + 31.00) (Fig. 13e)

Macroscopic facies:

This facies is characterized by its heterogeneous internal structure composed of a matrix sediment generally of silty-sand with gray-brownish tint, which includes fragments of other sediments in the form of clods, lenticular accumulations, and small angular or shapeless masses; these inclusions can be of a single sort (the most frequent), or be fragments of peat or sod clumps that sometimes include scraps of olive-greenish mineral substrate (example a, Fig. 13f), or be of several different natures (example b, Fig. 13e): brownish, carbonaceous black, or silty clayey olive-greenish peat clods.

Sample:

S20.

Zoarchaeological remains of faunal (identified by A. Savinetsky, bones / minimum number of individuals):

Sample S20
Pusa hispida (ringed seal)–2 / 1
Mammals indet.–13

Interpretation:

This can be interpreted as a facies of disintegration as in example a, involving deterioration of abandoned architectural features (collapse of walls and roofs, with elements progressively incorporated into the matrix); in this case it is necessary to envisage a rather long development, the duration of which it would be interesting to estimate. This heterogeneous facies can also have its origin in voluntary activity, as is probably the case for example b: throwing out sediment while digging the pit or leveling the space above the early features, refurbishing for installation of new features in the house, etc.

4.4.4.6
Indurated strata

Context:

Localized zones of weak extension connected with small pit features (see below: features C of Strat 1 and feature 4 of Strat 2). Another case represented (meters + 34 / + 36) shows one such subhorizontal indurated stratum in a lateral extension of 2.5 m. The upper part, with a thickness of about 20 cm, presents a clearly ribboned aspect; the induration affects equally the underlying sediment, which presents the aspect of a stratified midden.

example:

(+ 38.75 to + 39.15) = features C (Fig. 13g).

macroscopic facies:

Beige-orange sediment with colored deposits giving it a ribboned aspect, rather fine texture, very hard, sometimes the feature of the sediment a little granular, strong "rancid" smell.

Interpretation:

These strata are very likely hardened by impregnation with grease. Indurated strata of relatively small size form the base of features interpreted as food caches.

4.4.4.7
Strata with carbonized elements

Context:

Localized strata in features of variable dimensions (10 cm to several meters).

Example:

(+ 44.20 to + 44.80) (Plate 1b).

Macroscopic facies:

Several facies containing carbon have been encountered: a) lenticular deposits of sediment with a brown-beige, sandy-silty matrix enclosing charcoal and fragments of burned and calcined bone (dimensions of the elements: 0.5 to 2 cm); b) carbonized agglomerates or "clinkers," small, irregular and very hard chunks with the appearance of tar, black; c) fine gray-brown sandy sediment containing burned and calcined bone of large size (15 to 25 cm).

Sample:

S15.

Interpretation:

These are facies connected with hearth structures and hearth cleaning. A more detailed study of these facies would necessitate a more comprehensive study of that type of structure, particularly regarding spatial analysis and planimetric distribution of the different facies.

NOTE:

Full-size versions of the plates on the following pages (to pg. 54),
originally presented as A3 foldouts, are available to download from
www.barpublishing.com/additional-downloads.html

Facies of natural deposits

modern humus

humic silts and silty sands

fine and medium sands

coarse and gravely sands

gravels

solifluction and colluvium deposits

**Facies of anthropogenic strata
(sedimentary ethnofacies)**

house middens with plentiful coarse elements

organic strata with fine sandy-silty texture

roof and wall accumulation of sod and peat clumps

strata with elements of dismantling

strata indurated by impregnation of grease

carbonized and indurated agglomerates

reddened silty strata

carbonaceous strata

empty space / space filled with ice

structural and architectural elements
(whale bones and skulls, driftwood, stone)

architectural and structural elements
(whale bones and skulls, driftwood, stones)

strata included in identified structure

bone and wood charcoal

bone

baleen

sedimentological samples

details in fig. 13

Plate 1. STRAT 1 (mound EM XI); a) Natural sedimentary facies, including solifluction deposits, marine beach deposits, natural humic deposits. Ethnofacies, consisting of horizontally stratified and fine-textured house deposits, heterogeneous strata with old building materials, reddened strata, strata indurated by grease, dark-brown carbonized and indurated agglomerates, sod clumps from walls and roofs. b) Boundaries of sedimentary units, placement of architectural features, location of sedimentological samples.

+ 51   + 50   + 49   + 48   + 47   + 46   + 45   + 44   + 43   + 42   + 41   + 40   + 3

7 m

6 m

5 m

4 m

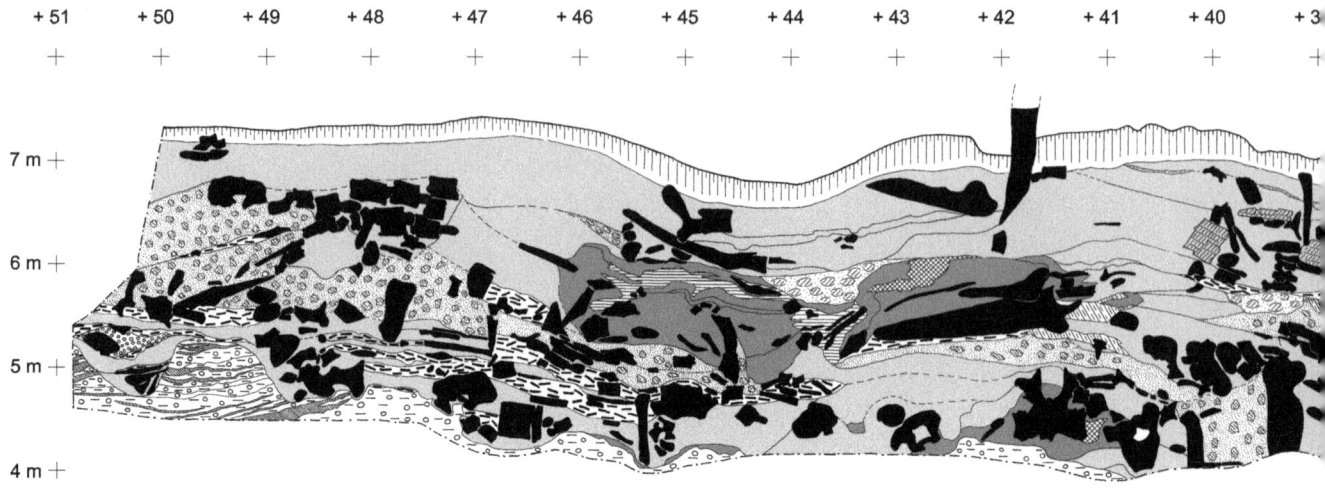

+ 51   + 50   + 49   + 48   + 47   + 46   + 45   + 44   + 43   + 42   + 41   + 40   + 3

+ 51   + 50   + 49   + 48   + 47   + 46   + 45   + 44   + 43   + 42   + 41   + 40   + 3

7 m

6 m

5 m

4 m

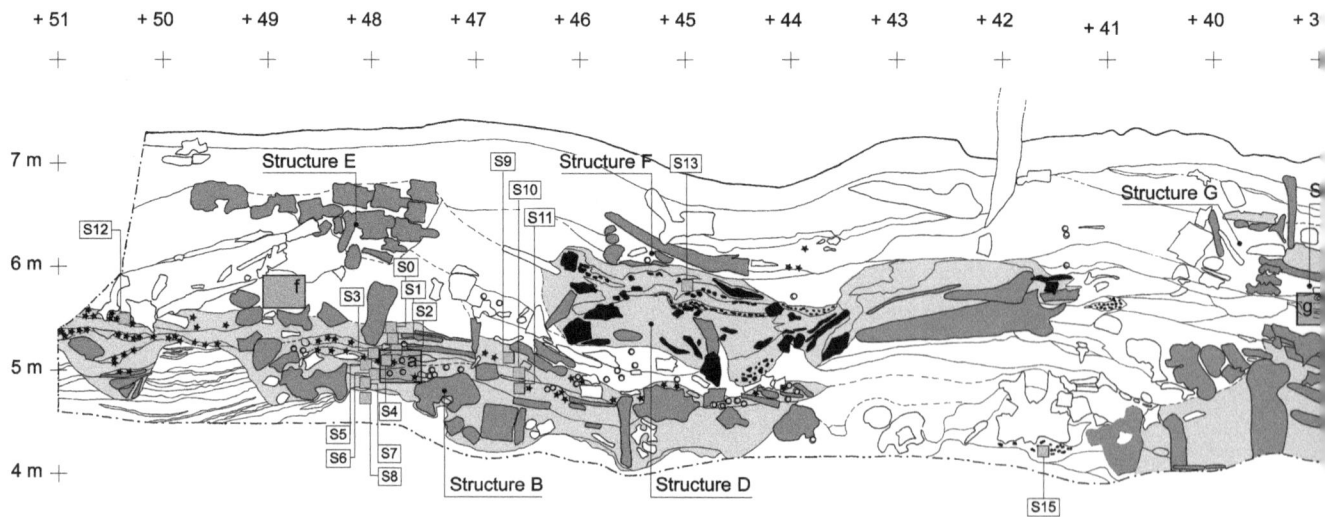

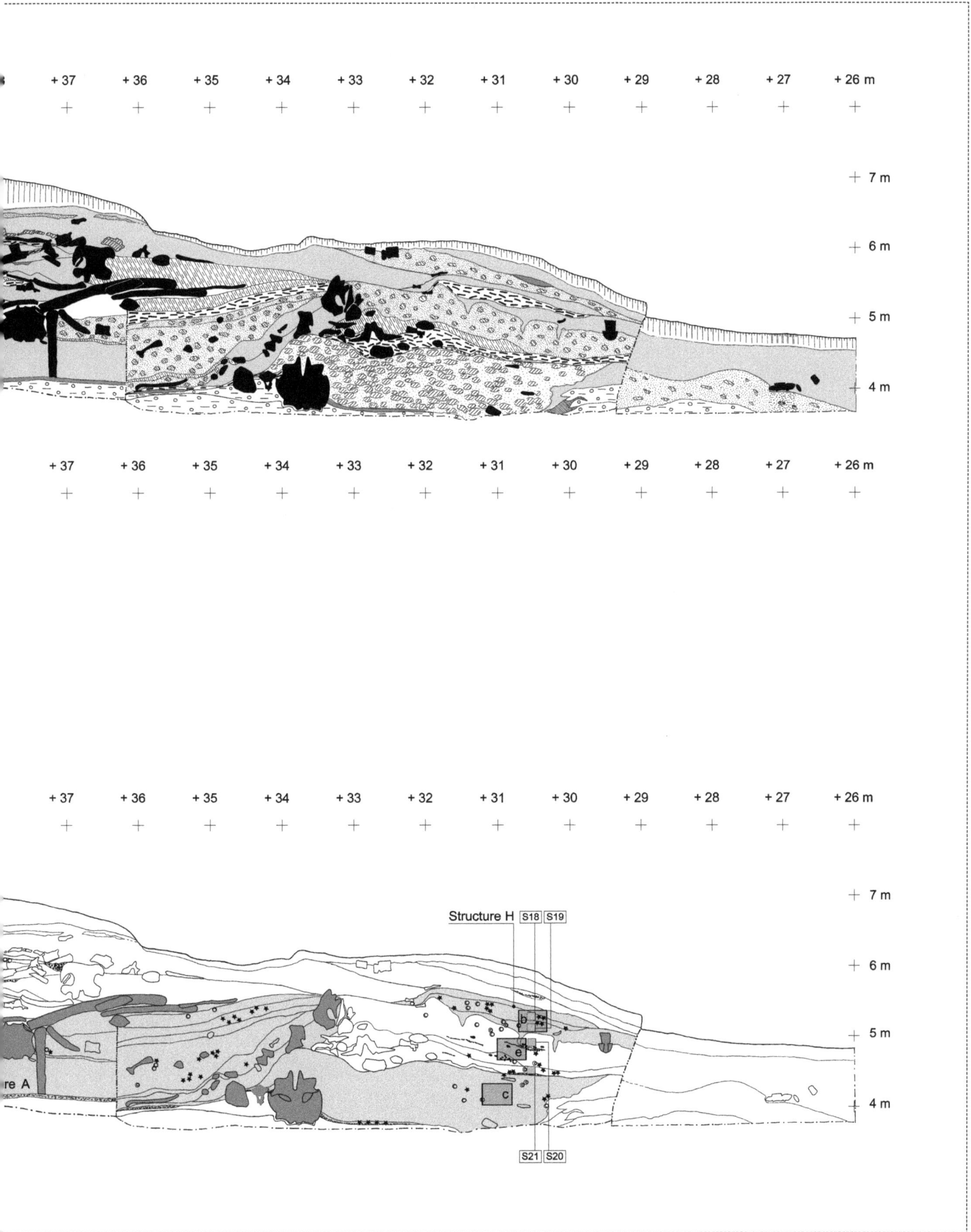

+ 37   + 36   + 35   + 34   + 33   + 32   + 31   + 30   + 29   + 28   + 27   + 26 m
+   +   +   +   +   +   +   +   +   +   +   +

+ 7 m

+ 6 m

+ 5 m

+ 4 m

+ 37   + 36   + 35   + 34   + 33   + 32   + 31   + 30   + 29   + 28   + 27   + 26 m
+   +   +   +   +   +   +   +   +   +   +   +

+ 37   + 36   + 35   + 34   + 33   + 32   + 31   + 30   + 29   + 28   + 27   + 26 m
+   +   +   +   +   +   +   +   +   +   +   +

+ 7 m

+ 6 m

Structure H   S18   S19

+ 5 m

e A   + 4 m

S21   S20

Plates 2a and 4a

▨	stone
⬗	wood
⬠	bone
〜	leather
●	C14 samples
x	chrono-typological artifact

Plates 2b and 4b

▬	long-bone and rib
◫	vertebra
◪	scapula
◗	mandible
◭	skull

Artifacts:

●	worked walrus ivory
▲	lithic artifact
◻	wood artifact
▽	reindeer antler artifact
○	bone artifact
✳	baleen artifact
☆	ceramic

Plate 2. STRAT 1 (mound EM XII); a) Architectural elements, including material such as driftwood, stone, whale bone. Location of radiocarbon samples. b) Whale bones, indicating whether skull, extended bones (long-bones and ribs), vertebra, scapula. Artifacts plotted three-dimensionally, indicating material (worked wood, ceramics, antler of reindeer and cervidae, walrus ivory, lithics). Small miscellaneous elements such as bones and baleen in sediments.

Plate 2a.

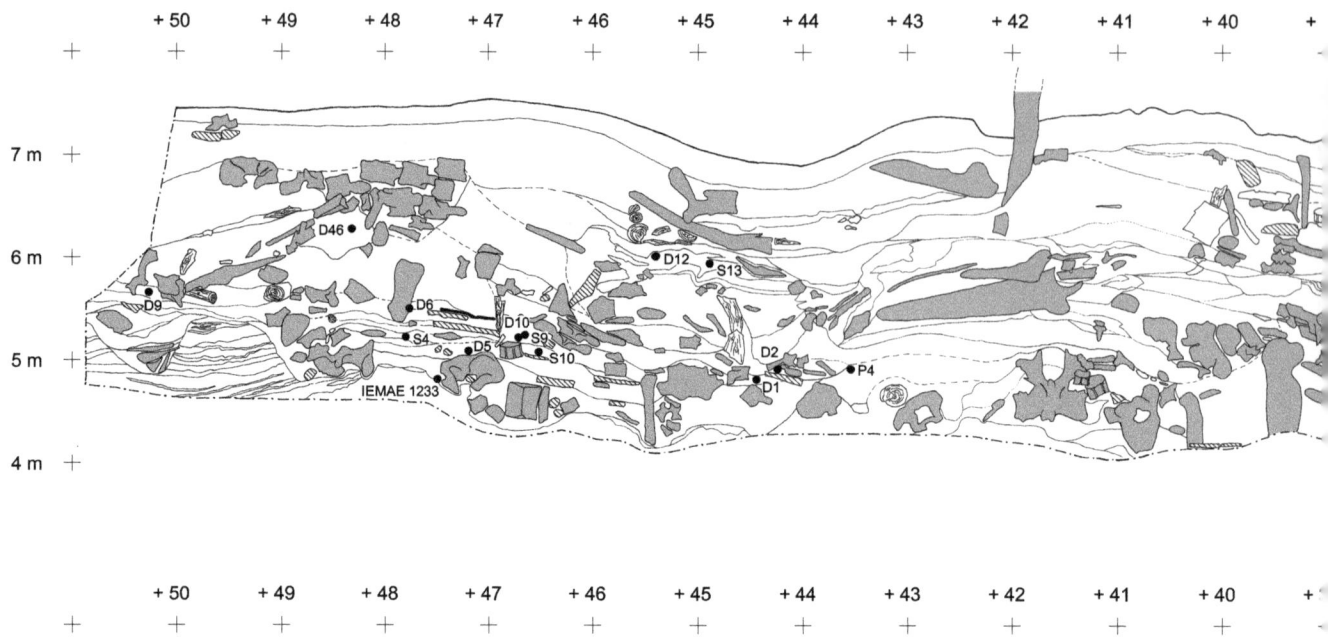

Plate 2b.

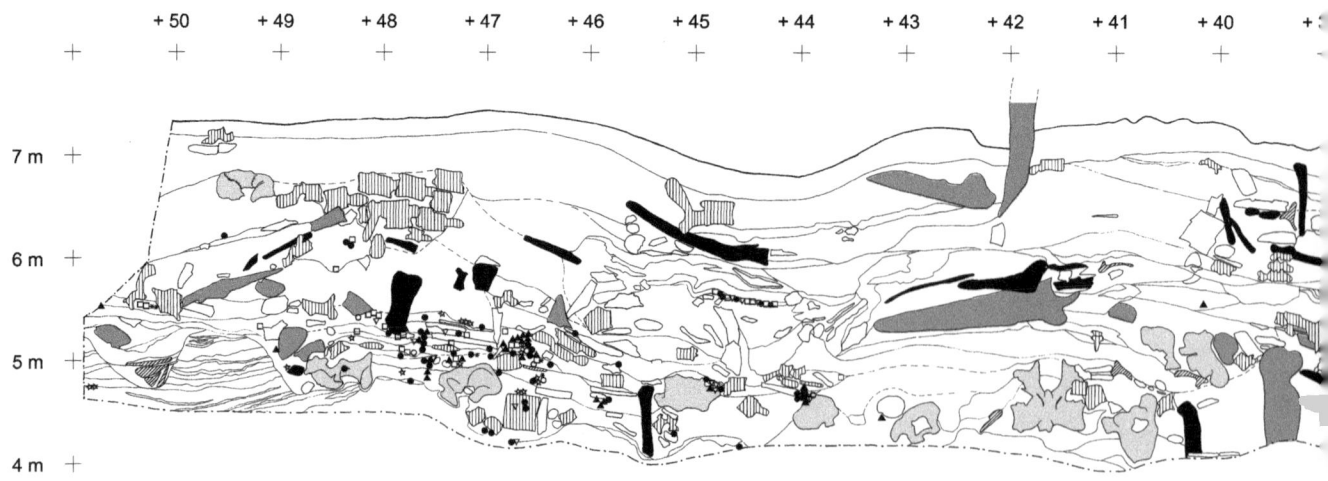

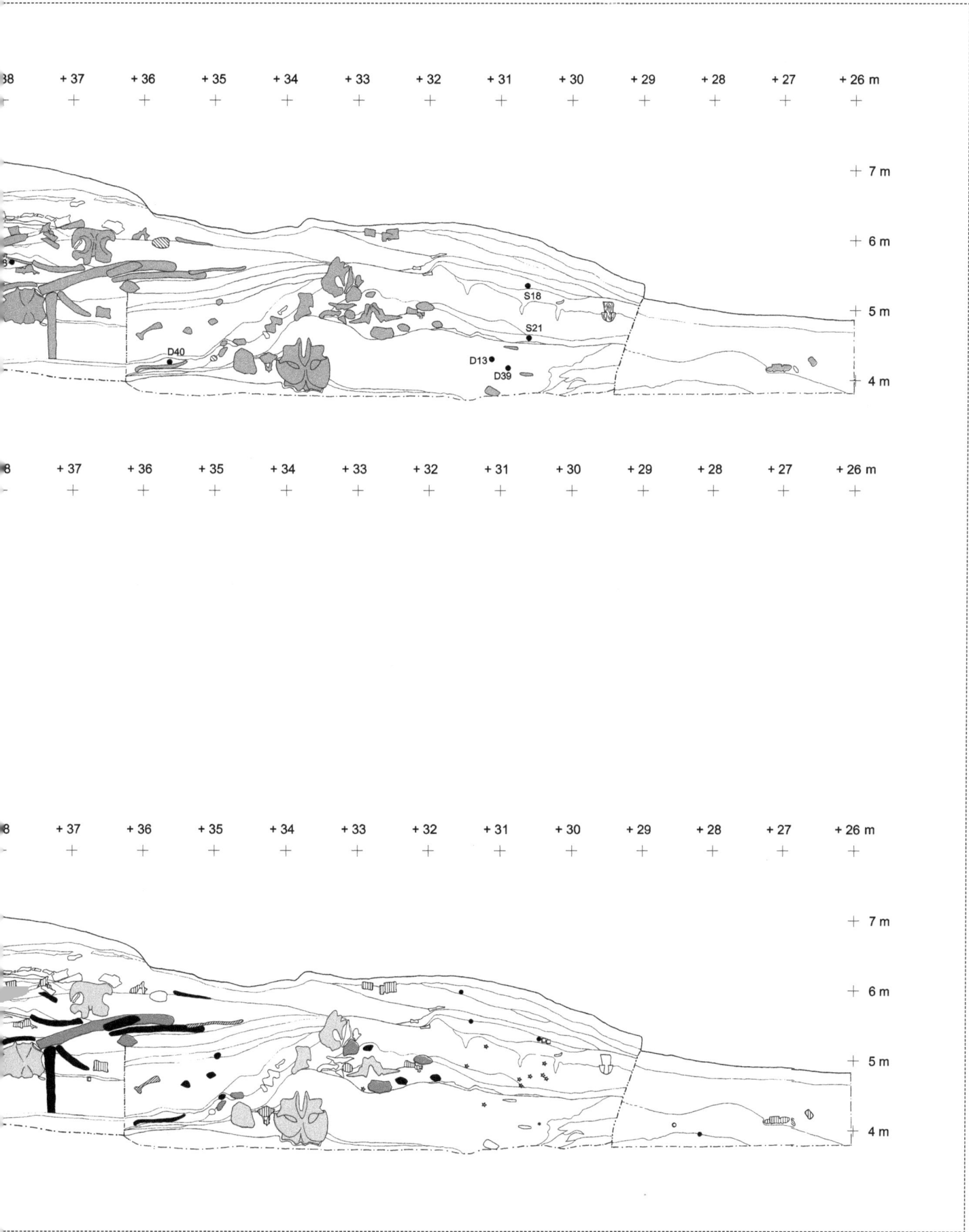

+ 37   + 36   + 35   + 34   + 33   + 32   + 31   + 30   + 29   + 28   + 27   + 26 m

+ 7 m

+ 6 m

+ 5 m

S18

S21

+ 4 m

D40

D13
D39

+ 37   + 36   + 35   + 34   + 33   + 32   + 31   + 30   + 29   + 28   + 27   + 26 m

+ 37   + 36   + 35   + 34   + 33   + 32   + 31   + 30   + 29   + 28   + 27   + 26 m

+ 7 m

+ 6 m

+ 5 m

+ 4 m

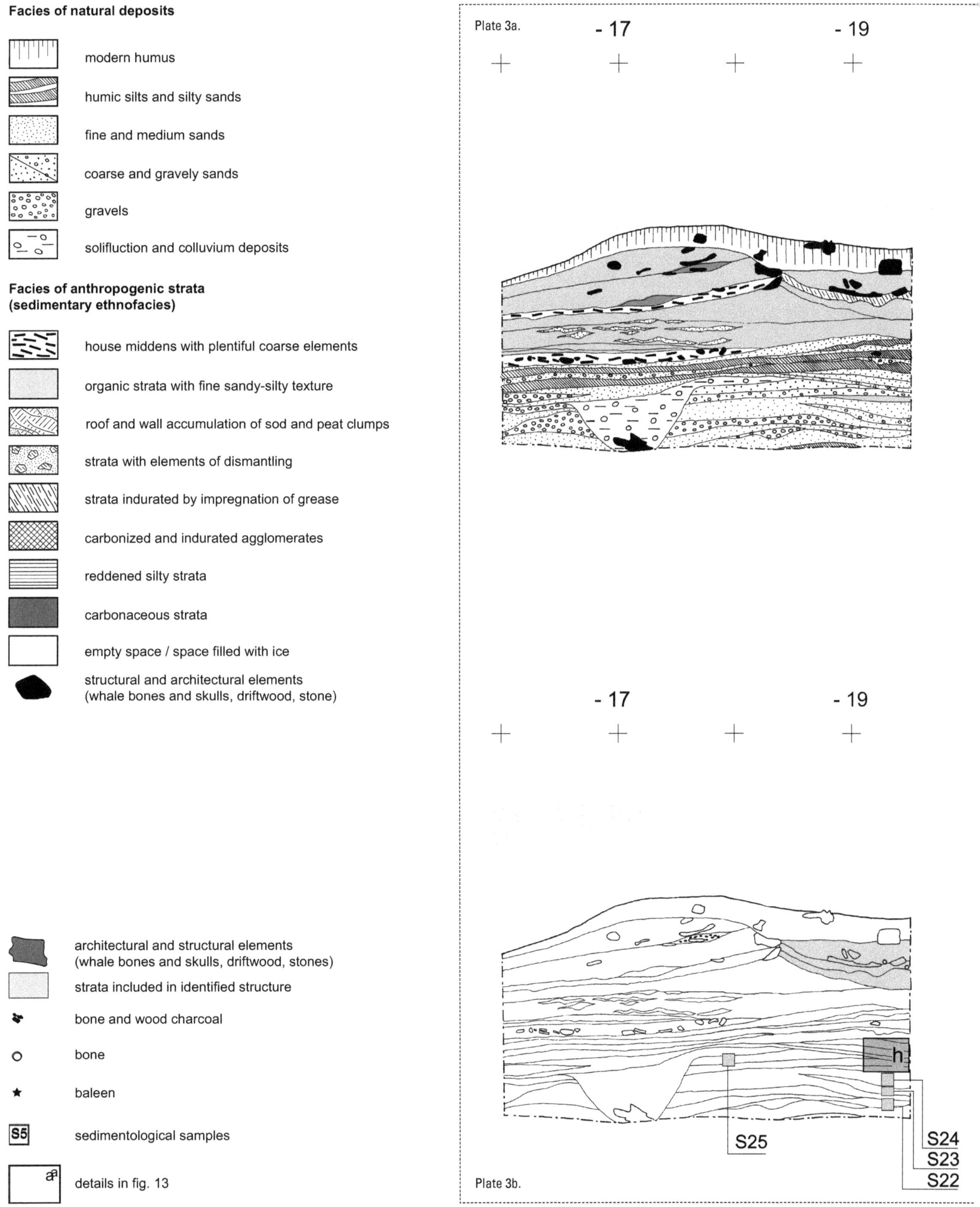

Facies of natural deposits

	modern humus
	humic silts and silty sands
	fine and medium sands
	coarse and gravely sands
	gravels
	solifluction and colluvium deposits

**Facies of anthropogenic strata
(sedimentary ethnofacies)**

	house middens with plentiful coarse elements
	organic strata with fine sandy-silty texture
	roof and wall accumulation of sod and peat clumps
	strata with elements of dismantling
	strata indurated by impregnation of grease
	carbonized and indurated agglomerates
	reddened silty strata
	carbonaceous strata
	empty space / space filled with ice
	structural and architectural elements (whale bones and skulls, driftwood, stone)

	architectural and structural elements (whale bones and skulls, driftwood, stones)
	strata included in identified structure
	bone and wood charcoal
O	bone
★	baleen
S5	sedimentological samples
a	details in fig. 13

Plate 3a.

- 17   - 19

- 17   - 19

Plate 3b.

S25   S24 S23 S22

Plate 3. STRAT 2 (mound EM XIV); a) Natural sedimentary facies, including solifluction deposits, marine beach deposits, natural humic deposits. Ethnofacies, consisting of horizontally stratified and fine-textured house deposits, heterogeneous strata with old building materials, reddened strata, strata indurated by grease, dark-brown carbonized and indurated agglomerates, sod clumps from walls and roofs. b) Boundaries of sedimentary units, placement of architectural features, location of sedimentological samples.

- 20

- 20

Structure 4

d

Structure 1

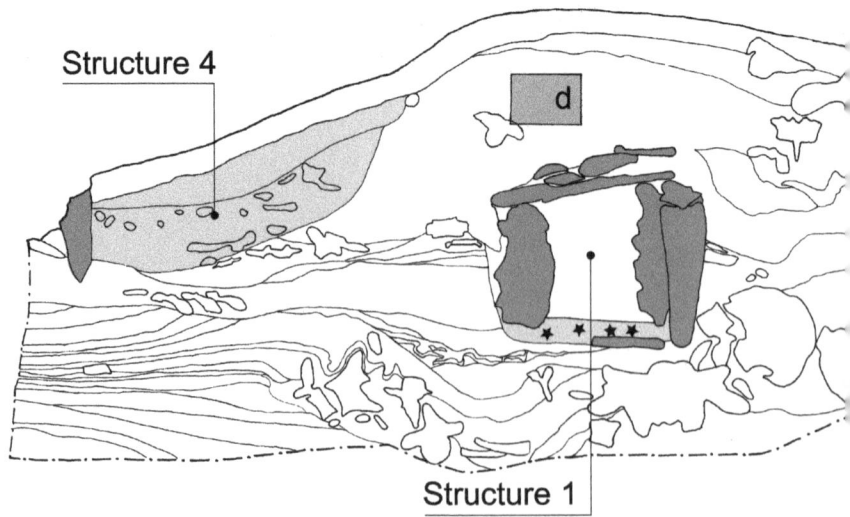

- 32 m

5 m

4 m

3 m

- 32 m

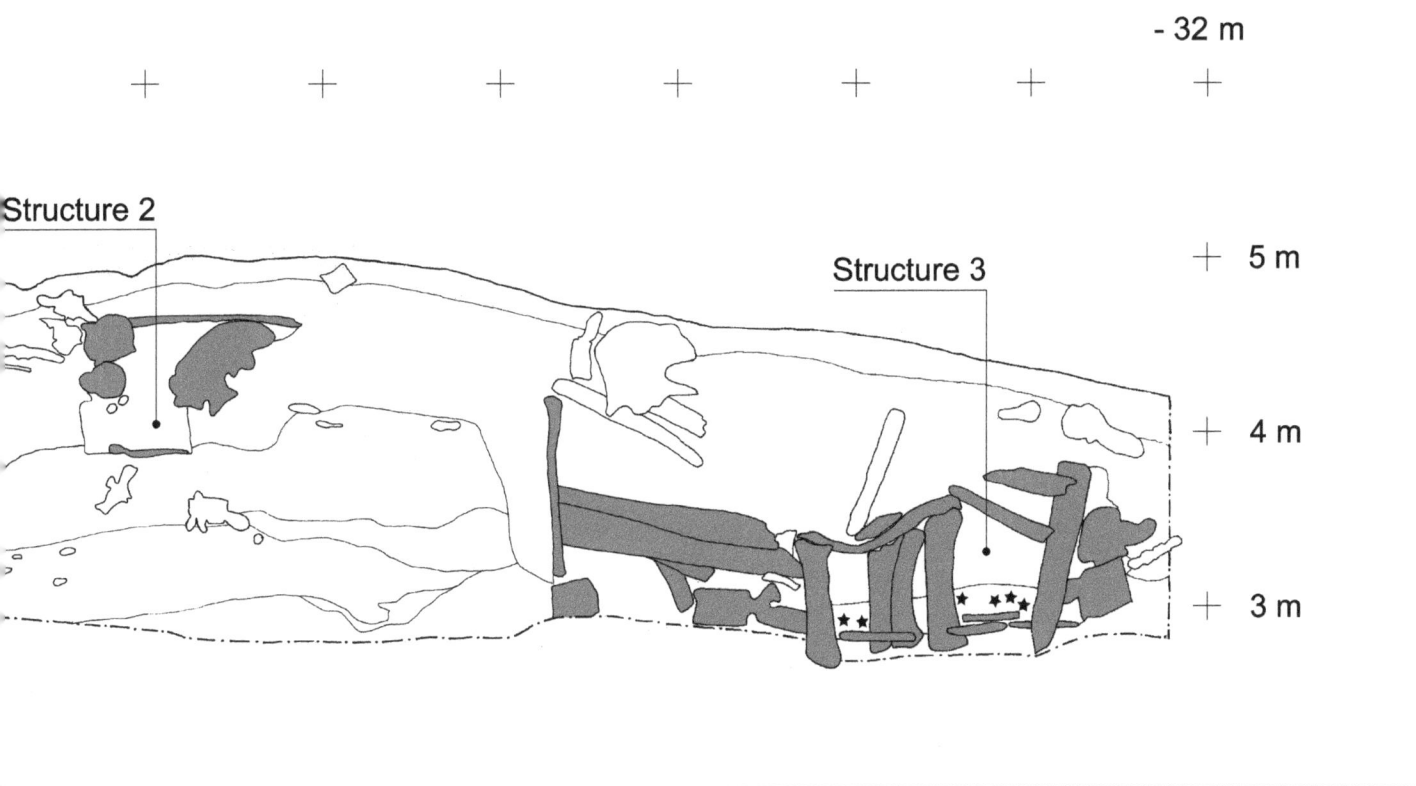

Structure 2

Structure 3

5 m

4 m

3 m

Plates 2a and 4a

- stone
- wood
- bone
- leather
- ● C14 samples
- x chrono-typological artifact

Plates 2b and 4b

- long-bone and rib
- vertebra
- scapula
- mandible
- skull

Artifacts:

- ● worked walrus ivory
- ▲ lithic artifact
- ▢ wood artifact
- ▽ reindeer antler artifact
- ○ bone artifact
- ＊ baleen artifact
- ☆ ceramic

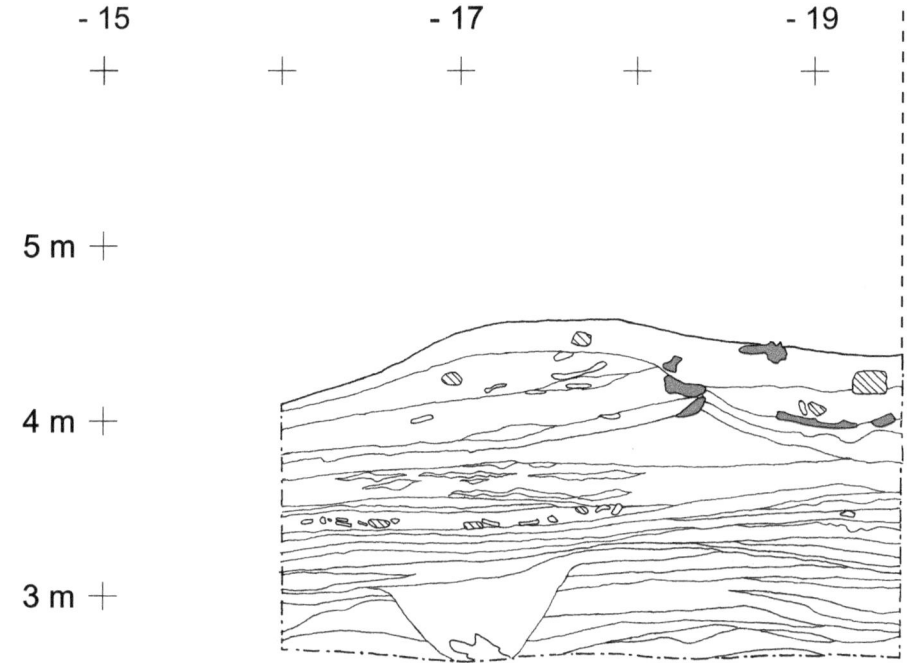

Plate 4a.

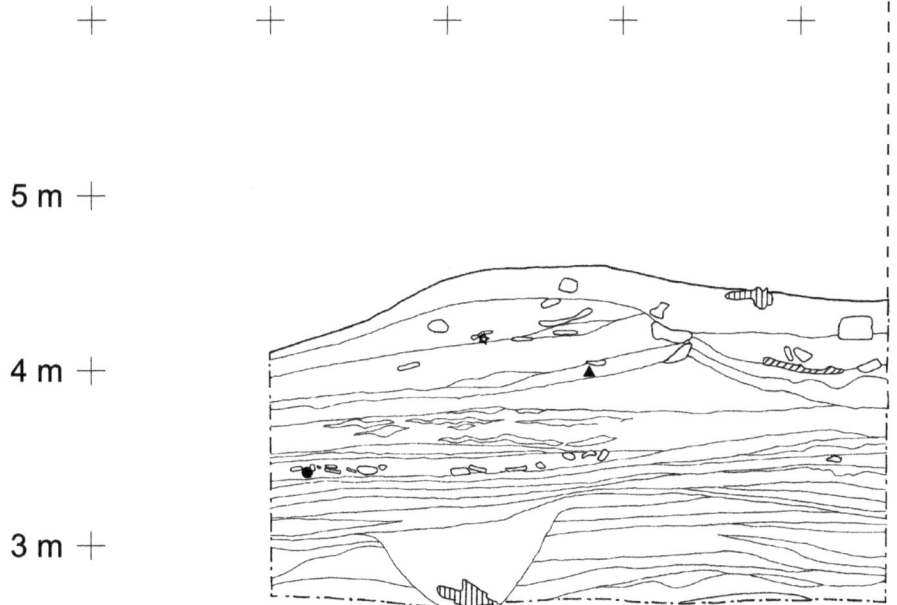

Plate 4b.

Plate 4. STRAT 2 (mound EM XIV) ; a) Architectural elements, including material such as driftwood, stone, whale bone. Location of radiocarbon samples. b) Whale bones, indicating whether skull, extended bones (long-bones and ribs), vertebra, scapula. Artifacts plotted three-dimensionally, indicating material (worked wood, ceramics, antler of reindeer and cervidae, walrus ivory, lithics). Small miscellaneous elements such as bones and baleen in sediments.

- 20

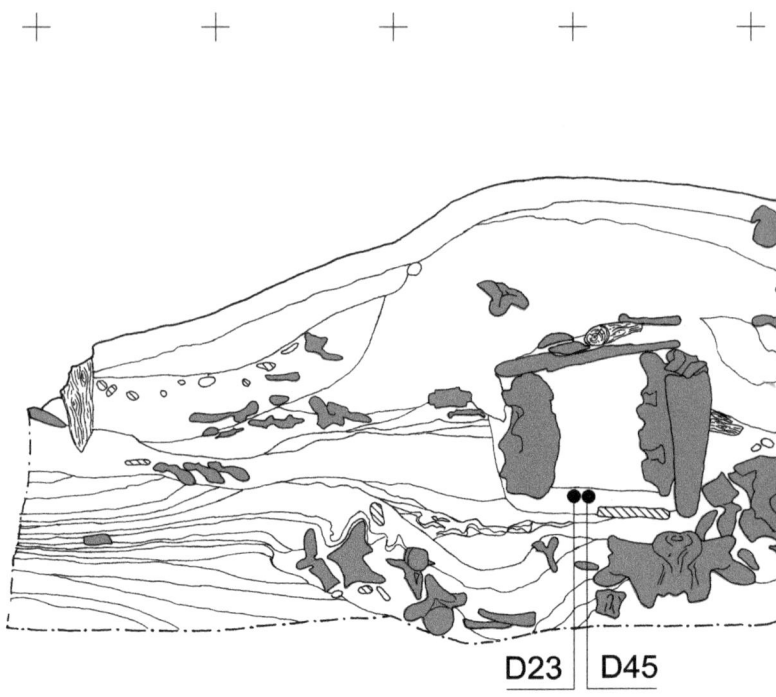

D23 | D45

- 20

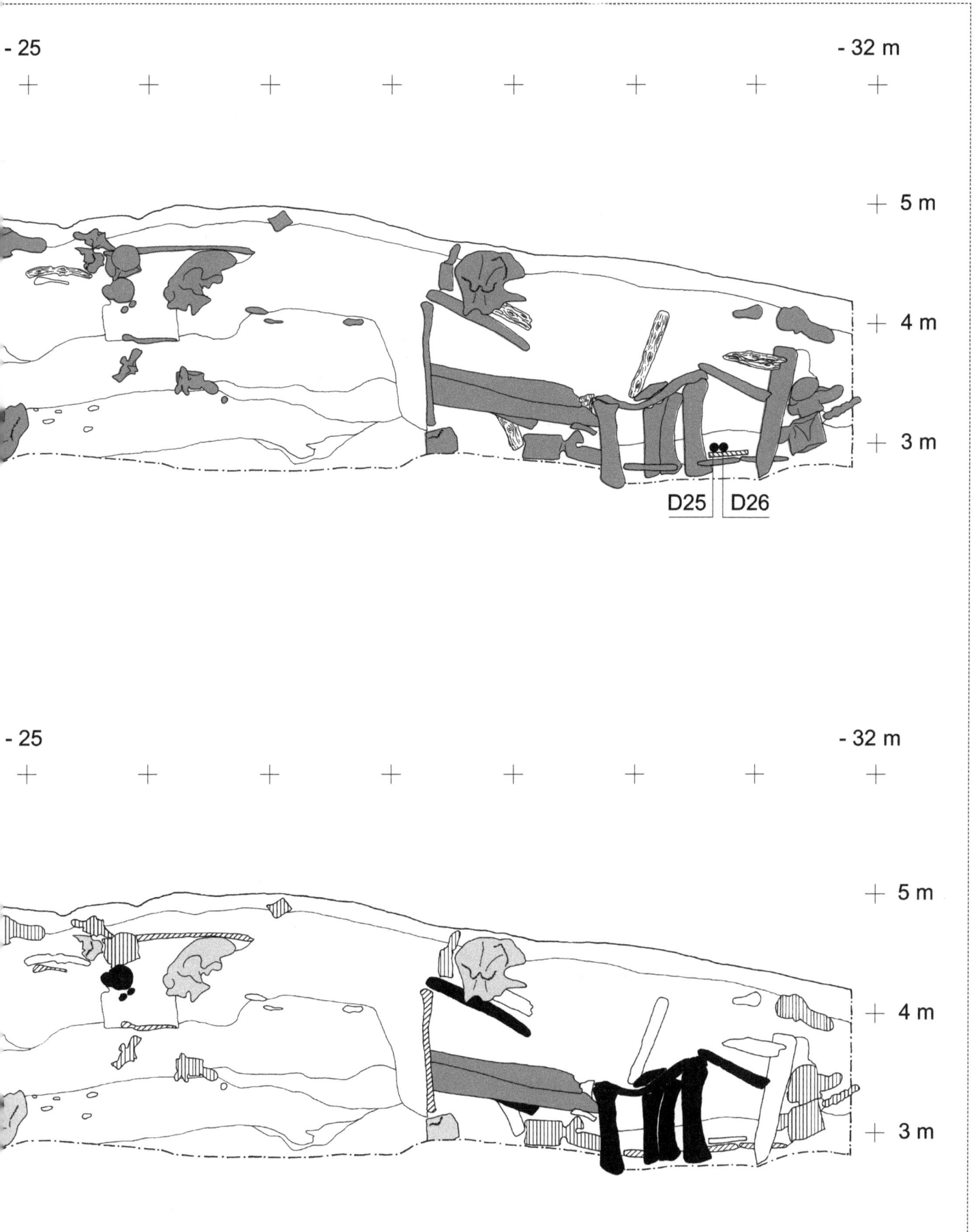

- 25

- 32 m

+ 5 m

+ 4 m

+ 3 m

D25 | D26

- 25

- 32 m

+ 5 m

+ 4 m

+ 3 m

4.5
STRATIGRAPHY AND GEOMETRY OF THE DEPOSITS; RELATION BETWEEN ANTHROPOGENIC SEDIMENTS AND ARCHITECTURAL ELEMENTS; ARCHAEOLOGICAL STRUCTURES.

From the documentation of the terrain conducted at 1:10, we have proceeded to a graphic synthesization of the data for each of the two stratigraphies on four documents at 1:40 (Plates 1 – 4):

In document n°1 (Plates 1a, 3a) the sedimentary facies were reported: facies of natural sedimentation (natural humiferous strata, organic silts, solifluction deposits, and marine beach deposits), and ethnofacies: "middens" of occupation with coarse elements, organic strata with fine texture, heterogeneous strata with elements of dismantling, reddened strata, strata indurated by grease and orange-colored borders (fossilization of leather or hide?), dark-brown carbonized and indurated agglomerates, sod clumps of the walls and roofs), empty space or space filled with ice; showing of the structural elements (whale bones, driftwood, and stone) in black permits visualizing their relatively great density in relation to the sediment as well as their zones of concentrations.

In document n°2 (Plates 1b, 3b) the limits of the totality of the sedimentary units recognized on the terrain and the situation of the structures (architectural or other) were reported, as was the positioning of the sedimentological samples and the detail elaborated at 1:5. Complementary data have been attached here: they concern, on the one hand, the distribution of baleen remains and small bones found in the plan of the cut at the time of elaboration of the terrain, the latter placing in evidence the occupation strata; and on the other hand, the carbonized elements (charcoal) and calcined elements (burned bone), which permit bringing to light combustion structures or the emptying of a hearth.

In document n°3 (Plate 2a, 4a) the nature of the architectural and structural elements placed in evidence were reported: whale bones, driftwood, stones, walrus hide. After a detailed analysis of the visible elements in the two stratigraphies (namely about 280 elements), representation of the elements is as follows: whale bone = 88%, driftwood = 8%, stone = 4%. In the same document, on the other hand, the positions the position of the samples analyzed by radiocarbon was noted, as well as that of those artifacts of chronologically diagnostic type.

In document n°4 (Plates 2b, 4b), on the one hand, whale bones were reported, placed to show what part of the skeleton they belong to: skulls, mandibles, long-bones (long-bones plus ribs), vertebras, scapulas. On the other hand, the artifacts (worked bone, ceramics, reindeer and cervidae antlers, walrus ivory, artifacts of baleen and lithic industry) recorded in tridimensional coordinates at the time of rectifying the cut, and projected onto the plan of the cut, were also reported. One can see the very strong concentration of artifacts in the occupation strata of Structure b of Stratigraphy 1.

4.5.1
STRATIGRAPHY 1

Strat 1 (Plates 1 and 2) sectioned about two-thirds of the diameter of the large mound designated EM XII (Figure 6; Photos 6, 24 and 25). The cut was 25 m in length, the anthropogenous strata between 2.5 and 3.5 m in thickness.

During the storm of August 20, 1998, waves removed the sediments crumbled at the foot of the erosion front, thus allowing examination of the stratigraphy of the natural substrate: Over the entire length of the cut, the substrate of the occupation deposit was composed of rather regular layers (80 to 100 cm thick) of olive-greenish sandy-silty-pebbly solifluction deposits. Below, the lower stratigraphic unit was lacustrine and deltaic deposits with domed and slump features, in every respect similar to those recognized farther to the west in the STRAT 3 cut.

4.5.1.1
Large architectural units, general aspect

There appears at first to be a rather generalized arrangement at the base of the sequence of anthropogenous deposits, made to appear so on one hand by careless excavation of the substrate, and on the other by the presence of vertical and horizontal architectural elements, with which whales' skulls are often associated. We shall relate the structural elements to the sedimentary facies. These elements of the base are localized in the lower 70 cm of the anthropogenous sequence, and the stratigraphy and geometry of the deposits lead one to think that the lower features could be contemporaneous. Later depositional events also can be recognized in various places: the feature of whale vertebras at + 47 and + 48 meters and locations of two superposed features at meter + 42, but it is at first rather difficult to establish chronological or functional links between them.

Architectural units, seriation of features and correlations between elements of architecture and sedimentary facies

Lower sequence

Structure A. This is the largest feature recognized in this cut (Plates 1 and 2, Figure 12, center section), extending a total of 12 m, from meter + 30 to + 42. The contact between the base of the element and the natural substrate is relatively flat; from meter + 34 to + 39 it can be seen in the form of a black organic border, and at meter + 32 by large strips of baleen arranged horizontally. At meter + 40, two slabs of schist mark the interface. One can also note reshaping of the sediment of the substrate by leveling or excavation. Two primary vertical supports (whale longbone and mandible) delimit the central part of the feature (a third support, not visible in the cut, should be located at meter + 35), which seems to appear as two covered rooms each about 2 m and symmetrically related to a central post at meter + 37. These two rooms, about a meter high, were covered by whale bone (mandibles and ribs, essentially) as a set of beams perpendicular to the axis of the cut that support a "ceiling" oriented parallel to the face. A part of these elements could not be represented in the profile, being in part collapsed in the embankment of the erosion front. Thin layers of orange-colored sediment (deterioration of leather or hide?) are associated with these horizontal elements of roofing. A part of these rooms must have remained empty

Photo 24. General view, from the beach, of Mound EM XII, two thirds of which are repeated by the Strat 1 stratigraphy.
Photograph by Bernard Moulin.

Photo 25. General oblique view to the west of Stratigraphy 1 during the course of elaboration.
Photograph by Bernard Moulin.

Photo 26. General view of Structure A from Stratigraphy 1, in the eastern part of the large Mound EM XII.
Photograph by Bernard Moulin.

after being abandoned since we have found them partially filled with ice. The eastern part (meters + 34 to + 35), on the other hand, must have suffered a later collapse, as was shown by the heterogeneous sediment concealing a double layer of orange sediment that would correspond to the deterioration of leather or skin; this last, associated with a series of horizontal elements of small size, rested almost directly on the stratified midden interpreted as the occupation level. On both sides of this double central opening interpreted as an occupation area (room), whale skulls can be seen at meters + 40 to + 41 and + 33 to + 34.

This large feature is situated at the east end of the large mound. East of the rooms of this feature (meters +30 to +33) it is possible to recognize a wall about a meter high made of an accumulation of sod and peat clumps. To the west, this feature probably leaned against other contemporaneous features and it is only possible to identify, at meter +40, a small zone composed of rather broken up sediment, rich in sods, which must have formed its west wall; this was evidently of smaller size than the wall on the east, which must have played a much more important isolating role. One notes that in comparison with the feature that will be described in connection with the Strat 2 cut (EM XIV; Pl. 3a), not even a roofing of sods has been observed above the "ceiling" of this feature. It is probable that at the time of later occupations – of which indications are present throughout the whole length – the top of the feature was partially truncated and leveled in order to create new surfaces. Correlating the architectural elements (in particular vertical and horizontal elements) with the sedimentary facies permits a proposed reconstruction of the feature (Fig. 20) with roofing of sods such as it was before leveling by later occupants.

Structure B. This feature (Plates 1 and 2, Photo 28), extends from meter + 44 to + 51, and is characterized by the following:
A. Four small depressions excavated into the natural substrate.
B. Whale skulls at the base of the anthropogenic sequence, of which two are associated with these depressions.
C. Vertical architectural elements of rather small height.
D. Large, superposed, horizontal architectural elements (driftwood beams, whale mandibles), positioned perpendicular to the cut at meters + 48 to + 49.
E. The superposition of organic strata (six in the best differentiated area at meters + 47 to + 48) – thin (5 to 15 cm), subhorizontal, well individualized (stratified middens, homogeneous middens with finer texture), and coherent for several meters' distance.
F. Slabs of stone and of a piece of walrus hide laid horizontally and associated with organic strata, at meters + 45 to + 47.
G. Finally, the extreme abundance of artifacts in these strata (Plates 2a and 2b).

The sedimentary sequence associated with this feature varies from 60 to 100 cm in thickness, topped by heterogeneous and poorly differentiated dismantlement strata. Two wall-like effects can be noted: the first, between + 48.50 and + 49.20, is marked by the interruption of the stratified midden present on both sides and by the superposition of four large horizontal architectural elements. The second partition effect is visible at +46.90: on both sides of a wooden post the strata change nature – midden with fine texture and slabs of stone to the west, midden with large elements to the east. The wall effect also seems to make itself evident higher in the cut, although it is difficult to define the precise nature of this feature. If the type

of sediment is appropriate to an area of occupation showing domestic activity, the absence of clearly preserved substructure inhibits understanding of the exact nature of the structure that is associated with this occupation area. The superposition of several successive strata and levels of slabs suggests a multiple or sequential occupation of this domestic space. The area of the feature situated between the two wall-like effects (+ 46.90 and + 48.50) exhibits the most developed succession of strata.

Upper sequence

Structure C. This feature, of much smaller size than those previously described, is located between + 38.40 and + 39.60 (Plate 1b). On the vertical plane of the cut it is composed of two piles of three whale vertebras, about 30 cm high, spaced at 1 m, on which a whale rib lies horizontally, the latter serving as support for a thick accumulation of stacked sod blocks. At the base of this rectangular feature is a vague depression filled with a double layer of beige-orange sediment, rather strongly indurated (probably by greases), that occupies the bottom of the depression and within which is interbedded a fine brownish sediment. An organic brown sediment tops this shallow basin. This feature can be interpreted as a food cache, the history of which is probably polyphasic.

Structure D. This is a large "combustion feature" that extends over nearly 5 m, from + 41.30 to + 46.20, its thickness in the center exceeding 1 m (Plates 1a and 1b). It can be subdivided into two subfeatures: to the west, a large basin, the borders diffuse, showing a succession of several strata more or less well differentiated; and to the east, carbonaceous deposits showing rather strong variations laterally, resting on a base made up of a large (2 m) whale mandible placed flat.

The basin-shaped structure (substructure west, + 43.30 / + 46.20) is made up of the following sequence, from bottom to top (Pls. 1a and 1b):
1. A lenticular stratum with a very carbonaceous matrix, enclosing some charcoal and numerous burned bones, a few centimeters high;
2. A sandy carbonaceous sediment, friable and rather pulverized;
3. In about forty centimeters of thickness a sand-silt sediment, carbonaceous, enclosing in a dispersed manner numerous whole and fragmentary large bones (20 x 20cm, 30 x 15cm), in particular vertebral sections, very strongly burned and calcined;
4. A thin stratum, well stratified, with a sandy-silty very carbonized matrix, enclosing numerous pieces of worked wood, bone, and ivory, partially burned;
5 A dense carbonaceous layer, black, pulverized, with large chunks of charcoal on top (10 cm);
6. An orange stratum, of rather irregular form, with internal color variations, of silty-sandy context, and pulverized appearance, with the inclusion of completely calcined bones (Photo 29);
7. A sandy-silty stratum, blackish-brown, more or less carbonaceous, heterogeneous;
8. At the end of the sequence, the fill of a small residual depression being characterized by a heterogeneous sediment enclosing charcoal centimeters thick and a reddened sediment.

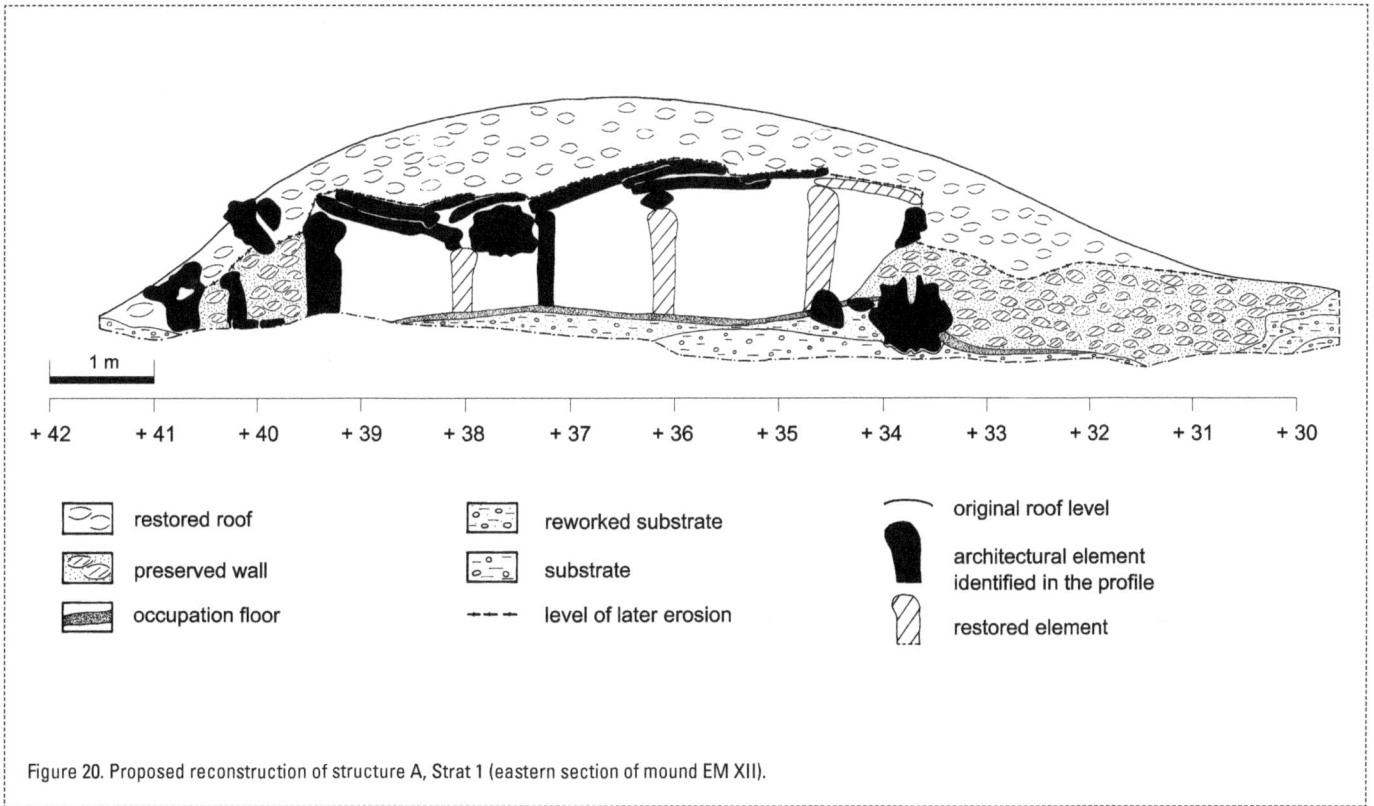

1 m

+ 42   + 41   + 40   + 39   + 38   + 37   + 36   + 35   + 34   + 33   + 32   + 31   + 30

restored roof

preserved wall

occupation floor

reworked substrate

substrate

level of later erosion

original roof level

architectural element
identified in the profile

restored element

Figure 20. Proposed reconstruction of structure A, Strat 1 (eastern section of mound EM XII).

0   0.5   1   1.5 m

Photo 27. Detailed view of Structure A of Stratigraphy 1 showing elements of vertical and horizontal architecture of whale bone (mandibles, long-bones, and ribs). Echelle horizontale = 1m. Photograph by Bernard Moulin.

Photo 28. Detail of the western part of Stratigraphy 1 (meters + 46 to + 50.50); the lower third corresponds to the well stratified zone (Structure B, sediment Samples S0 to S7), with a heavy concentration of artifacts, the accumulation of whale vertebras visible on the top correspond to Structure E. Photograph by Bernard Moulin.

Photo 29. Detail of the central part of the large combustion structure (Structure D, Strat 1) showing reddened silts and calcined bones covering carbonaceous accumulations. Photograph by Bernard Moulin.

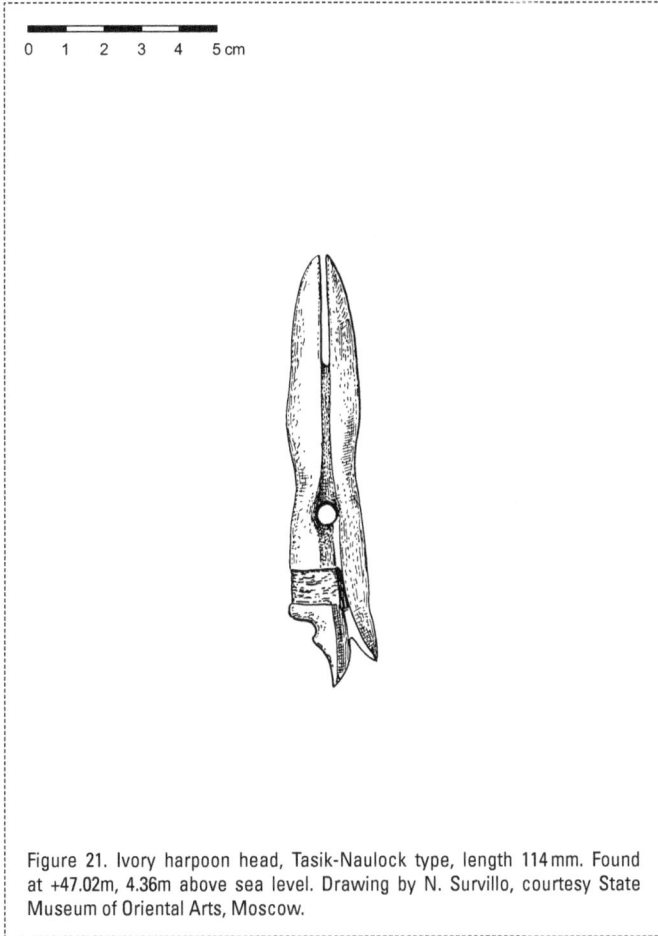

Figure 21. Ivory harpoon head, Tasik-Naulock type, length 114 mm. Found at +47.02m, 4.36m above sea level. Drawing by N. Survillo, courtesy State Museum of Oriental Arts, Moscow.

Photo 30. Stratigraphy 1, eastern part; detail of the well stratified occupation level (sedimentological Samples S18 to S20) from Structure H (meters + 30 / + 31). Photograph by Bernard Moulin.

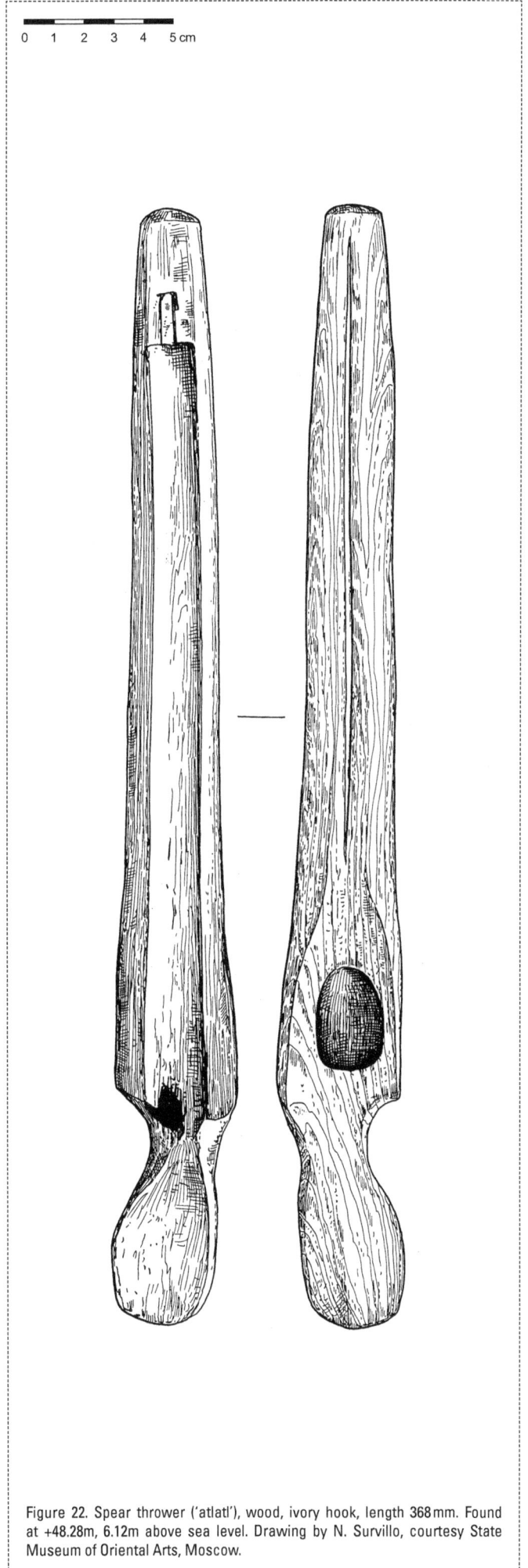

Figure 22. Spear thrower ('atlatl'), wood, ivory hook, length 368 mm. Found at +48.28m, 6.12m above sea level. Drawing by N. Survillo, courtesy State Museum of Oriental Arts, Moscow.

Atmospheric data from Stuiver et al. (1998); OxCal v3.4 Bronk Ramsey (2000); cub r:4 sd:12 prob usp[chron]

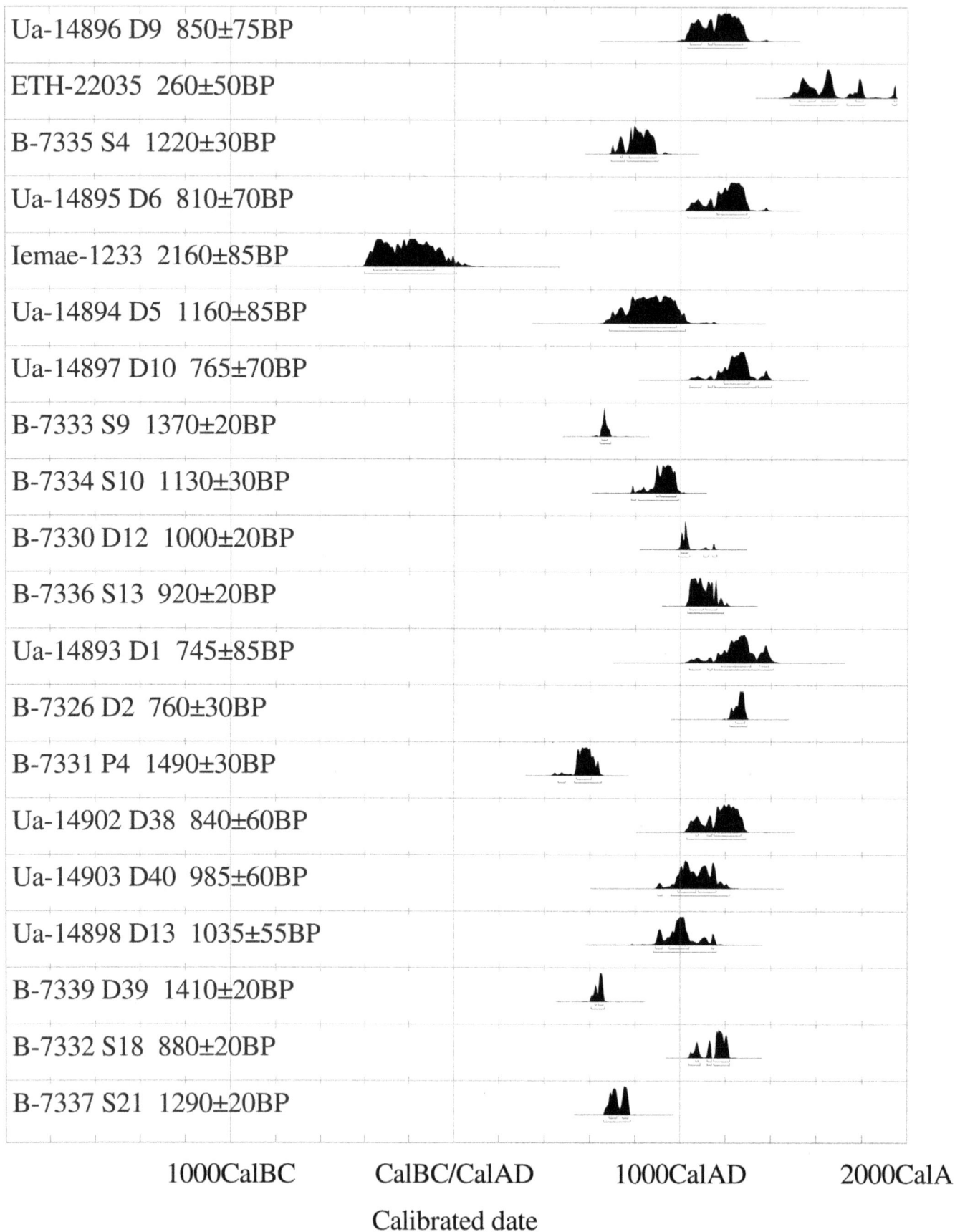

Ua-14896 D9 850±75BP

ETH-22035 260±50BP

B-7335 S4 1220±30BP

Ua-14895 D6 810±70BP

Iemae-1233 2160±85BP

Ua-14894 D5 1160±85BP

Ua-14897 D10 765±70BP

B-7333 S9 1370±20BP

B-7334 S10 1130±30BP

B-7330 D12 1000±20BP

B-7336 S13 920±20BP

Ua-14893 D1 745±85BP

B-7326 D2 760±30BP

B-7331 P4 1490±30BP

Ua-14902 D38 840±60BP

Ua-14903 D40 985±60BP

Ua-14898 D13 1035±55BP

B-7339 D39 1410±20BP

B-7332 S18 880±20BP

B-7337 S21 1290±20BP

1000CalBC   CalBC/CalAD   1000CalAD   2000CalA

Calibrated date

Figure 23. Calibrated dates from STRAT 1. The dates are arranged from top to bottom as they occur from +50.30 m to +30.60 m along the erosion front. For more details, see appendix, Figure 64.

The subfeature east (+ 41 / + 43.60) can be characterized in the following way:
1. A fine dark-gray sandy sediment enclosing gravels resting on a whale mandible placed flat;
2. In the western part (+ 42.60 / + 43.20) is a pile of black sediment, strongly indurated, of carbonized appearance, with irregular oulines;
3. At the eastern end of the mandible, a very carbonaceous area about 50 cm in extent encloses rather large burned bones. It is difficult to interpret this feature in a functional way with only elements of the data from the cut available. The abundance, in several strata of fill from this feature, of large bones (whale vertebras) where the spongy part is well represented as strongly burned and calcined, would suggest that, after having been impregnated with grease, they had been used as a combustible, as several ethnographic examples attest.

Structure E. This is situated between + 47.20 and + 49.60 (Plates 1b and 2b and Photo 28) and is characterized by the accumulation, over 80 cm thick, of a rather large number of whale vertebras. The interstitial sediment is not abundant, but it is a rather organic brown silty sand, not very compact. The whole has the form of a shallow basin and one can suppose that this was an excavated feature of which the opening was probably located about 50 cm below the present ground surface.

Structure F. This is a feature of small dimensions, situated in the upper third of the cut (Plate 1b) between + 45.00 and + 45.60. It is composed of elements of driftwood placed horizontally, and with axis perpendicular to the cut. A horizontal base and beginnings of lateral walls made of superposed elements of subcircular cross-section suggest something in the shape of a coffer with rectangular cross-section that is aligned perpendicular to the cut.

Structure G. This is a small feature (about 1 m) appearing in the plane of the cut (+39.20 to +40.20) in the following way: three whale bones placed horizontally and aligned perpendicular to the cut serve as support for clumps of sod and peat (Plate 1b). Vertical elements are located on both sides. This feature is superposed on the western half of feature C.

Structure H. This feature is situated at the eastern extremity of the mound (Plate 1b) in the slope zone (+ 29.40 to + 32.10). The stratification of the deposits is clear: above a thick bed composed of sod chunks and corresponding to the east wall of feature A, previously described, a bed of old building materials is enclosed between two occupation levels. The upper level is itself subdivided into two well-differentiated strata: the lower stratum is a grayish sediment, sandy to sandy-silty, with internal structure not very stratified; a wooden post wedged up with small pieces of wood and three post holes are associated with this stratum, which is itself covered by a gray-brown organic midden with internal stratified structure, rather compact, containing a large amount of animal hair, baleen, some feathers, abundant vegetal debris, as well as fragments of bone and ceramic (Photo 30). This structure can be interpreted as a light habitation feature (tent), placed at the east flank of the mound.

4.5.1.2
Chronology of STRAT 1
BY YVON CSONKA

Twenty samples from STRAT 1 were radiocarbon dated. They were collected in various archaeological features, between 30.6 m and 50.3 m along the line of the erosion front (see Plate 2a).

There were few traces of occupation floor and few artifacts in the large feature A in the lower sequence. The only suitable sample we could collect within the "house" gave a result of 960-1220 CalAD (Ua-14903) (all calibrations at 2 sigma; see Figure 23, Appendix, Figure 64 and Plate 2a). Two samples from the eastern wall cover of that same structure were dated to 605-665 (B-7339) and 880-1160 CalAD (Ua-14898). Another sample from a midden layer situated above this wall cover yielded a date of 660-780 CalAD (B-7337). The only logical aspect is that structure A is situated below occupations which occurred later. A sample collected just above the roof (its sod cover is missing) dates to 1030-1290 CalAD (Ua-14902), and another one above the eastern wall cover dates to 1040-1220 Cal AD (B-7332). Not enough diagnostic artifacts were recovered in the occupation layers to allow a chrono-typological assessment of the occupation. Artifacts found in displaced deposits in the rubble down-slope from feature A are fairly numerous, however, and most probably fell from the lower occupation floors. Nine harpoon heads were collected there, four of antler and five of ivory. The six less fragmented specimens are tentatively ascribed to Old Bering Sea (OBS) III (1 specimen, reworked), Late Birnirk (2), Punuk? (1), and Early Western Thule (2).

Within structure B, there was a well-stratified succession of midden layers between +46 and +48 meters along the erosion front, which contained numerous artifacts. The oldest radiocarbon date from the erosion front, calibrated to 400 BC-AD 10 (IEMAE-1233), comes from immediately underneath these layers. It may represent the relic of a first occupation in Old Bering Sea times. No artifacts were found associated with this sample, and OBS-style material is rare in the collections from the erosion front; but close to it, and in the same layer, was found a well-preserved ivory harpoon head of Tasik-Naulock type (Figure 21). Beside this early date, there are six others in this vertical corridor, the ranges extending between 640 CalAD (B-7333) and 1330 CalAD (Ua-14897, discounting the 7% probability of its being younger). Within 2 meters left and right of this succession of layers are three additional dated samples coming from the same lower and middle sequences, which cluster in the period between 1030 and 1410 CalAD (Ua-14896, Ua-14893, B-7326). A fourth sample, P4, contained fur (probably sea mammal) and its Δ 13C value of -17.5‰ was the lowest of all our samples. We may thus suspect a reservoir effect and suppose that this date should be corrected to a somewhat younger age than a straight calibration makes it appear (530-650 CalAD; B-7331). The vertical corridor situated between +46 and +48 meters along the front yielded by far the most artifacts, both in situ while cleaning the cut (105 out of 202 artifacts collected in situ in STRAT 1, see plate 2b), and in the sediments crumbled at the foot of the erosion front (224 artifacts). Very few of the objects whose location was recorded in three dimensions have diagnostic value, however. Those few that do are attributed to Birnirk, Punuk, and OBS III, in no particular vertical order.

Two other age ranges, 990-1040 (B-7330), and 1030-1190 (B-7336), derive from samples situated above structure B. The sample with the youngest date, was located less than one meter apart laterally, but 1.3 meter vertically, from the oldest sample; its calibrated date is 1480-1690 CalAD (ETH-22035; 74% probability at 2 sigma). The sample on which it was measured was found below the whale vertebras of structure E and belongs to the upper sequence. A well-preserved wooden spear-thrower with ivory hook was found associated with the sample (Figure 22).

The youngest and the oldest dates are both outliers that bracket the main occupation period. If one also eliminates B-7331, which is affected by reservoir effect to an unknown degree, there remains a group of 17 dates which cluster in an interval between 600 and 1400 CalAD. An OxCal "phase" model was used to estimate the boundaries and duration of this sequence. Such a model tightens the interval, with boundaries around 650 and 1300 CalAD, and a span with greatest probability at about 650 years. Our sampling strategy was highly dependent on the availability of suitable material (we preferred local wood such as Salix; for the determination of wood species in some of our samples, see Appendix, Figure 64), which was abundant only in midden layers, and on our interest in dating precisely such midden layers which contained numerous artifacts. We suggest that the part of the settlement around STRAT 1 is characterized by a sequence of occupations in the interval 650-1300 CalAD, preceded by faint traces of an earlier occupation, and followed by later occupations the traces of which are also more discrete – no large architectural units, no extensive midden layers. In any case, the interval 650-1300 AD may itself be subdivided, at least near structure A, into an earlier sequence of occupation, followed by the abandonment of the structure, and a subsequent installation at ca. 1200 CalAD on top of its roof, the sod cover but not the structural elements supporting it having been removed in the meantime. the fit between stratigraphic sequences and radiocarbon dating is, as could be expected in the very complex STRAT 1, far from perfect.

4.5.2
STRAT 2

4.5.2.1
General points

The example illustrated by the Strat 2 cut (Photos 31 and 32) is rather different from the preceding one. This cut, about 15 m long, passed through the whole length of the small, structurally simple mound (EM XIV). The detailed data are shown in Plates 3 and 4. A diagrammatic synthesis is presented in Figure 24. Correlations have been carried out between our elaborated stratigraphy of 1998 and the profile developed by N. K. Kiseleva in August 1990 (Dinesman & al. 1999: 19-20). Two large stratigraphic groups are clearly distinguished: a lower group (sedimentary sequences I to VII) in which natural dynamics dominated depositionally over anthropogenous processes (Photo 34), without assuming absence of the human element; an upper group (sedimentary sequences VIII to X), in which the sedimentary accumulation is essentially due to human activity. The interface between the two is marked by a sharp boundary (Photo 33), at which an artificial excavation in some places is clear.

4.5.2.2
Descriptive and first interpretations

Sedimentary Sequence I
This first, lowest, sequence was not reached in the present cut but was worked out by N. K. Kiseleva (her cm -201 to -210; Dinesman & al. 1999: 19-21); we correlate this facies with the deposits of colluvium and solifluction recognized over the whole length of Strat 1 – that is, the material that lies above the basal lacustrine and deltaic deposits and that constitutes the substrate of the occupation level.

Sedimentary Sequence II
The deposits of this sequence are made up of an organic sediment of peaty aspect with sandy intercalations, of which the top is located at the lower limit of our observations of 1998; they correspond to the strata between -163 and -201 cm in the work of N. K. Kiseleva (Dinesman al. 1999: 20).

Sedimentary Sequence III
Sequence II is surmounted by a sequence (III) dominated by sandy gravel: well-sorted yellowish sands, gravely sand and sorted gravel (Figure 12c); hydrodynamic sorting (by wave action) was preponderant in the deposition. The detrital mineral component predominates (Photo 34), although some deposits are distinguished by strong enrichment of organic matter (medium to fine yellowish sands with brown organic laminations). These sediments can be interpreted as deposits of the marine shore.

Sedimentary Sequence IV
At the top of this natural sequence (meters -17.70 to -18.60) a pit feature, from all evidence of human agency, with whale vertebras at the bottom, the heterometric fill a grayish silty sand with gravel. This pit can be correlated stratigraphically with other anthropogenous indications farther east in the profile: accumulation of whale vertebras at -22 m, whale skulls at -23 to -25 m, pit with fill of carbonaceous agglomerated material

	Stratigraphic sequence	C14 dates	Elevation / sedimentary facies	Type of deposit, dynamics of formation
UPPER GROUP	X			modern humus
	IX			food cache
	VIII	1300 – 1530 Cal AD (Ua-14905, 2 å) 1410 – 1475 Cal AD (B-7329, 2 å) 1400 – 1700 Cal AD (Ua-14900, 2 å) 1410 – 1440 Cal AD (B-7327, 2 å) 1440 – 1670 Cal AD (Ua-14901, 2 å)		dwelling structures (EH 25; EM XIV); clean excavation in the natural substrate. Superstructures with open spaces, and occupation strata; roofs of cumps of sod and peat.
LOWER GROUP	VII			marine beach affected by winds
	VI			discontinuous occupation stratum
	V			surface disconformity: erosional lacuna / marine beach, organic levels on top
	IV	970 – 1220 Cal AD (Ua-14899, 2 å) 980 – 1250 Cal AD (Ua-14904, 2 å)		occupation stratum collapsed by marine erosion, archeological structures, induration of sands
	III			marine beach
	II	1792+_85 BP (IEAMAE 906)		marine beach, humic intercalations
	I	2394+_90 BP (IEAMAE 898)		solifluction, terrigenous sedimentation

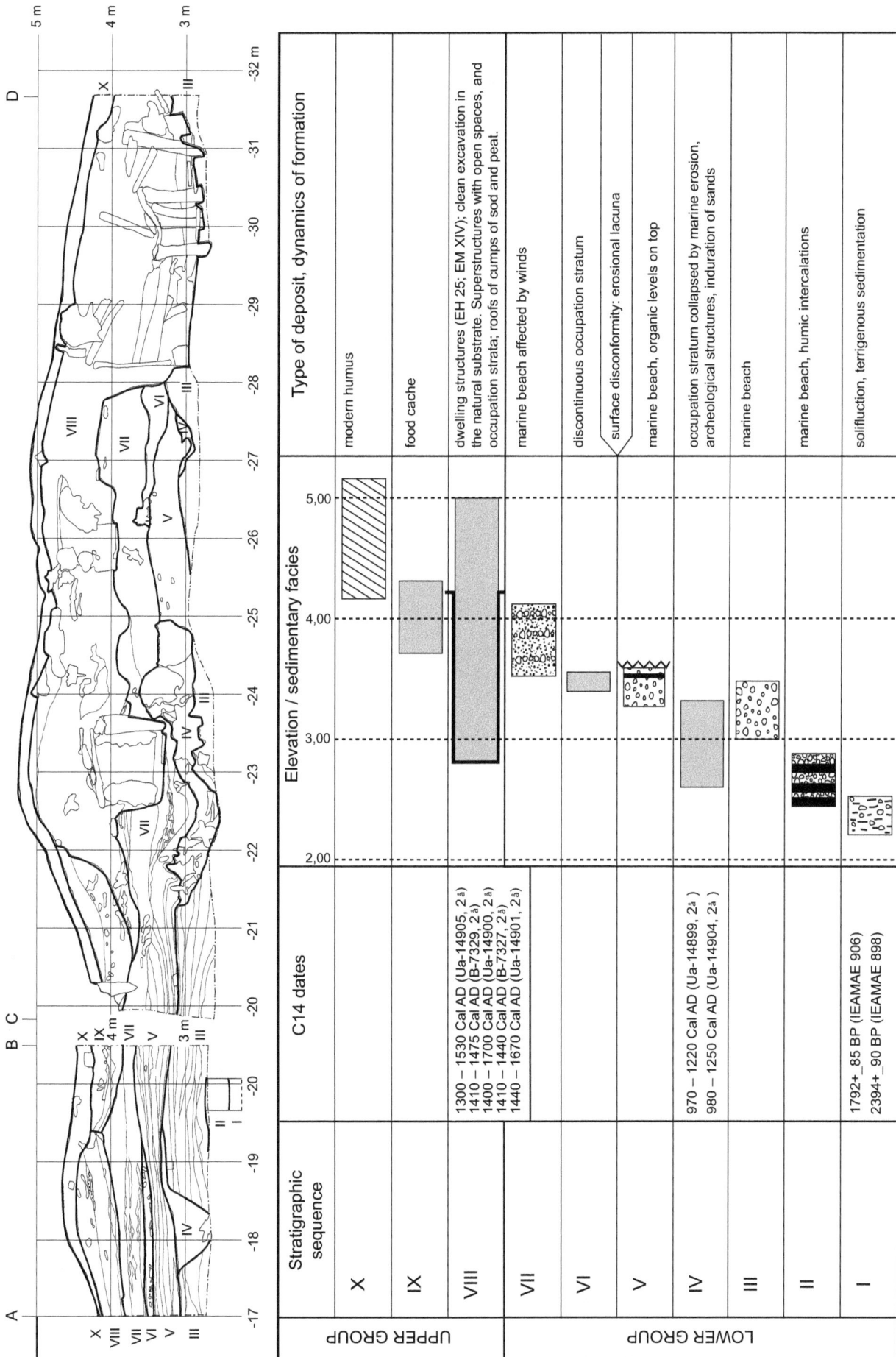

Figure 24. Chronological and stratigraphic synthesis of Strat 2. For each sedimentary unit (numbered I to X in the schematic profile) are given radiocarbon determinations, types of deposits and their elevations, and an interpretation of sedimentary dynamics involved.

at -27 and -28 m, and hearths. This group of elements suggests that remains of an occupation level, anciently disrupted by marine erosion, is interstratified between two sets of deposits emplaced by nature.

Next comes the second and more complex part of the lower group, which consists of sequences V to VII. It is also in the west part of the profile (meters -17 to -20) that the sequence is better stratified, where one can recognize the following succession, from bottom upwards.

Sedimentary Sequence V
At the base there are well sorted sands with gravel lenses, sealing the pit feature. A succession of three peat beds and interbedded thin sandy and sand-gravel deposits make up the second part of this sequence. The upper limit of sequence V is marked by a truncated eroded surface.

Sedimentary Sequence VI
This is an archaeological level (stratified midden containing numerous bones at meters -17 to -19) that can be correlated laterally with other indications of human activity: accumulation of lumps of sod (wall remains) at meters -27 and -28, in connection with whale vertebras (meter -22).

Sedimentary Sequence VII
To the west (meters -17 to -20), this sequence is made up of a brown-beige, sandy-silty stratum with intermittent light-gray, fine sandy interstratifications; farther east it is gravely sand (meters -25 to -28). This succession of natural deposits is again topped, and locally truncated, by anthropogenous deposits and arrangements of the upper stratigraphic group.

Sedimentary Sequence VIII
The second part of the cut, which begins with sequence VIII, recounts a more well defined story: a human presence is characterized by a series of excavations with subvertical sides that serve to support vertical architectural elements (whale skulls, scapulas, and mandibles), which themselves support horizontal elements, and then a roof made of sod chunks. We first describe the architectural features that make up sequence VIII, and then try to establish connections between them.

Structure 1 (-22.60 to -23.80 m). This is a feature in the form of a small coffer (1.2 by 1.2 m) delimiting an empty space. The two lateral walls are made of whale skulls in canted position; to the right side is connected a vertical long-bone, the upper concavity of which supports a whale vertebra. The base is constituted by a canted whale scapula. The vertical elements support a whale mandible placed horizontally, which in turn supports transverse elements. At the base is a slab of stone laid flat. The feature is excavated about 50 cm into the substrate and is covered by sods placed obliquely over about 60 cm, constituting a dome above the feature (Photo 35).

Structure 2 (-26.60 to -28.00 m). This is an empty space, 70 cm high and 60 cm wide, delimited to the east by a whale skull positioned obliquely, and to the west by a heap of whale bones, the latter serving as support for a horizontal rib. At the base a scapula is placed flat, some centimeters lower than the initial substrate. The group is fitted into a constructed sediment made up of an accumulation of sod clumps.

Structure 3 (-27.80 to -31.50 m). This feature, which extends over about 4 m, constitutes the east end of the mound. On the west there is a well-marked subvertical excavation (more than a meter) into the substrate. A whale scapula, in canted position and wedged by clumps of sod, makes up the western limit of the feature itself, close to the excavation. To the east of this scapula, two large whale mandibles, placed horizontally, mark the upper limit of an empty space and support a considerable accumulation of sod chunks (80 cm thick). Farther to the east, four long-bones and a mandible positioned vertically support elements placed flat that in turn support the upper accumulation of sod clumps. These elements are set in the natural sand substrate of the marine beach. At the base, on the sand substrate and between the two easternmost pillars, scapulas have been placed flat on which have accumulated stratified middens containing the remains of furs and numerous artifacts of walrus ivory, and interpretable as former beds. Above, the spaces are empty between the supporting features.

Relation of the features to each other. The three structures or features described belong to the architectural group christened EH 25. Documentation in 1998 records a cut with axis probably passing in the back part of a large house that extended over a dozen meters. Several successive photographs (Blumer 1997; Blumer & Csonka 1998), show how this erosion front appeared previously and to what degree the present marine erosion has acted destructively on this part of the site. In 1991, in the part east of the feature two large whale skulls marked the entrance to the house; several years later, the erosion front had moved back several meters and a large part of the habitation area is today destroyed. At the time of the storm of August 19-20 of 1998, most of the architectural elements of the area east of the feature were carried off by the sea. Structures 1 and 2 can be interpreted as "wall cabinets" adjacent to semisubterranean occupation spaces located initially more to the south, now eroded away.

Sedimentary Sequence IX
Structure 4. This is a pit located to the west of the three features that have been described (-19.20 to -22.00 m), and of which a large part has been carried off recently by marine erosion. It is a depression about 3 m wide and 40 cm deep, the deepest part of the apparent cache having been situated initially in front of the present profile. A basal stratum is indurated, beige-orange sediment surmounted by a level where rather abundant bones (whale scapulas in particular), are laid flat. The fill of the depression is a rather heterogeneous brownish, humic, sandy-silt. In front of the cut, several whale bones (skull, scapula) indicate the former south limit of this feature, which to the north is marked in the present topography by a small quadrangular depression (Figure 6). Structure 4 is placed chronologically later than the three features described above and is interpreted as a food cache.

Sedimentary Sequence X
This topmost sequence is modern humus.

Photo 31. Oblique view to the northeast of Mound EM XIV (Houses EH 23 and EH 25). Photograph by Bernard Moulin.

Photo 32. Front view, from the beach, of Mound EM XIV (Houses EH 23 and EH 25) elaborated in Stratigraphy 2. Photograph by Bernard Moulin.

Photo 33. Detailed view of the western part of Stratigraphy 2, showing the sedimentary succession from the lower group (stratigraphic sequences II to VII), to the natural top, surmounted by strata more organic than the upper group (sedimentary sequences VIII to X). Photograph by Bernard Moulin.

Photo 34. Stratigraphy 2, western part, detailed view of the sequence to the natural top of the lower group (sedimentary sequences II, III, and V). Photograph by Bernard Moulin.

Photo 35. Detail of the sod roofing covering Structure 1 (House EH 25) of Stratigraphy 2. Photograph by Bernard Moulin.

Photo 36. The late Patrick Plumet inspecting "structure 3" of STRAT 2 in 1991. These whale skulls are the ones which were dated by Dinesman et al. (1999 : 22, 46). They were removed by waves during a storm around 1993. Photograph courtesy of the late Patrick Plumet.

Photo 37. "Structure 3" within EH-25 in STRAT 2, in 1998. Compare with Photo 36 above : the large whale skulls stood just in front of this. At the bottom of the structure, lower right, one sees the remains of an anthropic layer which covers a floor of whale scapulae. Many artifacts were found in this layer (see Figure 26). Photograph by Yvon Csonka.

4.5.2.3
Chronology of STRAT 2
BY YVON CSONKA

Earlier sequences
From two radiocarbon determinations on organic materials (humic deposit and mammal bones) coming respectively from the base and from the top of sequence II (Dinesman et al. 1999:20), we infer calibrated ages between 750-355 CalBC (IEMAE-898; 2394 ± 90 BP) and 56-422 CalAD (IEMAE-906; 1792 ± 85 BP). Two samples were taken in sequence IV, in an additional cut a meter to the south of Strat 2. The assays yielded concordant dates, 970-1220 CalAD (Ua-14899, 2 sigma) and 980-1250 CalAD (Ua-14904, 2 sigma).

In a stratigraphic cut made in 1995 near the western end of STRAT 2, our Danish colleagues Hans-Christian Gulløv and Hans-Christian Kapel had dug deeper under the present beach, and dated charcoal from a hearth to 560-650 CalAD (written communication; AAR-2736, calibration at 1 sigma). This tends to indicate the existence in this part of the site, probably within sequence III, of a greater number of alternating episodes of marine transgression followed by human occupation than appear in STRAT 2 alone.

Sequence VIII, House EH-25
Dinesman et al. (1999:22,46) had dated a bowhead whale skull from EH-25 to 1272 ± 127 BP (IEMAE-0823), and concluded that the house into which this skull was incorporated had been constructed at that time (Photo 36)[1]. In 1998, we took samples from occupation layers clearly belonging to that same house.

One of them, consisting of several local wood twigs found side by side on the floor of structure 1, was split and dated in two different laboratories, yielding different results, 300 ± 65 BP (Ua-14900) and 460 ± 20 BP (B-7329). When calibrated, only the 2 standard-deviation intervals overlap slightly. Laboratory bias is not suspected. Lack of sample homogeneity could be an explanation – which would, in any situation comparable to this one, throw doubt on associations between dated samples and their immediate context. As it is, this discrepancy serves as a sobering reminder of the precautions that must be taken when interpreting radiocarbon dates from Neoeskimo sites (e.g. Morrison 1989).

Hypothesizing that the culturally derived layers from the floor of EH-25 pertain to a relatively short period of occupation, we have used a "phase" model with OxCal v3.4; a terminus ante quem of 1700 AD was added as a plausible additional hypothesis. The results indicate a concentration of probabilities between 1440 and 1490 AD. The weight of the two dates from the Bern lab in the assessment of the phase of occupation is better understood when looking at a calibration plot where the probability surfaces are equal (Figure 25). The reversal of the calibration curve in the interval 300-360 BP also contributes to deemphasize the significance of the two dates Ua-14900 and Ua-14901 in comparison with the three others.

Summing up, despite the facts that the house incorporated whale skulls dated to 1270 BP, and that two of the dates we obtained from occupation layers in EH-25 have 2-sigma calibrated intervals extending well into the seventeenth century, we think that occupation occurred during a relatively

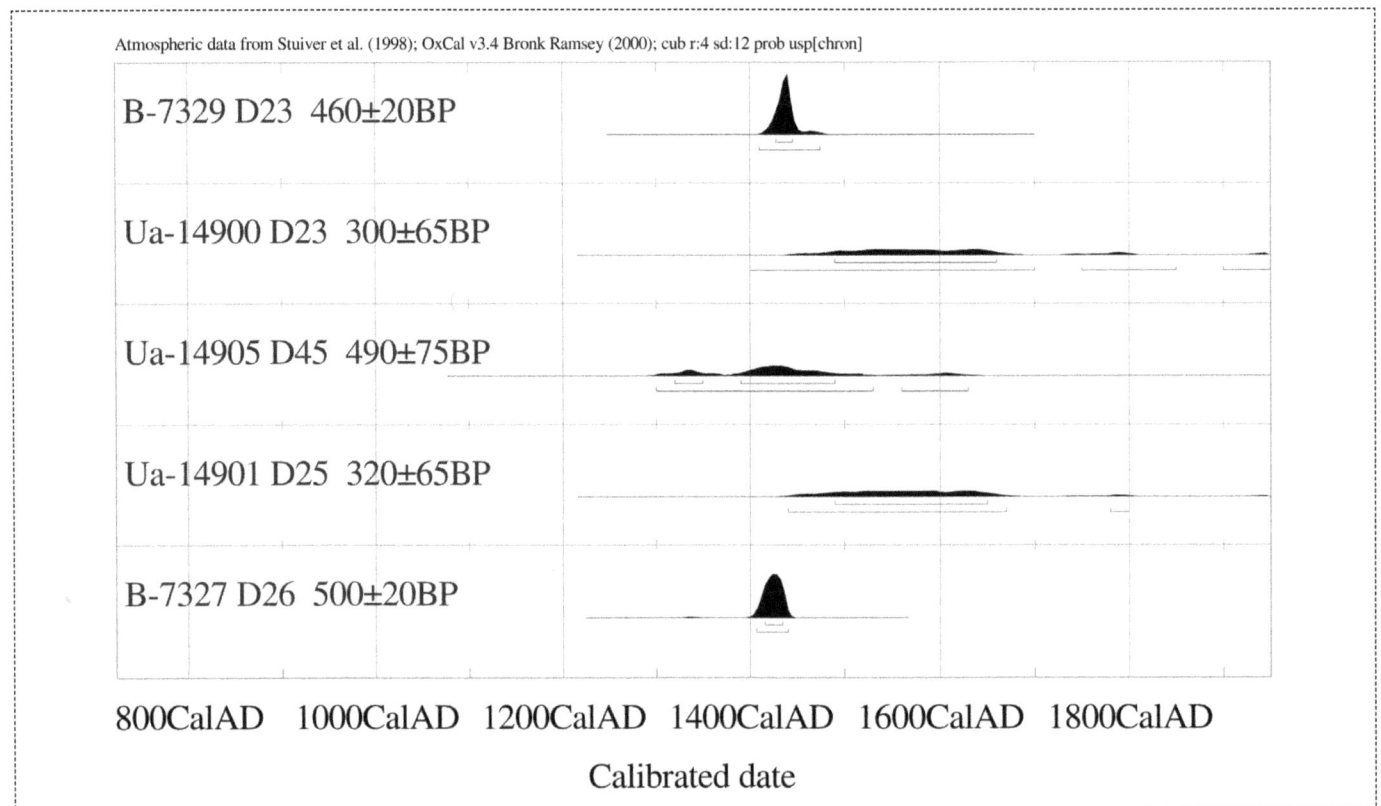

Figure 25. Dates from EH-25 with normalized probability surfaces (OxCal v.3.4).

[1] Uncalibrated and uncorrected for assumed Δ13C. Correcting by + 188 14C years for an assumed Δ13C value of -13.3 ‰ at PDB, subtracting 400 years for the reservoir effect, widening the sigma range by ± 50 years, and calibrating, provides a 2-sigma interval of 650-1300 A.D.

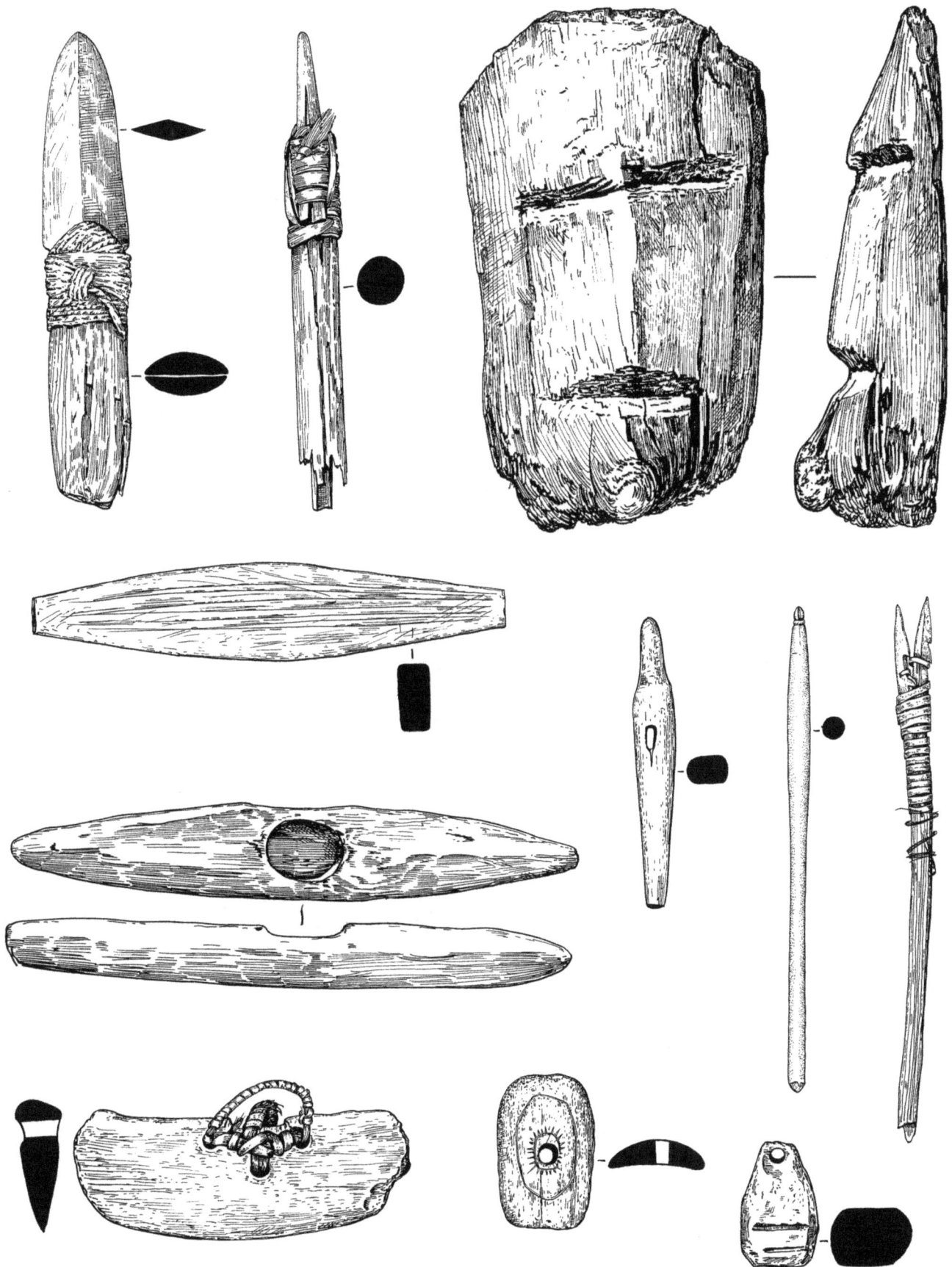

Figure 26. Artefacts from EH-25 (scale in cm). Drawing by N. Survillo, courtesy State Museum of Oriental Arts, Moscow.

short period (half a century?) during the fifteenth century AD. Some of the structural bones were already several centuries old when they were incorporated as construction elements into the construction. In this particular case, and although the assemblage unfortunately does not include any harpoon head, the style of the artifacts and their excellent preservation and light patina, hint at an age younger than those in other parts of the settlement, and are reminiscent of late Punuk and Western Thule (see Figure 26 and Photo 37). Sixty-three artifacts were recorded in situ in STRAT 2, most of them from the bottom layers of structures 1 and 3 (Photo 37). Of all the dwellings that were investigated in the settlement, EH-25 is the most recent, and it corresponds roughly to the abandonment of the cemetery as dated by Dinesman et al. (1999).[1]

Sedimentary sequence VI corresponds to an episode of human occupation, but was not dated. For sequence IV, two samples were dated, which yielded concording dates, 970-1220 Cal AD (Ua-14899) and 980-1250 Cal AD (Ua-14904).

4.6
SYNTHESIS AND CONCLUSION

Comparison of the two Mounds EM XIV and EM XII, and the dynamics of their formation in the Arctic context

Detailed study of these stratigraphies that cut through the two mounds (EM XIV and EM XII) shows two cases of rather distinct form:
On one hand, there is the case of a large mound (EM XIV) coalescing with other mounds (EM VIII and EM IX) where the boundary with the sterile substrate is clear, some times marked by small excavations. The sedimentation is essentially anthropogenous over the whole thickness of the mound, between 4 m and 7 m above sea level. The internal structure of the mound is distinctly complex: boundaries are often poorly marked and there is difficulty in recognizing an internal radiochronological seriation in the mound, where dates show that the densest occupation sequence is located in the interval 650 to 1300 AD.

On the other hand, Mound EM XII is of more modest size, its top 5 m above sea level and its present form resulting in large part from occupation sequence VIII. Its chrono-stratigraphy is better seriated, and there is evidence of alternating human and natural influences on its formation (Figure 24). Sequence VIII of Strat 2 (ca. 1440 and 1490 CalAD) corresponds chronologically with the upper sequence of Strat 1. The other periods represented in Strat 1 are also present in Strat 2, but in remnants of layers abraded by marine transgressions. We hypothesize that beginning as early as the seventh century AD the village at different periods covered both areas, but as the zone around Strat 2 was closer to sea level it was periodically washed out. Occupation sequence VIII is now exposed to storms, with erosion up to 3.5 m above sea level during the storm of August 20, 1998. Situated 3 m above sea level, its eastern part does not seem to have sustained prior erosion as is the case of occupations of some of the preceding phases (sequences IV and VI), both intercalated between sediments of the marine beach. Has sea level sustained phases of perceptible regression during the last two millennia? The question remains posed if one takes into account the data from the profile documented by Hans-Christian Gullov and Hans-Christian Kapel (written communication), where undeniable traces of occupation are located at 0.90 m above sea level.

---

[1] The cemetery is tentatively dated between about 2200 and 600 radiocarbon years BP, intentionally left uncalibrated by the authors (Dinesman et al. 1999: 2-3, Fig. 4.6.A, Table 4.15, and Appendix 2). Mason (1998: 225-226, 263) proposed conservative calibrations for these dates using a reservoir effect of 400 years; according to him, 56% of the graves (n=15) fall in the interval AD 800-1400. Dumond (1998: 118, 134) suggests other coefficients for correcting the reservoir effect, which would make the dates about a century younger still, that is, AD 900-1500. Radiocarbon ages in Dinesman et al. are not adjusted for any known or assumed Δ^{13}C.

The two examples studied permit us to propose an inventory of the sedimentary and post-depositional processes that led to the formation of the mounds as they appear today (Figure 27). The accretion of sediment of domestic origin seems to have taken place on the one hand during occupation phases – by accumulation of various elements within horizontal strata of several tens of centimeters thickness in the interior of houses (including remnants of beds, food remains, waste from handicraft activities such as wood shavings). On the other hand, during phases of abandonment, sediments of related origin were formed by dismantling of superstructural elements (including whale bones, timbers, and thick strata of badly differentiated sediment incorporating chunks of peat and sod). A more detailed understanding of these processes would necessitate more in-depth research and the contributions of biochemists in order to better determine the part taken by the post-depositional processes (Hall 1990) over the course of time in the particular context of the Arctic domain.

ACKNOWLEDGMENTS

This work could not have been accomplished without the contribution of a number of our colleagues. In the field there were Yvon Csonka, Reto Blumer, and others. For carrying out the work of analysis and elaboration, we have to thank the personnel of the Department of ARIA (Sion) for its material support, the staff of the Laboratory of Sedimentology of the College of Prehistory at the University of Basel (IPNA), in particular Philippe Rentzel and Ms Ritter, for taking charge of chemical analysis and the granulometry of fine fractions, Pierre-Alain Gillioz (Paris) for processing the granulometric data, Arkady Savinetsky (Moscow) for faunal analysis, as well as Bruno Moulin (†) and Susanna Kaufmann for their graphic work during production of the plates. This work has been financed by the FSLA. We have equally to thank Jacques Léopold Brochier and Owen K. Mason who have agreed to read this manuscript. Finally, my thanks go to Richard Bland, who translated this text from the original in French.

PRIMARY ANTHROPOGENOUS DEPOSITS

ARCHITECTURAL ELEMENTS
HOUSE FRAME: WHALE BONE, DRIFTWOOD
WALL AND ROOF: CLUMPS OF SOD, EARTH, AND PEAT
OCCUPATION FLOOR: STONES OF SCHIST AND GNEISS, WHALE SCAPULAS

- -

CONSTITUTION OF MIDDEN
WASTE FROM CRAFT ACTIVITY: WOOD SHAVINGS, IVORY, BALEEN
CULINARY WASTE: BONES OF SEA MAMMALS AND BIRDS, MOLLUSK SHELLS, BIRD FEATHERS
BEDDING RESIDUE: FUR, BIRD FEATHERS, MOSSES, TWIGS OF ERICACEOUS PLANTS
EARTH: VOLUNTARY OR INVOLUNTARY DRESSING OF OCCUPATION FLOORS INSIDE STRUCTURES

NATURAL AND ANTHROPOGENOUS SECONDARY PROCESSES

DEGRADATION CAUSING BURYING
SUPERSTRUCTURES PARTIALLY COLLAPSE AFTER ABANDONMENT
SPACE IS REARRANGED
REMAINING EMPTY SPACE FILLS WITH ICE

- -

POST-BURIAL DEGRADATION
CRYOTURBATION
SUBSEQUENT DEPOSITION
MARINE EROSION
PHYSICAL-CHEMICAL EVOLUTION OF SEDIMENTARY COMPONENTS: LEACHING, VERTICAL MIGRATION, ACCUMULATION OF PHOSPHATES, OILS, OTHER ORGANIC MATERIALS

Figure 27. Inventory of objects and processes contributing to formation of the Ekven mounds.

THE EKVEN SETTLEMENT: ESKIMO BEGINNINGS ON THE ASIAN SHORE OF BERING STRAIT

5.
PALEOCLIMATIC RECORDS IN THE EKVEN SITE: COMPARISONS WITH DATA FROM ALASKA [1]

OWEN K. MASON

5.1
INTRODUCTION

Ekven stratigraphic records correspond closely with the sea level history and paleoclimate proxy records from northwest Alaska. In brief, relatively stable, non-stormy conditions fostered the growth of a thick peat from 300 or 200 BC until AD 800 or 900, whereas after that time massive storms raked the Chukchi Peninsula coast and deposited a thick and sandy pebble layer – Unit (or "Sequence") V at the Ekven archaeological sites (Moulin, this volume: § 4.5.2.2 and Figure 24), which correlates with Unit 6 described by Dinesman et al. (1999). As was the case in Alaska, the Ekven coast witnessed heightened storminess from AD 800 to 1200 and during the Little Ice Age.

In specific detail, stratigraphic analyses by the International Research Expedition at the eroding bluff at Ekven record the episodic influence of climate-driven sedimentation through wind or marine agencies. Two types of deposits reflect climatic conditions: (a) gravels deposited by storm waves and (b) beach sand transported by wind. The Ekven sequence correlates closely with that of strata along the margin of Lopp Lagoon on the Alaskan shore less than 50 km distant. The following discussion of the Ekven data is based on the review of Dinesman et al. (1999) and on information in the immediately preceding chapter (Moulin, this volume).

A variety of geomorphic processes may produce stratigraphic records of past sea levels and reflect the interplay of eustasy, tectonism, and isostasy over periods of decades to centuries, as well as short term events such as storm surges and sea-surface temperature changes (Emery and Aubrey 1991, Douglas et al. 2001). In northeasternmost Asia, Late Pleistocene glaciation was limited to montane glaciers far distant from Ekven (Heiser and Roush 2001), so that isostatic factors can be discounted.

Tectonism may have had a cumulative effect on shoreline elevation over the course of the entire Quaternary (Brigham-Grette et al. 2001). However, in view of the formation of barrier and spits along the Chukchi Peninsula during the last few centuries, the effects of tectonism are apparently less profound than secular variations in climate such as storms that lead to the mobilization of clastic deposits.

5.2
OCEANOGRAPHIC FACTORS

The south-facing coast of Chukotka from Tunitlen to Dezhnevo (see Figure 4, p. 19) is comparatively straight, trending southwest to northeast; it is sheltered on the north by the Chukchi Peninsula and to the east and northeast by its eastern extremity, the Dezhnev massif. Thus, the coast can be affected only by waves from the south, a direction exposed to only a small portion of the maximum width of the Bering Sea. St. Lawrence Island, about 150 km to the south, partially shields the Ekven coast from southeast and southerly fetch. The longest window affecting the coast arises from winds from due south or southeast.

In general terms, the Ekven coast resembles the Seward Peninsula coast near Safety Sound, and the relatively protected nature of this coast may partially account for the preservation of coastal sites for much of the last 2000 years when northerly storms prevailed (Mason and Jordan 1993). However, the shift in storm tracks to the southwesterly direction after AD 1900 (Mason et al. 1996) could have endangered Ekven archaeological sites. A similar pattern may have prevailed during early periods of heightened storms, for example in the eighth to twelfth centuries AD and during the Little Ice Age.

[1] Editor's note: this chapter was originally published as Mason (2002) in a volume edited by Don Dumond and Richard Bland. We are grateful to Don Dumond and Owen Mason for their permission to reprint it in this volume.

Currents from the south prevail along the Bering Sea coast toward Ekven, producing a southwest-to-northeast littoral drift during fair-weather waves (Pavlov and Pavilov 1996: 19-28). About two-thirds of the flow through Bering Strait lies within the western part of the Strait (Coachman 1993) and variability in the volume of water transported is the greatest single agent controlling sea surface height in the Strait (Pavlov and Pavilov 1996: 40). This volume of water reflects shifts in the strength of geostrophic currents over the southern Bering Sea, in turn a consequence of the intensity and position of the Aleutian Low pressure regime (Overland and Pease 1982, Nieubauer 1988, Salmon 1992).

Present tidal range along the Ekven coast is less than 1 m; however, storms may elevate sea levels up to 3 m, as recorded by the archaeological crew during one event in August 1998 (Photo 16). Low level or average storm surges only reach between 1 and 1.5 m above mean high tide (Pavlov and Pavilov 1996: 40). The recurrence interval of the largest events is unknown, but low level surges may re-occur within three-to-seven- and eleven-year periods related to El Niño-Southern Oscillations, as reconstructed for the Nome region by Mason et al. (1996).

5.2.1
SEDIMENT BUDGETS

Comparatively few spits and barriers form along the southern Chukchi Peninsula; those that have formed are of smaller scale than on the Alaska shore or on the northern Chukchi Peninsula coast. The coast of that peninsula from Cape Chaplino to East Cape is apparently sediment-limited. Few of the rivers are large enough to contribute significant sediment to the littoral zone, and little sediment from the major system west of the Peninsula – the Anadyr River – is apparent on aerial photos.

Many of the beach ridge plains and spits along the Chukchi coast appear to have undergone considerable modification and re-assembly as eustatic sea level has risen during the Holocene (Ionin 1961). Although no chronometric controls – either geological and archaeological – are available, a few brief descriptions and speculative histories are available in the English-language literature, especially by Ionin (1961) and Zenkovich (1967). Beach ridge development is often correlated with submarine gravel bodies that were reshaped by storm waves (Zenkovich 1967: 290ff, Shcherbakov 1969: 129ff). At the approaches to the inner margins of Mechigmen Gulf, two recurved spits formed – one from northeast to southwest, and one from south to north (Zenkovich 1967: 389). Bluffs, updrift from the eastern spit, exhibit an active erosion face and likely fed comparatively recent east-to-west transport that constructed the eastern spit. Farther south at Cape Nygligan, two forelands or mainland-attached barriers form a reworked foreland (Zenkovich 1967: 431). At the mouth of Lavrentiya [St. Lawrence] Bay a very small triangular foreland has also formed; however, in the Ekven area the barrier bars are even smaller, barely discernible on aerial photographs of 1:60'000 scale.

5.3
EKVEN STRATIGRAPHY

Several issues confront any geoarchaeological analyst of the Ekven bluff and its superimposed archaeological sites (Csonka et al. 1999, Moulin and Csonka 2002, Moulin, this volume). The first concern involves the nature of the underlying sediments and the configuration of the bluff prior to settlement. The second concern is the paleo-climatic and occupation history evident in the sediments enclosing the site.

The presence of marine deposits underlying the archaeological materials indicates that the occupation was transgressive along the surface created by marine erosion of the bluff. This circumstance implies that settlement was either atop a now-eroded bench that was inset into the present lower bluff, or was on a paleo-beach. Sedimentological analyses identify two types of sand deposit (Moulin, this volume: § 4.3.2 and Figure 12): (a) beach sand and (b) wind-blown sand reflecting the presence of the beach; this latter depositional agency (b) is inferred for Unit or Sequence VII (Moulin, this volume: § 4.5.2.1 and Figure 24).

The Ekven bluff lies adjacent to the Bering Sea coast and its initial Unit I is composed of unconsolidated clays and silts identified as colluvium or solifluction that was produced by slope-related re-transport during the Pleistocene and continuing into the late Holocene (Moulin, this volume: § 4.2.2.1 and 4.5.2.2, Figure 12 and 24). In a single case, loam and rock debris was deposited over an extensive peat bed formed before 3955 ± 193 BP (IEMRZh-1078) (Dinesman et al. 1999: 26, 129); no marine influences are apparent. The colluvial materials were emplaced at lower sea levels prior to the Holocene; hence, the paleo-slope as observed by Dinesman et al. (1999: 26-27) was several tens of meters above sea level and considerably inland. Nonetheless, the colluvial sediments do not directly reveal pre-Holocene sea level position, although the upper contact of the slope does have some relevance to site formation history and its position relative to past sea level. A marked unconformity should underlie the entire archaeological site and should continue upslope.

The succeeding Unit II (Moulin, this volume: § 4.2.2.1 and Figure 24) describes an organic peat with interbedded, likely eolian-deposited, sand and is correlated with a geological exposure – described in Dinesman et al. (1999: 20ff) – at 160 to 200 cm below surface, or ca. 1 m above high tide. From 184 to 201 cm below surface, "thin peaty layers alternate with thin vague sand-peat interlayers and well-expressed sand interlayers." The sand layers are attributed to "periodic over[wash] of wave-action deposits" (Dinesman et al. 1999: 21), although a more convincing explanation invokes intermittent winds that raked an exposed beach. None of the sand beds is thicker than 1 cm. Storm deposition is evident from a higher bed, between 175-184 cm below surface, composed of "gray sand with eroded pebbles and walrus bones," a deposit correlated with an 1800-year- old (based on mammal bone) "well-expressed sand-pebble beach ridge" that built along much of the coast (Dinesman et al. 1999: 21).

Ekven Unit III (Moulin, this volume: Figure 24) consists of gravely, detrital sand, slightly altered by added organics and oxidation (from its yellowish color); this unit is attributed to marine agencies, but not necessarily related to high energy storms, instead reflecting fair-weather beach deposits. Ekven Unit IV includes re-worked cultural materials, whale baleen, other bone, and carbonaceous material; this may correspond to storm-deposited material. Similarly, culturally sterile Ekven Unit V consists of well-sorted sand interbedded with gravel – a good candidate for a storm bed and marked by an erosional truncation at its upper contact. Ekven Unit VI includes in situ cultural materials, while the superimposed Ekven Unit VII consists of sandy clay interstratified with sand beds deposited under the influence of south and southeast winds, as substantiated from sedimentological data. The episode of storm-produced winds was succeeded by Ekven Unit VIII including in situ cultural remains, with numerous structures dated between AD 1440 and 1490 (Moulin, this volume: Figure 24).

Several chronometric guideposts are available from the lower peat and interbedded sands at Ekven. The lowest peat interbedded with sand at the Ekven geological exposure designated 15/90 (about 1 m above sea level) is dated at 2394 ± 90 BP (Iemae-898) or, in calendar years at 1 sigma, between 789 and 356 BC. Only 25 cm higher in the section the bone of an unspecified mammal, likely sea mammal, was dated to 1792±85 BP (Iemae-906) (Dinesman et al. 1999: 20-21), which at 1 sigma, employing Dumond's (1998: 108) 512 ± 57-year marine carbon offset, calibrate within AD 1025-1241. However, if the bone was rather terrestrial mammal or even bowhead whale (requiring only a 200-year correction, cf. Dyke et al. 1996), the calibrated date might be as early as AD 30-425, a time more in accord with sea level trends in Alaska. Nonetheless, the intervening sand beds reflect several episodes of storms after 350 BC, with a stronger storm signal in the first millennium AD, possibly as late as AD 1000. The several thick, pebbly sand layers follow the several thin peats; these probably reflect the storms in the latter part of the first millennium AD.

Cultural charcoal dated and calibrated to AD 560-660 (AAR-2736) derives from a hearth "below the modern beach," based on Danish researchers Gulløv and Kapel in the mid-1990s (see above p. 68). The location of these materials is placed at 1.5 m above mean sea level (Yvon Csonka, written comm. 27 June 2001) and based on a photograph from Csonka et al. (1999: 104), is not substantially lower than the Ekven geologic sections. The hearths were possibly atop a surface produced by storms that eroded the underlying solifluction or colluvium (i.e., Unit I at the archaeological site) and are assumed to correlate with Unit II.

Within the Ekven archaeological site, using the geologic data points, the Unit II peat at 1 m above sea level represents a comparatively stable sea level position following the last centuries BC and the first centuries AD. Doubtless, the peat formed beyond the highest limit of storm waves that can crest 4 to 5 m above mean seal level (Csonka et al. 1999: 104). Unit III, termed a beach deposit, predates the occupation within Unit IV, which is dated within AD 970-1220 and AD 980-1250 – an average of AD 1000-1150. Hence, the emplacement of Unit III must have occurred after AD 700 and before AD 1000, or 1150 at the latest. Since Unit IV beds reveal reworking, it is likely that storms continued during this period

as well. Subsequently, a major storm episode is recorded in the following period, Unit V, but it is difficult to assign any firm age – after AD 1000, possibly after AD 1200. Records from western Alaska would support the younger range, with cultural materials ca. AD 1000, and storms probably occurring after AD 1100-1150 but before AD 1200. Unit VI is undated, but is younger than AD 1250 and older than AD 1440. Eolian activity in Unit VII is likely associated with storms during the Little Ice Age.

5.4 GEOLOGICAL IMPLICATIONS OF THE EKVEN STRATIGRAPHY

Stratigraphic sections in the vicinity of the Ekven barrier record storm events during the early first millennium AD. The sequences fine upward, alternating between gravel and sand beds emplaced by storms, and sea-transgressed detrital peats that are the remains of stabilized and vegetated surfaces. The dating of the profiles is based primarily on whale bone obtained from shallow cores in the Ekven area (Dinesman et al. 1999: Fig. 2.5). While the bones provide a poor basis for inferring past mean eustatic sea level, considering their origin as clasts transported by storm waves, they do inform us about past storm-elevated sea levels. From the discussion in Dinesman et al. (1999: 29ff), the surface elevation of the Ekven bar is uncertain; apparently it is above sea level. The salt tolerance of the peat is also uncertain, as is its elevation in relation to sea level. The transect profiles are described as on "the surface of beach ridges" (Dinesman et al. 1999: 33); from this I infer that the surface is at maximum storm elevation and that peats are likely swale or non-salt-tolerant vegetation.

Several Ekven geologic sections, interbedded with dated sea mammal bones, provide temporal reference points for the reconstruction of storm history (Dinesman et al. 1999: 29ff), employing the calibrations of Stuiver et al. (1998), and the old-carbon corrections of 200 ± 100 years for bowhead whale (Dyke et al. 1996) and 459 ± 32 years for gray whale and seal (Dumond and Griffin 2002). The earliest storm, in evidence more than 1.7 m below ridge surface (Sect. 10/89), pre-dated a complex anthropogenous deposit of gravely, pebbly sand with abundant plant and animal detritus – baleen, whale skin, fish scales (cf. Dinesman et al. 1999: 31) – that contained a vertebra from a bowhead alive between 542 BC and AD 22 (2228 ± 114 BP [Iemae-814]). Subsequently (within Sect. 9/89), at 122-125 cm below surface and following at least two additional storms, a gray whale was alive between AD 720 and 1212 (1896 ± 107 BP [Iemae-856]). A discrete storm bed ("a layer of free-flowing pebbles") at 54-58 cm below surface in Sect. 11/90 (Dinesman et al. 1999: 31, 129) contained a whale rib dating to AD 1498-1884 (635 ± 83 BP [Iemae 508]). Within the last several centuries, the Ekven bar has stabilized, as reflected by peat formation and only intermittent addition of eolian sand. Peat, at 10-15 cm below surface, formed above ringed seal remains dated to AD 1434-1673 (1231 ± 63 BP [Iemae-855]).

The more than 1 m elevational differences between whale and seal samples indicate differences in depositional environments and the idiosyncrasies of individual storms that rarely extended across the entire Ekven barrier bar (cf. Dinesman et al. 1999: Fig. 2.5). Thus, two exceptionally large storms occurred during the life of the gray whale, AD 720-1212. Several smaller storms accompanied by a rise in eustatic sea level resulted in the surface that contains the ringed seal that may have died as late as AD 1673. Another whale dated to AD 1498-1884 (635 ± 83 BP [Iemae-908]) that is now 54-58 cm below surface but 2.4 m above sea level, probably died in the early sixteenth century AD, considering the seal age. While the reference datum of the sections with regard to mean high or low sea level is unclear in Dinesman et al. (1999), the elevations of carcasses almost certainly reflect storm-elevated sea levels, not eustatic (ice volume) levels.

5.5
SEA LEVEL RECORDS OF CHUKOTKA AS COMPARED TO ALASKA

A bewildering array of geomorphic reconstructions is offered by Dinesman et al. (1999: 40-41), including a series of rapid eustatic sea level fluctuations from a +7 m high stand to a −7 m low stand during the middle Holocene. In the absence of Chukotka field experience and only limited access to the Russian literature, I offer only tentative comments. Russian researchers infer two periods of higher sea level: One in the early Holocene, the other from 4000 to 2000 BP. The early Holocene transgression hypothetically attained levels 5 to 7 m above present sea level (Gasanov 1982, Svitoch 1973), and occurred between 7000 and 6000 BP, leading to the formation of spits and beach ridges in the regressive period from 5000 to 4000 BP. Following 4000 BP, colluvium should have been deposited on spits and coastal land forms. The processes responsible for this colluviation are unclear in the discussion in Dinesman et al. (1999). Presumably, a regression in the high sea level after 4000 BP should have allowed the preservation of deposits of the earlier high stand – but unfortunately none is preserved. This argument based on negative evidence is unsatisfying, and it is easier to argue that sea level was lower than present before 4000 BP. As discussed below, this is the situation inferred for northwest Alaska only 100 km across Bering Strait.

The dearth of geomorphic data continues during the next millennium after 4000 BP. As Dinesman et al. (1999: 41) observe, the Ekven research "suppl[ies] no data on changes in the shoreline in the period 4000-2500 years BP." Significantly, however, dated peat and marine mammal bone can be employed to infer that sea level was 1.5 to 2 m below present at 2500 BP (Dinesman et al. 1999: 41-42). One seemingly definite reference point is the presence ca. 4000 BP of a fresh water, lowland tundra on the basin of the present Dezhnev lagoon. To explain this, Dinesman et al. (1999: 41) envision either a decline in sea level or a blockage by dunes or barrier; considering other sea level data points the latter is the more likely possibility. Supporting data for a lower sea level are found in the Laptev Sea cores described by Bauch et al.

(2001), who provide no evidence of two Holocene high stands but instead infer that near modern sea levels were attained by 5000 years ago. Diatom evidence of sea level transformation occurs within Chukchi Sea cores and is inferred for the early Holocene (Polyakova 1990).

5.5.1
COMPARISONS WITH THE ALASKA MAINLAND AND ARCTIC SHELF

Data from a variety of depositional environments (i.e., peats on barrier islands and deltas, lagoon margins) record 6000 years of sea-level history over the 1000 km from Lopp Lagoon near Cape Prince of Wales and Bering Strait to Point Barrow – a coast with little or no co-seismic or isostatic adjustments (Jordan and Mason 1999; Mason and Jordan 2001). As Hopkins (1967) recognized, progradational beach ridges from northwest Alaska indicate the near-stabilization of sea level c. 5000 years ago, termed the Krusensternian transgression. As mentioned, cores from the Laptev Sea indicate a contemporaneous stabilization of sea level (Bauch et al. 2001: 136). The late Holocene history of sea level indicates that at 3700-3000 BC sea level stood at 1.5 m below present, rose to 1.0 m below present between 2000 and 1600 BC, and increased to 0.5 m below present between 400 and 200 BC (Jordan and Mason 1999, Mason and Jordan 2001). Considering the limited materials from the Ekven lagoon, it is noteworthy that the data show such a strong parallel.

Storms along the Seward Peninsula occurred during three principal periods, as described in Mason and Jordan (1993), Mason et al. (1995, 1997), with chronology based on radiocarbon determinations from archaeological and geological contexts (Mason 1999). Storms truncated nearly every spit and beach ridge complex on the Alaska coast between 1600 and 1000 BC, during AD 750-1200 and from AD 1600 to 1900. Neoglacial sediment input into the western Arctic Ocean has an inferred age of 3500 to 1500 years BP and is preserved within a core several hundred km north of Bering Strait (Darby et al. 1994).

5.5.2
BACKGROUND FOR ALASKA SEA LEVEL AND STORM HISTORIES

The microtidal, north-facing Chukchi Sea (with diurnal variation of less than 0.5 m) is a 1000-km-long embayment of the Arctic Ocean, located north of the Bering Strait at 65° N latitude (Naidu and Gardner 1988). The south-facing Bering Sea is a compartment of the North Pacific. Although ice-covered usually from late October to late June, Chukchi and Bering Sea coasts are wave-dominated and often subjected to fall-season storm surges that reach several meters above sea level (Wise et al. 1981). Due to a combination of low tide-range and abundant, mobile clastic material (both terrestrial and shelf), the coasts are sensitive proxies for atmospheric processes.

Kotzebue Sound and Seward Peninsula are moderately active seismologically as part of the Brooks Range province (Thenhaus et al. 1982). Seismic activity is sporadic in the Chukchi Sea; a 6.4-magnitude quake occurred off Chukotka more than 300 km northwest of Cape Espenberg (Fujita et al. 1990). No co-seismic elevation changes are reported, as is evident in the consistent elevation of 125,000 year-old shorelines from Isotope Stage 5e at no more than 10 m above sea level (Brigham-Grette and Hopkins 1995). The low coastal hills did not support glaciation during the late Pleistocene or Holocene, so that no isostatic factors need be considered.

5.5.3
THE ALASKA DATABASE

Fourteen of the more than 20 northwest Alaska beach ridge complexes located north of the Yukon River yield temporal data useful in establishing geomorphic history and storm frequency. Complexes vary in orientation and in number of ridges; cumulatively, at least 489 ridges can be enumerated, a mean of 33 in a range of 5 to 114. Higher numbers of ridges are preserved on many coasts due to a succession of lower intensity storms or during intervals with long intervals between storms. The highest number of ridges occurs at Cape Krusenstern, with at least 114 preserved, not including composite and lake-margin ridges. Point Spencer contains more than 100 ridges but lacks any dating control. Next-highest Sisualik has about 70 ridges, while Cape Espenberg has 35 that include at least six composite dunes.

Ridge formation reflects fetch and storm duration, circumstances also affected by the percentage of ice cover. Locations with multiple orientations have higher numbers of ridges (e.g., Cape Krusenstern). Predictably, the maximal number of ridges occurs in the middle stretches of the Chukchi Sea, not at the margins that are subject to variable (i.e. increased) ice conditions or limited fetch.

Of the total of 275 14C ages that pertain to the late Holocene depositional history of western and northwestern Alaska beach ridges (cf. Mason and Ludwig 1990; Mason and Jordan 1993, Mason et al. 1997), only 34.5% (n=95) were collected specifically with geological aims. Archaeological samples comprise the overwhelming majority of the dates and provide only upper limiting ages – e.g., at the St. Lawrence Island cemetery and houses and the Cape Krusenstern houses drawn on by Mason and Ludwig (1990). All ages were dendro-calibrated to calendar years to adjust for 14C variability following Stuiver et al. (1998), applying a 510 ± 57-year offset to shell samples (Dumond 1998); however, a 459 ± 32-year offset might be more accurate (cf. Dumond and Griffin 2002) to account for the ingestion of anomalously old marine carbon. Ages are reported in two sigma ranges, using probability distribution to refine age determinations, which are cited as cal BC or cal AD. Approximately 35 14C ages bracket coastal changes in the late first millennium AD.

5.5.4
LATE HOLOCENE STORM HISTORY
ON THE CHUKCHI SEA COAST OF ALASKA

Between cal AD 800 and 1150, nearly all beach-ridge sets from the Yukon River delta to Point Barrow were subject to erosional truncation that produced disconformable ridges, due to a major shift in storm frequency and direction that caused substantial erosion and sediment remobilization along the Chukchi Sea (Mason and Jordan 1993, Mason et al. 1995, 1997). Storms produced substantial changes during the Little Ice Age, as well. At the south after cal AD 700-1000, the Yukon River witnessed a major avulsion and the creation of a new delta lobe (Mason and Dupre 1999), while several storm ridges were added south of these. Storm facies, redeposited peat, dated to the first millennium AD also occur on the Bering Sea shelf (cf. Mason and Jordan 1993).

The most complete records of coastal evolution are from Capes Krusenstern and Espenberg, respectively located on the north and south shores of Kotzebue Sound. Both north and south coasts experienced net erosion during the late first millennium AD. However, on the southern coast – Seward Peninsula from Espenberg to Wales – sand transported higher onto the back beach was incorporated into dunes by persistent high, onshore winds during fall and winter. Within decades from AD 900 to 1100, high dunes had built along the entire northwest Seward Peninsula coast (Jordan 1990). Contemporaneously, storms cut numerous inlet channels through the Shishmaref barrier islands. Composite gravel ridges were built along north-facing coasts at Point Barrow, Cape Krusenstern, Kotzebue, and on Choris Peninsula (Mason and Jordan 1993), with stratigraphic evidence at archaeological sites of powerful storms affecting north-facing coasts on St. Lawrence Island (Mason and Ludwig 1990) and on southern Kotzebue Sound from Deering (Reanier et al. 1998) to Kotzebue. Soil development indicative of surface stabilization reflects decreased storm activity in the thirteenth century AD (Mason et al. 1997).

Cape Espenberg, the depositional sink for the northern Seward Peninsula littoral cell, experienced 4 to 6 m of vertical dune growth landward of eroding beaches and atop older, low dunes separated by wide swales – this was formed during AD 200-750 when storms were less frequent and of less magnitude (cf. Psuty 1988). Two episodes of intense storms are recorded at Espenberg by shell beds (more than 1-1.5 m above mean high water) dated to cal AD 750-950 and cal AD 1050-1150, but are separated by a non-stormy interval of dune stabilization and soil formation between cal AD 950-1050. Most dune building from cal AD 750-1150 reflected high onshore sand supply under the influence of North Pacific-derived storms that produced oblique waves and alongshore sand transport, unlike earlier stormy episodes in the Neoglacial, 1600-1200 cal BC (Mason and Jordan 1993), that produced little or no progradation by their predominant onshore waves.

South-facing Cape Krusenstern expanded partially by cannibalizing older ridges, as is evident in the repeated southeastward displacement of clasts after major truncations (Mason and Ludwig 1990). Storm erosion at Cape Krusenstern involved several responses. First, high intensity northwesterly storms truncated earlier ridges on its northwest margin between cal AD 750 and 950, and produced a high, composite gravel ridge cal AD 1050-1200. The intervening century, cal AD 950-1050, witnessed the transport of sand, pebbles and cobbles, and the addition of several ridges to the southwest edge of the beach ridge complex. The poorly dated Sisualik spit, down drift about 50 km from Cape Krusenstern, probably also experienced a combination of erosion and southeastward progradation between cal AD 750 and 1150. A partially inverse relationship prevailed between the northern Seward and southern Lisburne Peninsulas. Differences in storm trajectories (variability in direction and duration) probably explain such responses; whereas northwesterly storms predominated between AD 700 and 900, recovery during fair weather periods allowed progradation to the southeast.

5.6
THE BIG PICTURE: HOLOCENE PALEO-CLIMATES FROM SLOPES AND BOGS NEAR EKVEN

Cool, wet conditions fostered peat formation on the Cape Dezhnev massif as early as 7500 BP – possibly a millennium earlier, based on the Uelen peat bog north of the Ekven site (Dinesman et al. 1999: 35ff). A shift to warm and dry conditions occurred during the period 6500 to 3800 BP, based on high decomposition rates and the lack of mineral additions to the peat. Around 3800 BP peat decomposition slowed, which may "indicate more severe thermal conditions ... lower summer temperatures ... [and] a certain increase in the precipitation" (Dinesman et al. 1999: 39). Between 3800 BP (ca. 2200-2000 BC) and 2200-2100 BP (the last centuries BC), colluviation resulted in the deposition of a 20 cm thick loam within the Uelen peat bog. By AD 1, a wetter climate was re-established, as indicated by peat formation and "increased surface humification" (Dinesman et al. 1999: 40).

Coastal bluffs next to Ekven (Dinesman et al. 1999: 25ff, Fig. 2.4) reveal landscape-scale processes in the strata (20-50 cm thick) of sand, pebbles and / or peat and rock debris that accumulated during several episodes of colluviation. Three episodes of peat formation represent surface stabilization: (a) ca. 4000 BP; (b) ca. 2800-2200 BP and (c) ca. 1500 BP. This sequence of alternations in colluviation followed by peat formation is paralleled in the archaeologically dated sequences at Iyatayet near Cape Denbigh and Onion Portage (Mason and Gerlach 1995a) and by stabilized surfaces (O soil horizons) within Cape Espenberg sand dunes (Mason and Jordan 1997). By AD 1, colder conditions once again prevailed along the Ekven coast; similar shifts to cooler climates are recorded in beach ridge chronologies and glacial records across northern Alaska (Mason and Jordan 1993; Mason 1999). The last two millennia of slope processes are not dated at Ekven, although one section (5/89) offers promise for a full record (Dinesman et al. 1999: 26, Fig. 2.4). If the record parallels that of northwest Alaska, I would expect that periods of decades to several centuries of warmth during the second to seventh centuries AD were followed by a lengthy cooler episode AD 750-1000. Subsequently, one or two centuries

of maximum warmth occurred around the thirteenth century AD, while an abrupt return to cooler conditions marked the several-hundred-year-long Little Ice Age that commenced c. AD 1300 and lasted some centuries. (Mason and Jordan 1993; Mason and Gerlach 1995a; Mason and Jordan 1997; Mason 1999).

5.7
HEMISPHERIC CORRELATIONS

Comparisons with other regions of the world show numerous correlations with the heightened storminess, colluviation and surface stabilization in northwest Alaska and on the Chukchi Peninsula that were discussed above. The early Medieval period of coastal reorganization in northwest Alaska co-occurs with evidence of hemisphere-wide colder temperatures (Grove and Switsur 1994; Krupnik 1993; O'Brien et al. 1995). Heightened storms co-occurs, and are perhaps correlative, with increased precipitation producing Brooks Range glacial expansion (Ellis and Calkin 1984) and wider Alaska tree-rings (Graumlich and King 1998), as well as a major reorganization in the Yukon River (Mason and Dupré 1999). Farther afield, eastern Asian paleoclimatic records reveal numerous correlative geomorphic transformations (cf. Mason 1999 for detailed review). Two examples include the development of a massive chenier (or storm) ridge in north China (Wang and Ke 1989) and intensified Yangtze and Huang Ho flooding (Gong and Hameed 1991, cf. Mason 1999 for fuller review of East Asian evidence). Massive Bering Strait erosion during the Early Medieval period corresponds to several North Atlantic glacial expansions (cf. Grove and Switsur 1994).

Increased storminess reflects a global atmospheric pattern with intensified meridional circulation, a circumstance evident in heightened salt concentrations in Greenland ice cores (O'Brien et al. 1995). Several decadal Bering Strait cold intervals between AD 700 and 1800 are closely paralleled in a fine scale 18O record reported by Dansgaard et al. (1975). Parallels notwithstanding, one should not expect that every stormy episode in northwest Alaska was or will be paralleled on the Chukchi Peninsula; for example, during the twentieth century AD storms in Chukotka (especially in the early 1920s) were out of phase with those on the Seward Peninsula (Krupnik 1993: 142-143; Mason et al. 1996). Only a concerted program of inter-disciplinary Quaternary research will enable researchers from both sides of Bering Strait to discern fine scale patterns.

5. PALEOCLIMATIC RECORDS IN THE EKVEN SITE: COMPARISONS WITH ALASKAN DATA

6.
POTTERY FROM THE EKVEN SETTLEMENT[1]

AGNÈS GELBERT

6.1
INTRODUCTION

During excavation campaigns conducted in 1997 and 1998 in the Ekven site (in Chukotka) several hundred pottery sherds were found. The material, collected by the Swiss team, consists of 921 sherds, collected in four different parts of the settlement (Blumer and Csonka 1998, Csonka, Moulin and Blumer 1999):

- 739 sherds come from surface collections in the erosion front (EEF). This material, found out of context, represents more than 80% of the studied corpus and covers a very extended time period, from 0 to 1700 A.D. (cal.)

The rest of the material comes from three test pits[2]:

- 86 sherds from ER1, a whale skull structure assigned to Late Prehistory (1500-1700 AD);
- 76 sherds from EH21, a semi-subterranean dwelling ruin attributed to Punuk and Thule;
- 20 sherds from EH13, a semi-subterranean dwelling ruin probably more recent than EH21.

The material is very fragmented, and of varying quality. A large number of sherds are very crumbly, some are exfoliated, and the inside or outside surfaces of a large number of fragments are missing. Many sherds are completely covered with a carbonate incrustation, which renders the observation of the surface features very difficult.

6.2
AIMS OF THE STUDY AND METHODOLOGY

The study of ceramics has been widely neglected in Beringian prehistoric sites, particularly in Siberia. This gap can be partly explained by the roughness of the sherds (especially when compared to the other types of artefacts to be found there) and by their morphological and ornamental uniformity, which is ill-adapted to the classical typological methods used in the study of ceramics.

I therefore suggest, for the Ekven pottery, a study based both on a typological analysis of the final products, and on the reconstruction of the different steps of the "chaîne opératoire". This is a preliminary study, the main aim of which is to characterize the variability of the ceramics production found on the site.

After observing the 921 sherds from the EEF, ER1, ER21 and EH13, I have selected all the elements that may yield information concerning morphology, decorations and technology. I have not sorted the material according to dimensions and I have only left out the sherds which, because of a bad state of conservation, or because they were too small, were impossible to interpret. About 35% of the material was thus left aside, and the final corpus is made up of 620 sherds (Figure 28).

LOCALISATION	EEF	EH21	EH13	ER1	TOTAL
N° OF SHERDS ANALYZED	506	50	20	44	620
N° OF SHERDS LEFT OUT	233	26	0	42	301

Figure 28. Studied corpus.

The morphological, ornamental, and technological data collected on this material has allowed me to characterize different techno-morphological types of pottery.

---

[1] Editor's note: this chapter was originally published as Gelbert Miermon (2006) in a volume edited by Don Dumond and Richard Bland. We are grateful to Don Dumond and to Agnès Gelbert Miermon for their permission to reprint it in this volume.

[2] See p.12. The location of ER1, EH21 and EH13 can be seen on figure 6.

In the absence of stratigraphical assignment, the question was to ascribe the artefacts to specific cultures and periods. I have attempted to answer this question by exploring several paths:

- The analysis of the distribution of morphological, ornamental and technological types on the erosion front. In this zone, the material was collected in two-meter wide corridors, some of which corresponded to identified archaeological structures. Thus, corridors 51 to 56 match the erosion zone of a recent habitation. I have tried to determine whether this zone might offer certain ceramic characteristics.

- The analysis of the distribution of morphological, ornamental and technological types in the ER1, EH21 and EH13 test pits. Unfortunately, the small number of sherds found in these structures affects the reliability of the results obtained.

- A comparative analysis of the Ekven ceramics and material found in Alaska. This analysis has been conducted only on the basis of bibliographical data which offers some kind of typological and technological descriptions.

6.3
POTTERY MORPHOLOGY

It was possible to refit only a very small number of sherds, and no complete shape. In order to analyze the morphological variability of the vessels, it was thus necessary to use isolated sherds, from different parts of the pot. The typology was mainly established on the basis of rim sherds, which allow for a characterization of the upper profile of the vessel, the rim diameter, the shape of the rim and of the lip.

6.3.1
DESCRIPTIVE SYSTEM

1. The orifice
The characterization of the orifice of the vessel was determined from rim sherds, by evaluating the "a" angle, between the rim axis and a horizontal line (Fig. 29). I have thus distinguished between two main categories of vessels:
R: restricted vessels, where "a < 90°"
U: unrestricted vessels, where "a = 90°"°
In the unrestricted vessels category, three types are revealed (Fig. 29):
U1. extremely unrestricted vessels, where "a >135°
U2. slightly unrestricted vessels, where "a = 135° = 95°
U3. nearly vertical-sided vessels, where "a = 90°"

2. The neck
In the category of restricted vessels, two types are found:
R1. vessels without a neck
R2. vessels with a neck

3. Dimensions
The only dimensions which it was possible to define were the diameter of the rim and the thickness of the wall. However, the rim sherds were sometimes narrow and often irregular, so that the measures concerning the diameter are only estimates.

4. The base
No base sherd was clearly identified in this corpus. Quite frequently, on very fragmented material, it is impossible to distinguish round base fragments from body fragments. As there were no flat nor conical base sherds, nor foot fragments, we may consider that all the vessels in the corpus have a round base.

5. The body
Only one sherd has angled shoulders while all the others have more or less convex continuous profiles, from globular to cylindrical.

6. The rim
All the rims have parallel or slightly divergent sides. Two groups are distinguished, based on their angle from the wall of the vessel (Fig. 30):
Ri1. straight rims
Ri2. everted rims

7. The lip
Undecorated lips (L1) have various shapes (Fig. 30):
L1/1 flattened
L1/2 flattened with an inward bulge
L1/3 flattened with an outward bulge
L1/4 bevelled
L1/5 rounded
L1/6 rounded with an inward bulge
L1/7 rounded with an inward and outward bulge
L1/8 rounded with an inward edge
L1/9 roof-shaped

8. Appendages
In the studied corpus, only two sherds have appendages. One has a pierced suspension lug (Fig. 31) on the rim, the other bears the trace of a vertical handle on the upper part of the body.

6.3.2
ANALYSIS IN THE DIFFERENT ARCHAEOLOGICAL UNITS: EEF, EH21, EH13, AND ER1

6.3.2.1
EEF
The material found in the erosion front contains 99 rim sherds, but the typology (Fig. 32) was established on the basis of only 94 sherds which provided sufficient morphological information. Two categories are found in EEF, restricted and unrestricted vessels:

RESTRICTED VESSELS (R)

They are less numerous in the studied corpus (22 out of 94), and are divided into three types (Fig. 32):

R1. Restricted vessels without a neck (Fig. 33, a-d)
21 rim sherds out of 22 fit into this category. They are medium- to large-sized vessels, the rim diameters of which range continuously from 13 to 36 cm. Their average thickness is approximately 9 mm. The rims of these vessels is usually straight (n = 16), more rarely everted (n = 5). When the lip is not ornamented (10 sherds out of 16), it has varied morphologies: flattened (n = 5), flattened with an inward

Unrestricted vessels (U)
$a \geqslant 90°$

Restricted vessels (R)
$a < 90°$

Extremely
unrestricted(U1)
$a > 135°$

Slightly
unrestricted (U2)
$135 \geqslant a > 90$

Nearly
vertical-sided (U3)
$a = 90°$

Inside

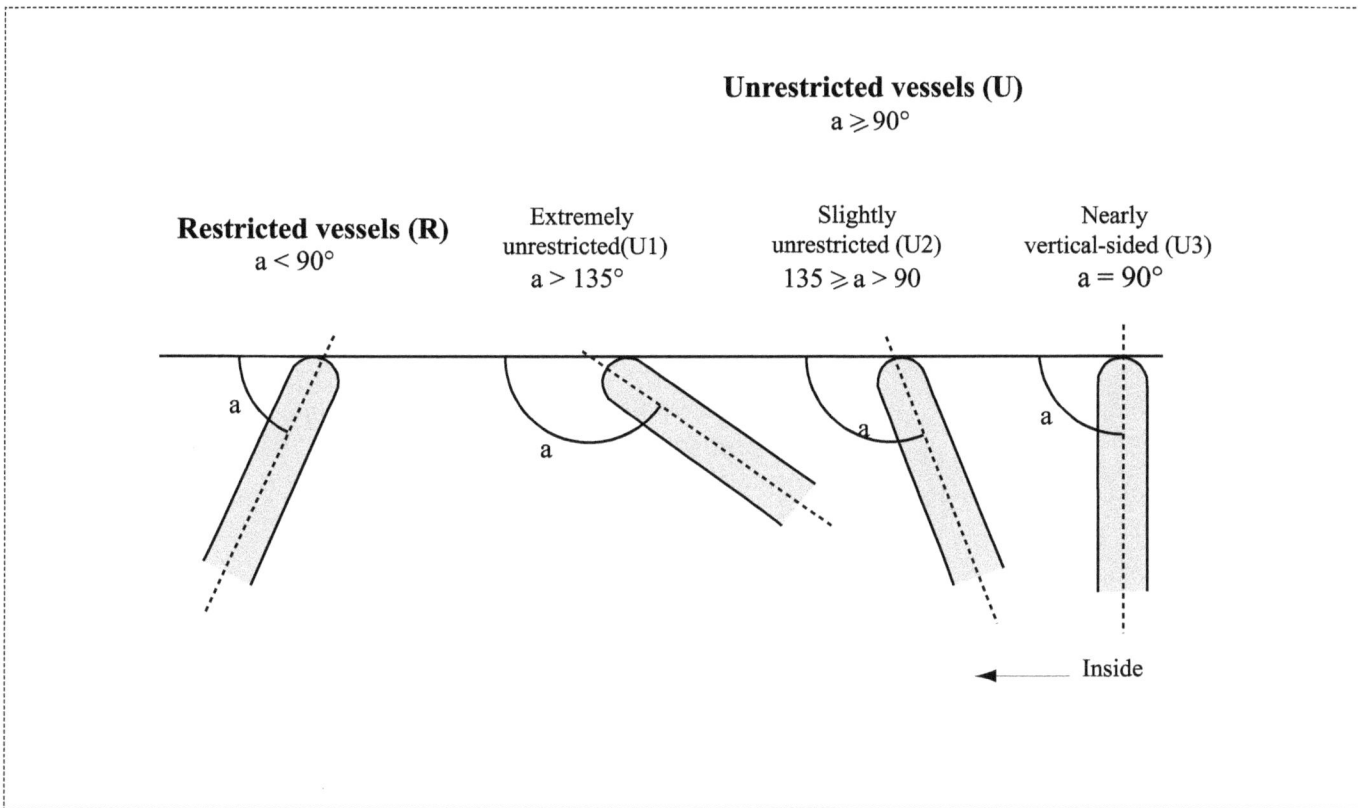

Figure 29. Characterization of vessel upper profiles.

Straight rims	L1/1	L1/2	L1/3	L1/4	L1/5
	L1/6	L1/7	L1/8	L1/9	
Everted rims		L2/1	L2/5		

Figure 30. Morphological types of rims and lips.

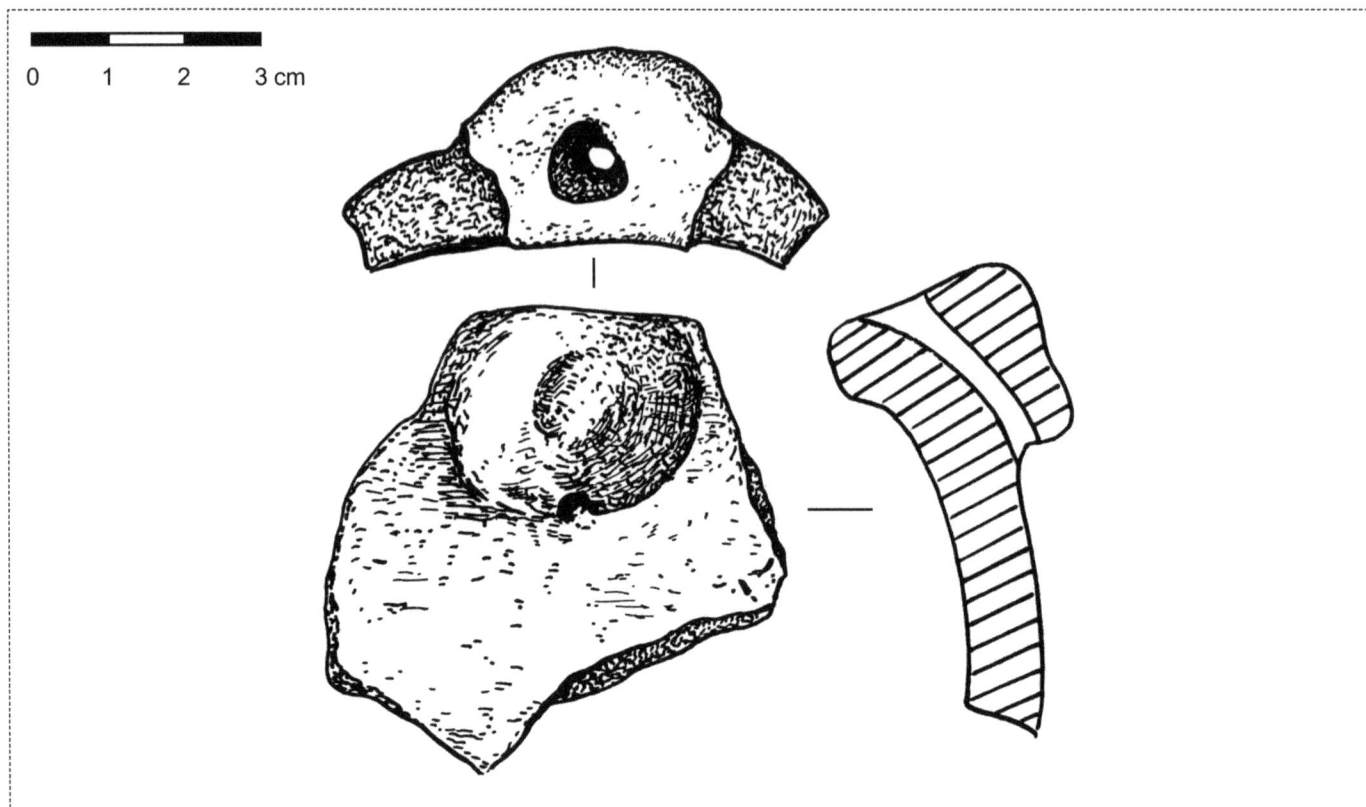

Figure 31. Rim with a pierced suspension lug. Drawing by N. S. Survillo.

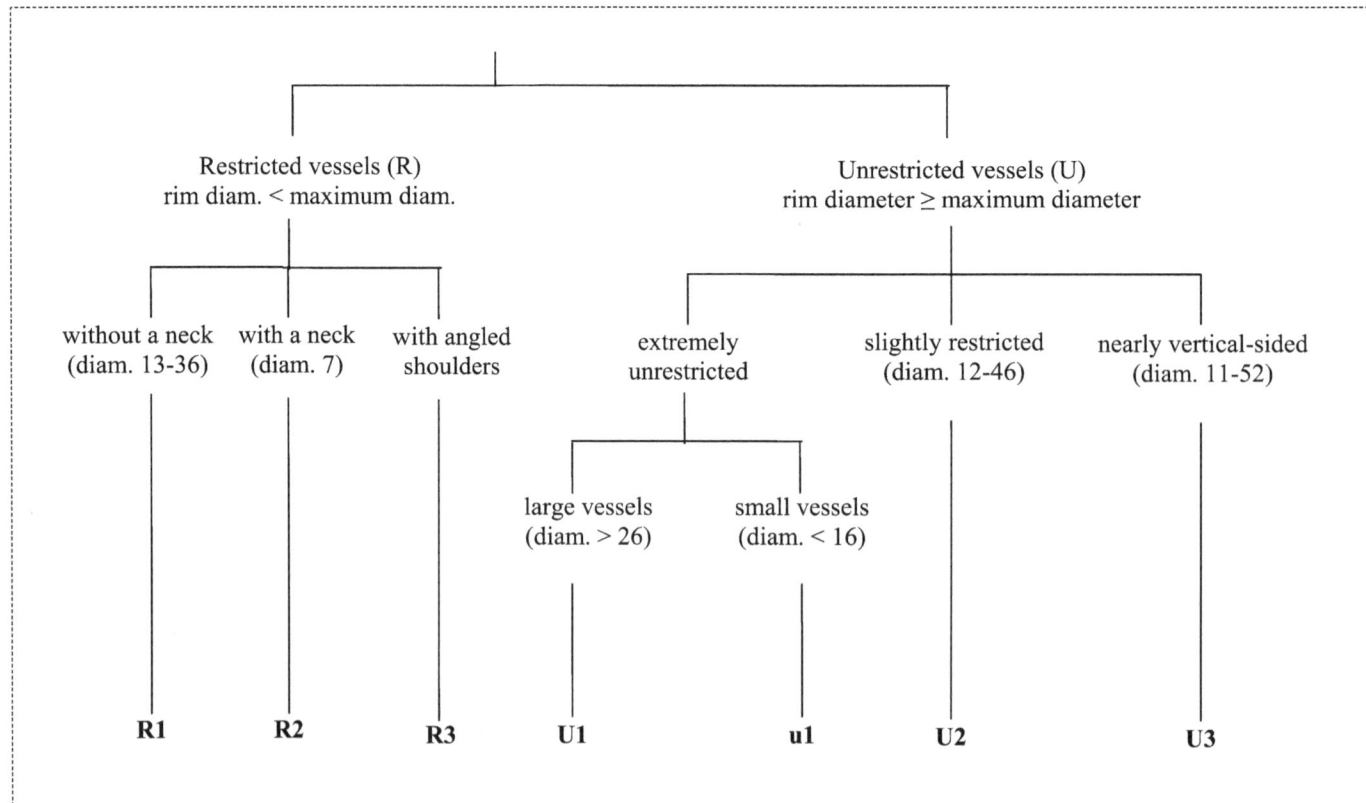

Figure 32. Typology of Ekven ceramics.

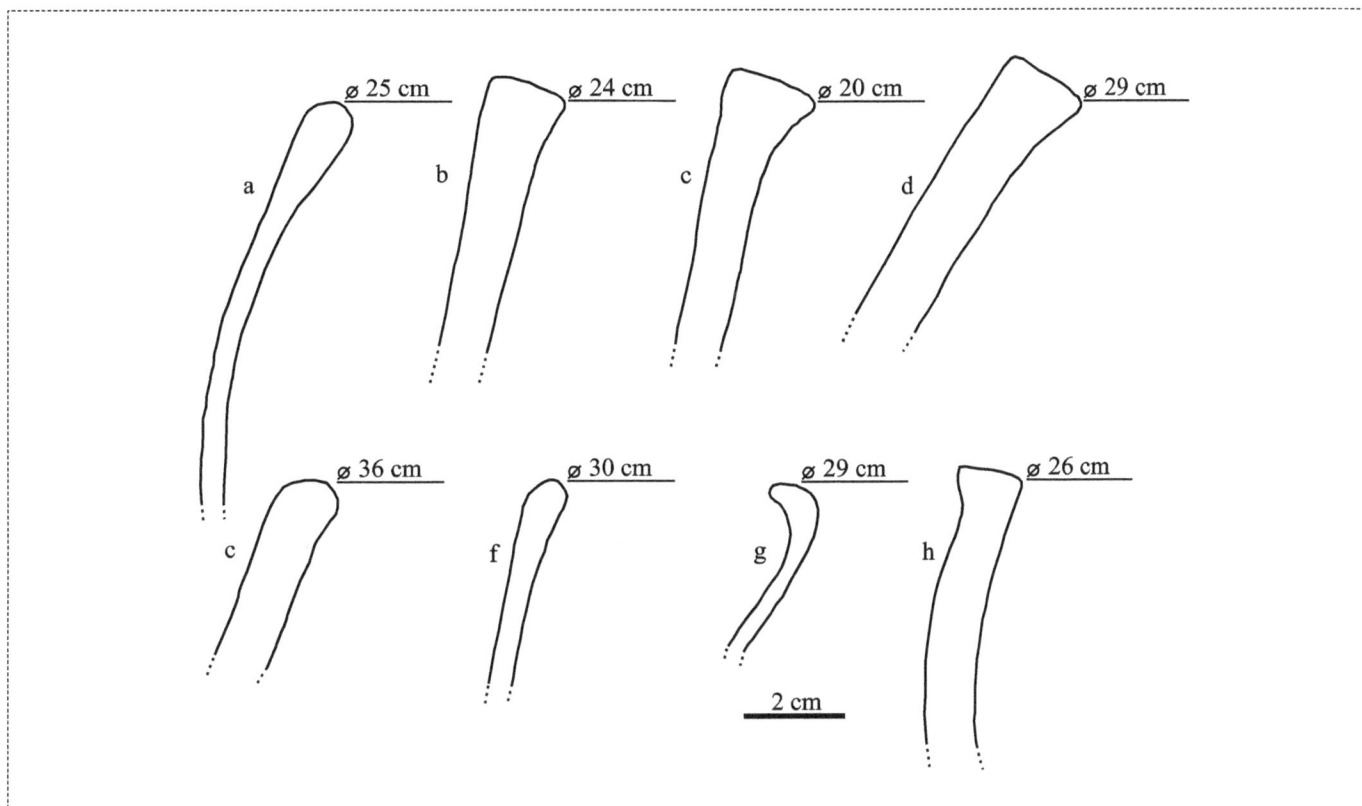

Figure 33. Rim profiles from restricted vessels. a-f: straight rims; g-h: everted rims.

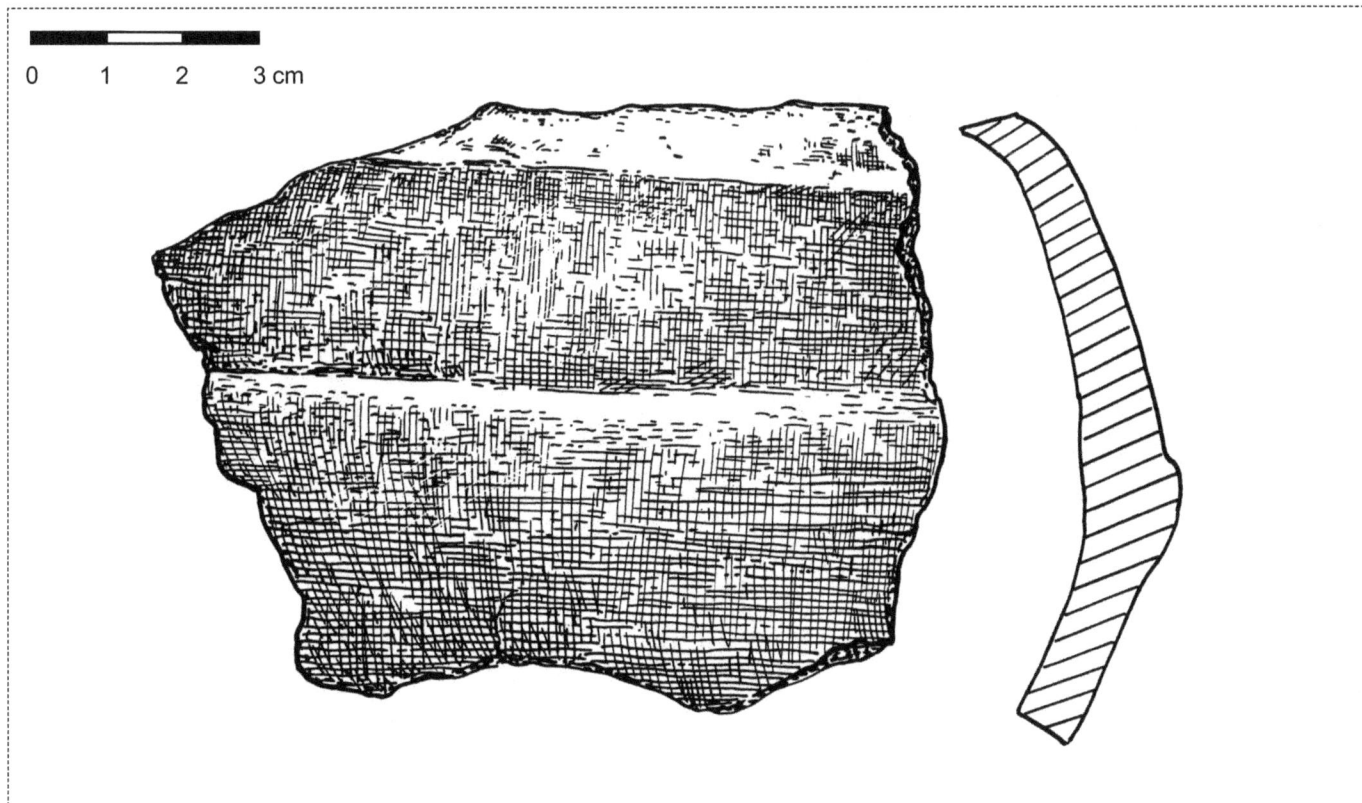

Figure 34. Sherd with an angled shoulder. Drawing by N. S. Survillo.

bulge (n = 4), rounded (n = 3), rounded with an inward bulge (n = 2) or roof-shaped (n = 1).

R2. Restricted vessels with a neck
Only one neck sherd was identified in the erosion front. This fragment, 8-mm thick, belongs to a vessel whose rim diameter is approximately 7-cm wide. The undecorated lip is flattened.

R3. Restricted vessels with angled shoulders
Only one sherd of this type was identified in EEF (Fig. 34).

UNRESTRICTED VESSELS (U)

They are a majority in the studied corpus (72 sherds out of 94) and are divided into three types (Fig. 32):

U1. Extremely unrestricted vessels (Fig. 38, a-d)
This type is made up of 13 rim sherds which are divided into two clearly differentiated dimensional sub-types:
U1.1 Small vessels
Only 3 rim sherds belong to this sub-type, the rim diameters of which range from 13 to 15 cm. Their average thickness is 12 mm. Their rims are always straight and their lips ornamented.
U1.2 Large vessels
This sub-type includes 10 rim sherds, the rim diameters of which range from 27 to 38 cm. Their average thickness is 15.7 mm. Their rims are straight and their lips, undecorated, have varied morphologies: flattened (n = 3), flattened with an inward bulge (n = 5), bevelled (n = 1) or roof-shaped (n = 1).

U2. Slightly unrestricted vessels (Fig. 38, e-g)
34 rim sherds belong to this type. The rim diameters vary continuously from 13 to 46 cm. Their average thickness is 12.6 mm. Their rims are straight, 26 lips are undecorated and of varied morphologies: flattened (n = 4), flattened with an inward bulge (n = 11), bevelled (n = 2), rounded (n = 4), rounded with an inward bulge (n = 3) or rounded with an inward and outward bulge (n = 2).

U3. Nearly vertical-sided vessels (Fig. 38, l-p)
25 rim sherds belong to this type. The rim diameters vary continuously from 11 to 52 cm. Their average thickness is 9.7 mm. The rims are always straight, and 20 undecorated lips have varied morphologies: flattened (n = 5), flattened with an inward bulge (n = 10), flattened with an outward bulge (n = 1), rounded (n = 1), rounded with an inward edge (n = 2) or roof-shaped (n = 1).

Judging from this data, there is no exclusive correlation between the overall morphology of a vessel and that of the lip and each type of vessel has varied lip shapes (Fig. 36). However, the flattened lips with an inward bulge are the more frequent on restricted vessels and flattened and rounded lips are proportionally better represented on restricted ones.

The thickness of the rim is more clearly related to the morphological type of the vessel (Fig. 38). We can thus distinguish between the restricted and the nearly vertical-sided vessels, which have thin rims (average thickness below 10 mm), and the extremely or slightly unrestricted pots, which have thicker rims (average thickness between 12 and 16 mm).

TYPE	NUMBER	RANGE	MEAN	STANDARD DEV
R1	21	4-18	9.3	3.27
R2	1	8	-	-
U1	3	8-17	12	3.74
U1	10	10-24	15.7	4.57
U2	27	7-27	12.6	4.18
U3	22	5-14	9.7	2.14

Figure 35. Thickness (mm) of the different pottery types in EEF.

LIP SHAPE / VESSEL TYPE	L1/1	L1/2	L1/3	L1/4	L1/5	L1/6	L1/7	L1/8	L1/9	TOTAL
R1	5	4	-	-	3	2	-	-	1	15
R2	1	-	-	-	-	-	-	-	-	1
U1	3	5	-	1	-	-	-	-	1	10
U2	4	11	-	2	4	3	2	-	-	26
U3	5	10	1	-	1	-	-	2	1	20

Figure 36. Relationship between vessel type and lip shape in EEF.

6.3.2.2
EH21

Out of the 8 rim sherds found in this test pit, only 6 deserve a morphological classification. They all come from unrestricted vessels, belonging to types U2 or U3.

U2. slightly unrestricted vessels (Fig. 39, h-i)
5 sherds found in EH21 belong to this type. The rim diameters vary from 16 to 45 cm and their thickness from 5 to 11 mm. The rims are always straight, and 4 undecorated lips have varied morphologies: flattened (n = 2) or flattened with an inward bulge (n = 2).

U3. nearly vertical-sided vessels (Fig. 39, q)
In EH21, only one sherd belongs to this type. Its rim diameter is 32 cm and it is 8-mm thick. The rim is straight and the lip, undecorated is flattened with an inward bulge.

6.3.2.3
EH13

Only 3 rim sherds were found in this test pit. They all come from unrestricted vessels, belonging to types U2 or U3.

U2. slightly unrestricted vessels (Fig. 39, j)
This type includes two rim sherds, whose diameters are 12 and 17 cm and whose thickness are 4 and 7 mm. Their rims are straight and one lip is flattened and the other flattened with an inward bulge.

U3. nearly vertical-sided vessels (Fig. 39, r)
Only one sherd belongs to this type. Its rim diameter is 17 cm and its thickness 12 mm. The rim is straight and the undecorated lip is flattened with an inward bulge.

6.3.2.4
ER1

Only 10 rim sherds were collected in this test pit, among which 8 fragments enabled me to distinguish three morphological types, R1, U2 and U3.

R1. Restricted vessels without a neck (Fig. 33, e-f)
This type includes 3 sherds whose rim diameters vary from 30 to 36 cm, and thickness from 6 to 11 mm. Their rims are straight and 2 lips are undecorated: one is flattened and the other is flattened with an inward bulge.

U2. Slightly unrestricted vessels (Fig. 39, k)
This type includes 2 sherds whose respective rim diameters are 21 and 22 cm and whose thickness are 7 and 9 mm. The rims are straight, one has a flattened lip and the other a rounded lip with an inward bulge.

U3. Nearly vertical-sided vessels (Fig. 38, s)
3 sherds belong to this type. Their rim diameters vary from 23 to 29 cm and their thickness from 12 to 13 mm. Their rims are straight and the undecorated lips are flattened (n = 2) or rounded (n = 1).

6.3.3
DISTRIBUTION OF THE MORPHOLOGICAL TYPES

No particular scheme of grouping is revealed by an analysis of the distribution of the various morphological types along the erosion front (Fig. 37). Most types of vessel are to be found in any part of EEF. Unfortunately, no rim sherds were collected in corridors 51 to 56, which are thought to contain more recent artefacts.

Due to the very small number of rim sherds collected in the test pits, it is also difficult to compare them fruitfully with those found in the erosion front (Fig. 38). One can nevertheless note that all the vessel shapes analyzed in the test pits fit into the typology devised from the EEF sherds. Also, that no restricted shapes are to be found in EH21 and EH13, and that no extremely unrestricted vessel was identified in the test pits. Nevertheless, as these shapes were present in very small numbers in EEF, their absence in the test pits may not reflect a real lack but might be explained by the limited quantity of sherds of any type collected there.

UNITS	EEF	EH21	EH13	ER1	TOTAL
R1	21	-	-	3	24
R2	1	-	-	-	1
U1	13	-	-	-	13
U2	34	5	2	2	43
U3	25	1	1	3	30
TOTAL	94	6	3	8	111

Figure 38. Distribution of pottery types in the archaeological units.

6.4
POTTERY DECORATION

6.4.1
DESCRIPTIVE SYSTEM

Decorations are all impressed on soft clay and located only on the external wall[1] and on the top of the lip. On the external surface of the body, the decorations are all curvilinear, composed of concentric circles or spirals (Fig. 40).

The designs all fit into the same general pattern and the variations observed do not allow for any classification. The occurrence of these body decorations depends on the fashioning technique which is used and will thus be analyzed in the next part of the study, dedicated to technological traits. On the lip, different decoration types are distinguished according to the tool used and the design. Four different stamped decorations were identified in Ekven (Fig. 41):

- D1: diagonal lines, impressed with an edged tool on the outward side;
- D2: herringbone pattern, impressed with an edged tool;
- D3: herringbone pattern, fingertip impressed;
- D4: diagonal lines, impressed across the top with an edged tool;
- D5: curvilinear designs, paddle impressed.

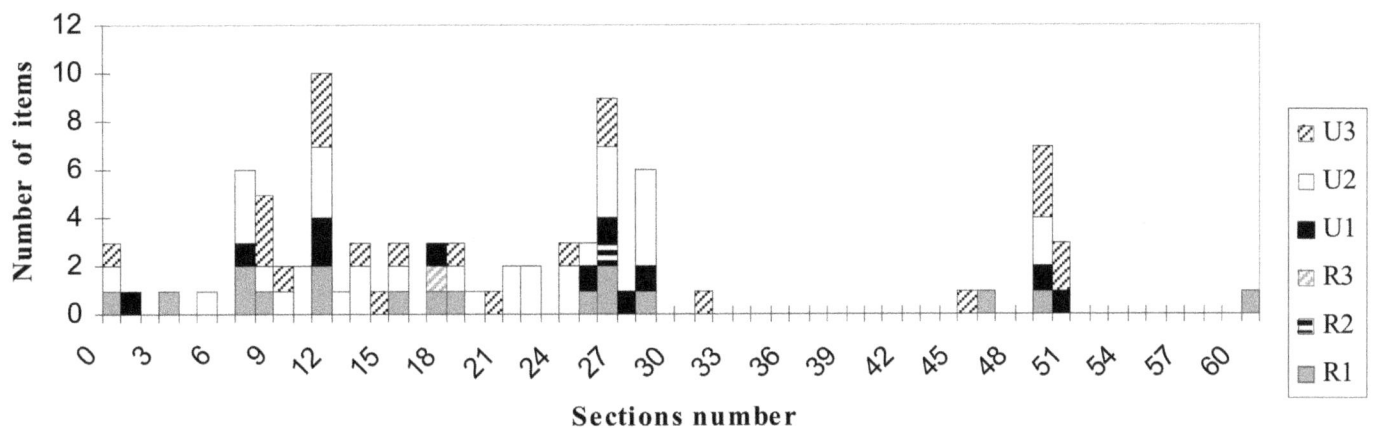

Figure 37. Distribution of morphological types along the erosion front.

---

[1] As I couldn't make a distinction between base sherds and body sherds, it was not possible to determine what exact surface the decorations covered.

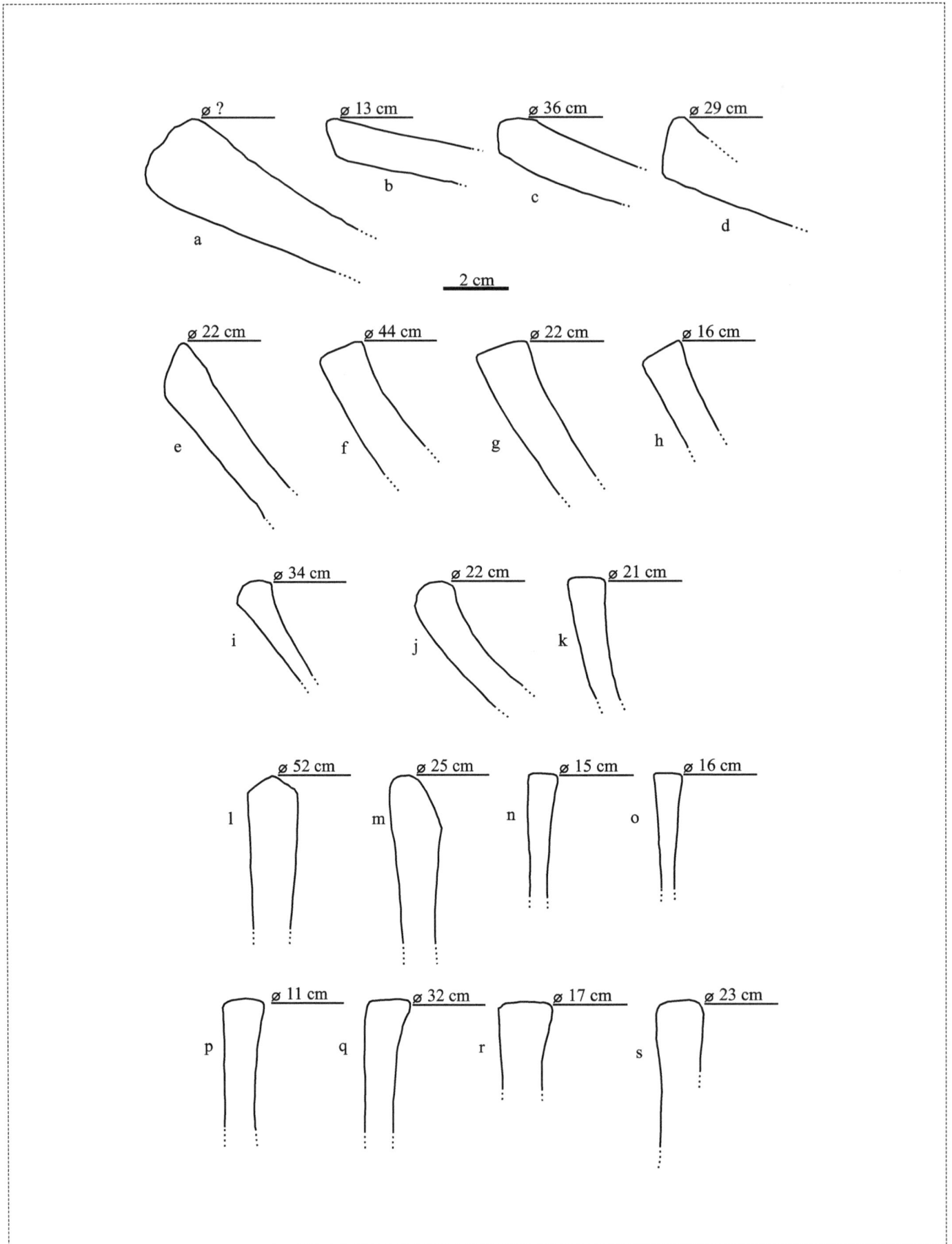

Figure 39. Rim profiles from unrestricted vessels. a-d: extremely unrestricted; e-k: slightly unrestricted; l-s: nearly vertical-sided.

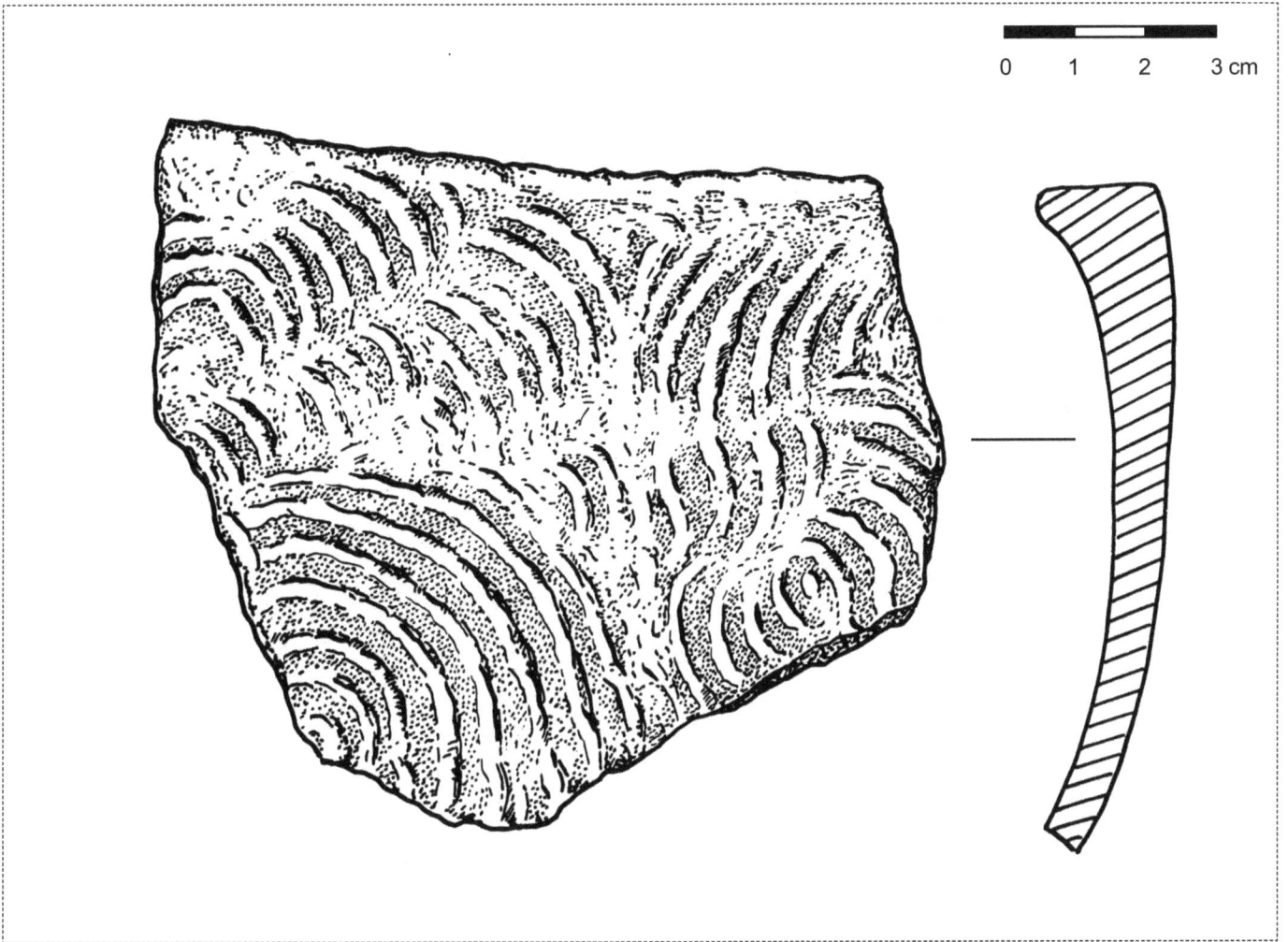

Figure 40. Curvilinear decoration on the external side of a sherd. Drawing by N. S. Survillo.

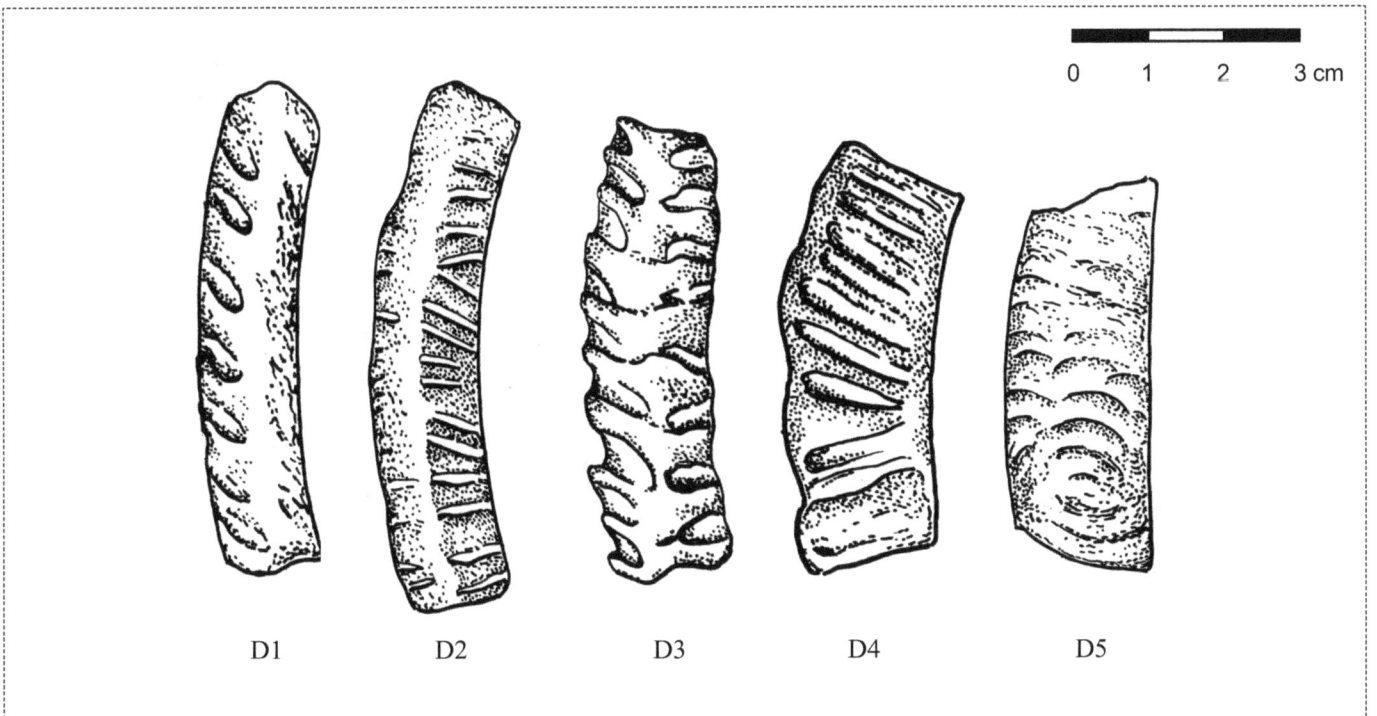

D1   D2   D3   D4   D5

Figure 41. Different types of stamped decoration observed on the top of the lip. Drawing by N. S. Survillo.

6.4.2
ANALYSIS IN THE DIFFERENT ARCHAEOLOGICAL UNITS : EEF, EH21, EH13, AND ER1

6.4.2.1
EEF

There is a far smaller number of decorated lips on all the pottery types (Fig. 42), except on the extremely unrestricted small pots (u1), represented by three items which all have a stamped lip.

LIP DECORATION / VESSEL TYPE	UNDECORATED	DECORATED	TOTAL
R1	15	6	21
R2	1	-	1
U1	-	3	3
U1	10	-	10
U2	26	8	34
U3	20	5	25

Figure 42. Correlation between vessel type and lip decoration in EEF.

Each type of vessel bears a variety of designs (Fig. 43), and no correlation is observed between the morphology of the pot and its lip decorative motif. For all vessel types, the more current type is the curvilinear stamped decoration (D5).

DECORATIVE MOTIF / VESSEL TYPE	D1	D2	D3	D4	D5	TOTAL
R1	2	-	2	-	2	6
U1	-	1	-	-	2	3
U2	3	1	-	2	2	8
U3	1	2	-	-	2	5
TOTAL	6	4	2	2	8	22

Figure 43. Correlation between vessel type and decorative motif in EEF.

6.4.2.2
The test pits

Only two decorated rim sherds were found in the test pits, one in EH21 and one in ER1. The rim from EH21 belongs to a slightly unrestricted vessel and has a herring-bone lip decoration, impressed with an edged tool (D2). The rim sherd from ER1 is assigned to a restricted vessel (R1) and presents diagonal lines, impressed with an edged tool on the outward side of the lip (D1).

6.4.2.3
Distribution of decorative types

As far as I can judge from the small corpus studied, there is no particular pattern of distribution of decorative motifs along the erosion front (Fig. 44).

The data is too limited to attempt a comparison between the erosion front and the test pits. It is only possible to note that the two decorated sherds found in ER1 and EH21 do not have different designs but are included in the general decorative typology observed in EEF.

6.5
POTTERY MANUFACTURE

The study of the pottery sherds allowed me to reconstruct three main steps of the "chaîne opératoire" : the preparation of the clay body, the forming techniques and the finishing techniques. It also provided some clues concerning the firing of the vessels.

6.5.1
CLAY PREPARATION

6.5.1.1
Descriptive system

I first proceeded to a simple visual examination of the corpus and then selected samples which I observed with a binocular microscope.

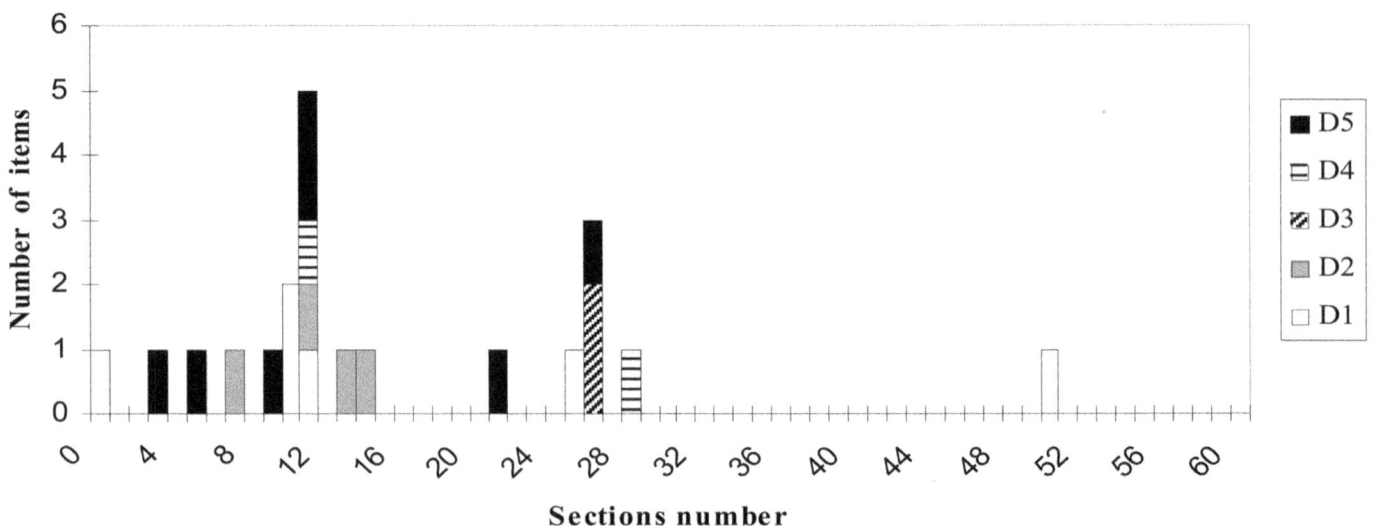

Figure 44. Distribution of lip decorations along the erosion front

Two main types of inclusions are distinguished in the sherds: mineral and organic temper. Minerals are differentiated according to morphology and size. It is thus possible to distinguished subangular from subrounded mineral inclusions and coarse inclusions (2 mm) from fine inclusions (< 2 mm). For the organic temper one can distinguish between, on the one hand, non-identified fibers which look like grass, hair or baleen and, on the other hand, easily identified feathers.

From a visual evaluation it is also possible to separate pastes with a very high density of non plastic inclusions from pastes with a low density of such materials.

7 different types of paste can be observed in Ekven:
- P1: with a low density of subangular coarse minerals and unidentified fibers (grass, hair or baleen);
- P2: with a low density of subangular coarse minerals and feathers;
- P3: with a low density of unidentified fibers;
- P4: with a low density of feathers;
- P5: with a high density of subrounded coarse minerals;
- P6: with a high density of subangular coarse minerals;
- P7: with a high density of subangular fine minerals;

6.5.1.2
Analysis in the different archaeological units (EEF, EH21, EH13, and ER1) and distribution of the paste types

P1 paste, with a low density of subangular coarse minerals and unidentified fibers, is found most frequently in the erosion front where around 74% of the studied sherds belong to this group (Fig. 45). P2 paste, with a low density of subangular coarse minerals and feathers, and P6, with a high density of subangular coarse minerals, are relatively common, observed each on more than 6% of the fragments. Other paste groups, P3, P4 and P7 are rare and represent less than 5% of the material from EEF.

The same pattern is observed in test pits EH21, EH13 and ER1, where paste P1 is also the most common (Fig. 45) and where the other groups are under-represented.

PASTE / UNIT	P1	P2	P3	P4	P5	P6	P7	TOTAL
EEF	334	30	18	22	12	29	7	452
EH21	31	7	2	1	-	1	-	42
EH13	9	-	-	-	-	1	-	10
ER1	27	2	-	1	5	2	1	38

Figure 45. Distribution of paste types in the archaeological units.

6.5.1.3
Petrographic characterization

M.A. Courty has analyzed 12 thin sections from ceramic samples collected in EEF. Several petrographic types were distinguished which give a better idea of the nature of the mineral inclusions initially present in the clay and added intentionally (Fig. 46).

PETROGRAPHIC TYPE	COARSE FRACTION	FINE FRACTION
1.1A	Two modes: (1) very fine quartz sands (80-100 µm) (2) subangular mica schist and granito-gneiss sands (15%; 4-8 mm)	Ferruginous clay (morainal?)
1.1B	Two modes: (1) very fine quartz sands (80-100 µm) (2) subangular mica schist and granito-gneiss sands (15%; 4-8 mm)	Schistose clay (morainal?)
1.2A	Two modes: (1) very fine quartz sands (80-100 µm) (2) quartz sands (30%; 4-8 mm)	Ferruginous clay (morainal?)
1.2B	Two modes: (1) very fine quartz sands (80-100 µm) (2) quartz sands (20%; 2-8 mm)	Ferruginous clay (morainal?)
2.1	40% subangular quartz ferruginous sands 80 µm-4 mm	Ferruginous clay (morainal?)
2.2	40% subangular quartz sands 80 µm-8 mm	Coarse ferruginous clay (morainal?)
2.3	40% subangular quartz sands 80 µm-8 mm	Coarse clay (morainal?)
3	Two modes: (1) fine metamorphic quartz sands (80-500 µm) (2) metamorphic quartz sands and ferruginous sandstone (20%; 2-8 mm)	Brown-red silty clay (morainal)
4	30% quartzite and subrounded to subangular 3-8 mm (beach or alluvial sands)	Dense black crackled (rich in iron) (coastal plain?)
5	30% micro-gabbro and diabase (etc.) 1-8 mm (beach or alluvial sands)	Dense black crackled (rich in iron) (coastal plain?)

Figure 46. Petrographic analysis of thin sections from EEF.

Figure 47a.

Figure 48b.

Figure 47b.

Figure 49a.

Figure 47c.

Figure 49b.

Figure 48a.

Figure 50.

6.5.2
FORMING TECHNIQUES

6.5.2.1
Descriptive system

A visual examination of surface features on all the pottery sherds enabled me to recognize 4 technological groups (Fig. 47-50). For each one I have identified the forming technique based on the diagnostic attributes. No experimentation was conducted for this study and the interpretations of surface features are based on experimental and ethnographical data already available (Balfet et al. 1989, Gelbert 1994, 2000, Huysecom 1994, Rice 1987, Rye 1981). A cautious approach is thus necessary.

1. Group A. Drawing/Paddle and anvil technique

The vessels in this group have been roughened by "drawing" and/or "pinching" from a lump of clay.

Diagnostic surface features: no joins of coils or slabs are visible on the sherds and they all have a homogenous mass. The material being of mediocre quality and the finishing quite rough, one can indeed suppose that the use of coils or slabs would have left visible traces on the final product.

The vessel was then shaped with the paddle and anvil technique, with an engraved paddle (group A1) or with a non-engraved paddle (A2).

Diagnostic surface features: the external surface of the sherds from group A1 are covered in curvilinear paddled decorations (Fig. 47, a). This feature shows that the technique used was that of paddling with an engraved paddle, made of wood or of ivory[2]. Sherds from A2 have a plain external surface, without striations but some large diagonal grooves are visible on a few sherds (Fig. 47, b). These grooves were not made by scraping the clay but rather look like an impression made with the edge of a tool. They may be an impression made by the edge of a paddle.

In both groups the paste is compact and there are subrounded impressions on the internal surface (Fig. 47, c). These features indicate that an anvil was used. Their shape suggests that a round tool, such as a pebble or a sherd, was used.

2. Groupe B: Paddling over a convex basket mold

The roughout has been fashioned from a lump of clay either directly over the mold or before being pressed onto the mold.

Diagnostic features: No joins of coils or slabs are visible on the sherds and they all have a homogenous mass.

The vessel was shaped by paddling over a convex basket.

Diagnostic surface features: The external surface is covered with curvilinear paddled decorations (Fig. 48, a) and the internal surface with matting impressions (Fig. 48, b). The wall has a very regular curve and the paste is compact.

3. Group C: Modeling

The vessels in this group have been roughened and preformed by "drawing" and/or "pinching" from a lump of clay.

Diagnostic surface features: No joins of coils or slabs are visible on the sherds and they all have a homogenous mass; both sides reveal irregular depressions which look like finger prints; the curve and thickness of the wall are irregular, the paste is not compact (Fig. 49, a-b).

4. Group D: molding into a concave basket mold

The roughout has been fashioned from a lump of clay either directly into the mold or before being pressed in the mold. Diagnostic surface features: No joins of coils or slabs are visible on the sherds and they all have a homogenous mass. The vessel was shaped by pressing the clay into a concave basket.

Diagnostic surface features: The external surface shows matting impressions (Fig. 50); the curve and thickness of the wall are regular; there are no traces of paddling on the internal surface.

6.5.2.2
Analysis in the different archaeological units (EEF, EH21, EH13, and ER1) and distribution of the forming techniques

In the erosion front, group A (paddle and anvil) dominates and represents 73% of the sherds (Fig. 51). Among these, 35% were shaped with an engraved paddle (group A.1). 17.5% of the sherds were made by paddling over a basket mold (group B) and only 7% by modeling (group C). Finally, the technique of molding into a concave basket mold (group D) was identified on 13 sherds only, 7 of which come from the same vessel.

In the EH21 test pit, among the 50 examined sherds, a large majority belongs to group A (44 sherds), out of which 19 sherds were fashioned with an engraved paddle. Groups B and C are also represented by a few fragments (Fig. 51).
In the EH13 test pit, the sherds also mainly belong to group A (17 sherds, 9 of which belong to A1). 2 sherds fit into group B (Fig. 51).

Among the 44 sherds of the ER1 test pit, 40 belong to group A (14 of which, to A1) and 4 to group B (Fig. 51).

GROUP	A1	A2	B	C	D	TOTAL
EEF	174	190	87	36	13	500
EH13	9	8	2	0	0	19
EH21	19	25	4	2	0	50
ER1	14	26	4	0	0	44
TOTAL	216	249	97	38	13	613

Figure 51. Distribution of forming techniques in the archaeological units.

[2] Paddles engraved with the same motifs as those on the sherds were indeed found in Ekven.

Whatever the considered ceramic unit, the main forming technique is paddle and anvil (group A). The technique of molding into a concave basket mold (group D) is not to be found in any of the three test pits, and modeling (group C) appears in only two sherds in EH21; nevertheless, considering the small number of sherds found in the test pits, this is not necessarily very meaningful as it concerns technological groups which are also a minority in the erosion front.

All five technological groups are present all along the erosion front, and no particular grouping was observed (Fig. 52).

6.5.3
FINISHING TECHNIQUES

6.5.3.1
Descriptive system

Surfaces vary according to two criteria:
the surface microtopography is more or less flattened, due to the varying extent of the smoothing on the wet paste. The lack of striation indicates that a hard tool was used.
a gloss indicates that a very light polishing of the internal and/or external surfaces took place

Taking into account the combination of these two criteria on the internal or external sides of the sherds, I have established 4 types of surface treatment:
- light smoothing
- light smoothing and light polishing
- neat smoothing
- neat smoothing and light polishing

6.5.3.2
Analysis in the different archaeological units: EEF, EH21, EH13, and ER1

I have been able to determine the finishing techniques used in only 320 sherds from EEF. Among these, 234 (about 73%) reveal a light smoothing and light polishing (type b), either on both sides or on the external surface of the sherd (Fig. 53). 7 fragments only (about 2% of the corpus) show a neat smoothing and light polishing (type d) either on both sides or on the external surface. 11 sherds (about 3.5%) were neatly smoothed on both sides (type c). Finally, 68 fragments (about 21.5%) were only lightly smoothed (type a).
In EH21, 11 sherds belong to type a, 18 to type b, 4 to type c and 3 to type d (Fig. 53).
In EH 13, 2 sherds belong to type a, 5 to type b, 3 to type c, and 4 to type d (Fig. 53).
In ER1, 13 sherds belong to type a, 15 to type b, and only 1 to c. Type b is not represented (Fig. 53).

Whatever the considered structure, a majority of the sherds were lightly smoothed and lightly polished. Nevertheless, neatly smoothed sherds were indeed found in Ekven, even though they are in small numbers.

FINISHING	A	B	C	D	TOTAL
EEF	68	234	11	7	320
EH21	11	18	4	3	36
EH13	2	5	3	4	14
ER1	13	15	1	-	29

Figure 53. Distribution of finishing in the archaeological units.

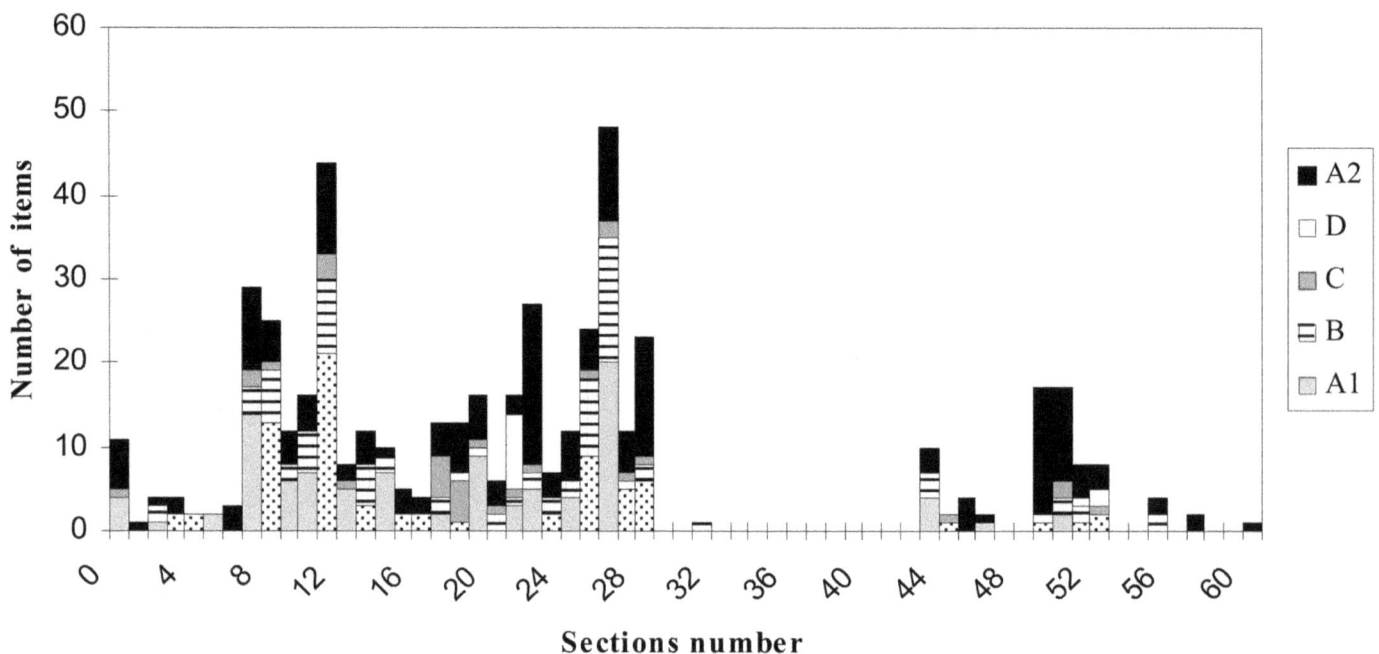

Figure 52. Distribution of forming techniques along the erosion front.

6.5.4
FIRING

Sherd colors vary from light yellowish brown (10YR 6/4)[3] to black (2.5YR 2/0), with a large variety of shades, several of which may be found on a single sherd (light brownish gray - 10YR 6/2; very pale brown - 10YR 7/3; grayish brown - 10YR 5/2; dark brown - 7.5YR 3/2; dark gray - 7.5YR 4/0). Many factors other than firing can determine the color, such as paste composition, or taphonomic processes. The firing mode can therefore not be determined based on this criteria alone. However, the variety of shades and the traces of fireclouds suggest a bonfire, where the fuel was in direct contact with the pots.

The core of the sherds is usually darker than the sides, which may indicate that the firing time was short (partial oxydation) but can also be explained by the high density of organic material in the paste.

6.6
THE "CHAÎNES OPÉRATOIRES"

Firstly, there is no correlation between the temper used and the forming technique (Fig. 60-63) Each forming technique was practiced with different types of paste, characterized by varied combinations of mineral and/or organic inclusions. Only the technique of molding in a concave basket mold (group D) has been conducted most frequently with a P6 type paste, which contains a high density of subangular minerals. It must be said that this group is represented solely by a few sherds, possibly from the same vessel.

There is also no link between the forming technique and the finishing (Fig. 54-57) Only neat smoothing is found exclusively in the paddle and anvil technique (group A2). Nevertheless, other finishing techniques are observed in this group.

FINISHING / FORMING TECHNIQUE	A	B	C	D	TOTAL
GROUP A1	18	127	-	-	145
GROUP A2	21	41	11	7	80
GROUP B	16	45	-	-	61
GROUP C	12	13	-	-	25
GROUP D	1	8	-	-	9

Figure 54. Correlation between finishing and forming technique in EEF.

FINISHING / FORMING TECHNIQUE	A	B	C	D	TOTAL
GROUP A1	3	12	-	-	15
GROUP A2	6	4	4	3	17
GROUP B	3	1	-	-	4
GROUP C	-	-	-	-	0
GROUP D	-	-	-	-	0

Figure 55. Correlation between finishing and forming technique in EH21.

FINISHING / FORMING TECHNIQUE	A	B	C	D	TOTAL
GROUP A1	2	4	-	-	6
GROUP A2	2	3	-	1	6
GROUP B	-	2	-	-	2
GROUP C	-	-	-	-	0
GROUP D	-	-	-	-	0

Figure 56. Correlation between finishing and forming technique in EH13.

FINISHING / FORMING TECHNIQUE	A	B	C	D	TOTAL
GROUP A1	6	10	-	-	16
GROUP A2	6	2	1	-	9
GROUP B	1	3	-	-	4
GROUP C	-	-	-	-	0
GROUP D	-	-	-	-	0

Figure 57. Correlation between finishing and forming technique in ER1.

No correlation can be established between the vessel type and the different steps of the "chaîne opératoire". Thus, as the material from the erosion front shows, a wide variety of tempers (Fig. 58), and forming techniques[4] (Fig. 59) are found on a same type of vessel.

VESSEL TYPE / PASTE TYPE	R1	R2	R3	U1	U2	U3
P1	17	1	1	5	25	22
P2	1	-	-	3	5	-
P3	1	-	-	4	1	1
P4	1	-	-	-	1	-
P5	1	-	-	1	1	1
P6	-	-	-	-	1	1

Figure 58. Correlation between vessel type and paste type in EEF.

VESSEL TYPE / FORMING TECHNIQUE	R1	R2	U1	U2	U3
GROUP A1	6	-	3	10	6
GROUP A2	11	-	8	16	13
GROUP B	1	1	1	7	5
GROUP C	1	-	1	1	1

Figure 59. Correlation between vessel type and forming technique in EEF.

One should thus note the great variety of the "chaînes opératoires" for the making of ceramic in Ekven, which results from the combination of the variables identified at each step of the production.

6.7
COMPARATIVE ANALYSIS BETWEEN EKVEN AND ALSAKA

As I did not have access to the small bibliography on Siberian ceramic[5], I have centered my comparative analysis on the ceramic from Alaska. This analysis is based on several more or less recent works: Arnold and Stimmell 1983, Collins 1937, Dumond 1998, Ford 1959, Harritt 1994, Lucier and VanStone 1992, Oswalt 1955, Stimmell 1994)

Morpho-functional types

The main morphological types observed in Ekven have all been described in the Neoeskimo sites in Alaska.

Restricted vessels (R1) are reported at Point Hope, in the Seward Peninsula and near East Cape, associated to a "Barrow Curvilinear Paddled" type present from Birnirk to Thule (Harritt 1994: 419, Oswalt 1955: 36). This form has also been described in ceramics from St Lawrence Island attributed to Old Bering Sea (Dumond 1998).

Restricted vessels with angled shoulders (R3), called "situla-shaped" seem to be a recent shape, associated only with the Thule stage from 1000 A.D. (Oswalt 1955, Stimmell 1994: 42-43).

"Barrel-shaped" pottery, which are nearly vertical-sided vessels (U3) are also documented in various Neoeskimo sites of Alaska: in the Old Bering Sea ceramics of St Lawrence Island (Dumond 1998), in the Birnirk site (Ford 1959: 202-203), in the site of Nunagiak attributed to Punuk (ibid: 202) and in different sites attributed to Thule such as Utkiavik (Ford 1959), Walakpa (Stanford 1976: 57) and in the sites of the Seward Peninsula (Harritt 1994: 418-421).

Extremely unrestricted vessels (U1) and slightly restricted vessels (U2) are also described in different regions and periods: in Old Bering Sea pottery, from the Hillside site of St Lawrence island (Dumond 1998), in the Birnirk site (Ford 1959: 203), in Nunagiak, where it is assigned to Punuk (Ford 1959: 202) and in Thule contexts (Ford 1959: 197 et 201; Stimmell 1994).

I have found no reference to necked vessels in the literature. The neck fragment found in Ekven doesn't allow for a reconstruction of the overall shape of the body.

Apart from the situla-shaped pottery which may be associated to Thule, the types found in Ekven are thus documented in Alaska in the entire Neoeskimo. In some cases, these shapes are associated with flattened or conical vases. The rounded vases found in Ekven have long been considered as characteristic of Old Bering Sea (Oswalt 1955). However, they have since been documented for more recent periods and up to the late prehistory (Harritt 1994: 165).

By ethnological analogy, the Bering Strait pots have been considered to belong to two main functional categories: cooking pots and lamps which are almost always found together in the Neoeskimo sites. Morphologically, the Ekven vessels may be interpreted as belonging to these two functional types. The restricted (R1, R2 and R3) and nearly vertical-sided (U3) vessels of Ekven, the average wall thickness of which is below 10 mm (never more than 18 mm), correspond to the cooking pots. Many sherds are incrusted with a layer of soot which seems to indicate that they were in contact with fire.

The extremely (U1) and slightly (U2) unrestricted pots, with wall thicknesses averaging 13.5 mm and up to 27 mm, may be interpreted as being oil lamps. Their morphology is similar to that of the shallow saucer-shaped lamps described for St Lawrence Island (Collins 1937: 168, Dumond 1998) and for Utkiavik, Nunagiak and Birnirk (Ford 1959: 201-203, Stimmell 1994: 42). In these sites, round and oval shapes have been noted. In Ekven, the presence of these two types cannot be ruled out, even if no fragment is big enough to ascertain their existence. As Dumond wrote concerning the lamp sherds

---

[3] Color code taken from Munsell, 1988.

[4] The angled-shoulder vessel seems to have been fashioned in two steps, since a join is visible in the carene. However, as there was only one fragment of this type, it was not possible to determine the exact forming technique.

collected in Hillside, it can be said about Ekven that "none of them displays absolutely clear evidence of interior burning, and it is possible that they include at least some vessels other than lamps (…)" (Dumond 1998 : 40).

Concerning the morphology of the lips, there is a degree of variability in the Alaskan ceramics. Most are rounded, flattened and some have an inward bulge (Ford 1959 : 203, Dumond 1998 : 41, Oswalt 1955). No specific morphology can be clearly associated with a particular culture or period.

Decoration

There is very little information concerning lip decoration in Alaska. As in Ekven, undecorated lips are the most common. Diagonal lines across the top and Herringbone patterns (types D2, D3 and D4) are described for Birnirk (Stimmell 1994 : 41) and Thule (Ford 1959 : 202, Oswalt 1955) wares.

Body decoration is the element best described in the ceramic studies conducted in Alaska. Curvilinear impressions seen in Ekven are clearly integrated into the "Barrow Curviliear Paddled" type observed from Birnirk to historic contact (Oswalt 1955 : 36, Stimmell 1994), and to the "Ahteut Curvilinear Paddled" type assigned to Thule (Oswalt 1955 : 36). They have been found in various sites in coastal Alaska from the Colville River mouth to Cape Denbigh (Oswalt 1955 : 36), in Ahteut (Oswalt 1955 : 36), in the sites of the Seward Peninsula (Harritt 1994 : 418-421), in Walakpa (Stanford 1976 : 57) and near Point Barrow (Ford 1959 : 204). These motifs are clearly distinguished from corrugated decorations, characteristic of Old Bering Sea (Dumond, 1998 ; Ford 1959 : 204, Oswalt 1955 : 32).

Temper

As in Ekven, varied combinations of organic (feathers, grass or hair) and mineral (sand, gravel or crushed rocks) temper is to be found in all the ceramic corpuses of Alaska (Arnold and Stimmell 1983, Dumond 1998, Ford 1959 : 201-204, Harritt 1994 : 163-164 and 418-421, Oswalt 1955, Stimmell 1994). These combinations vary in a single chrono-cultural stage, so that they cannot be considered as valid comparative criteria.

Forming techniques

To my knowledge, no precise study of surface features has been conducted for Beringian ceramics. Nevertheless, certain elements hint at the existence in Alaska of the main forming techniques recognized in Ekven.

The use of the paddle and anvil technique (group A) may only be identified thanks to the curvilinear decorations impressed on the external side of the sherds. Only type A1 (with an engraved paddle) has thus been identified in the literature. The paddle and anvil technique seems to have been used at

every stage of Neoeskimo. Curvilinear decorations are indeed found on "Norton Linear Stamped" and "Norton Check Stamped", "St Lawrence Corrugated", "Barrow Curvilinear Paddled", "Ahteut Curvilinear Paddled" and "Nunivak Check Stamped" types (Oswalt 1955). Several authors suggest the hand was used as an anvil (Dumond, 1998 : 38, Oswalt 1955 : 34). However, the lack of a more precise description of surface features, in particular on the inside wall, makes it impossible to confirm this hypothesis. The main question is to determine if the described pots were first fashioned by modeling and then shaped by paddling, as in Ekven ; or if the paddle was only used to decorate a preformed pot. Oswalt suggests that certain types were fashioned by coiling (Oswalt 1955), a technique which is absent in Ekven. Concerning the plain wares associated to paddled types, we can only suggest the use of the paddle and anvil technique with non-engraved paddle (group A2).

Molding on a basket also exists in Alaska and can be identified thanks to the matting impressions described on the pottery. However, it is sometimes difficult to infer from the literature whether the impressions are on the inside or outside walls, and thus to distinguish concave (group D) from convex (group B) molding.

Oswalt states that convex molding was used in Thulean ceramics in Ahteut (Oswalt 1955 : 35). Internal matting impressions were also observed for the same stage in the Seward Peninsula (Harritt 1994 : 163 and 419), and on more ancient vessels in Birnirk (Ford 1959 : 204).

Concave molding, ethnographically documented (description by Curtis in Lucier and VanStone 1992 : 7) appears in Late Prehistoric sites in Kotzebue Sound (Lucier and VanStone 1992 : 11-12). Stimmell also refers to the existence of external matting impressions on more ancient Birnirk wares (Stimmell 1994 : 42).

Though modeling has often been mentioned concerning Alaskan ceramics (Oswalt 1955), there is no clear enough description of the surface features to confirm these interpretations.

Finishing techniques

Most descriptions of Alaskan pottery mention a light smoothing ; only one evokes polishing, in Birnirk and Late Neoeskimo wares (Stimmell 1994). However, as the polishing observed in Ekven is very light, it is possible to imagine that the authors simply did not describe it.

[5] Publications in Russian by Dikov, Arutiunov, and Sergeev.

PASTE / FORMING TECHNIQUE	P1	P2	P3	P4	P5	P6	P7	INDET.	TOTAL
GROUP A1	127	11	13	3	3	3	7	7	174
GROUP A2	103	15	5	14	7	15	-	31	190
GROUP B	71	3	-	5	2	-	-	6	87
GROUP C	31	1	-	-	-	-	-	4	36
GROUP D	2	-	-	-	-	11	-	-	13

Figure 60. Correlation between paste type and forming technique in EEF.

PASTE / FORMING TECHNIQUE	P1	P2	P3	P4	P5	P6	P7	INDET.	TOTAL
GROUP A1	11	3	1	-	-	-	-	4	19
GROUP A2	16	4	1	1	-	1	-	2	25
GROUP B	4	-	-	-	-	-	-	-	4
GROUP C	-	-	-	-	-	-	-	2	2
GROUP D	-	-	-	-	-	-	-	-	0

Figure 61. Correlation between paste type and forming technique in EH21.

PASTE / FORMING TECHNIQUE	P1	P2	P3	P4	P5	P6	P7	INDÉT.	TOTAL
GROUP A1	6	-	-	-	-	-	-	3	9
GROUP A2	7	-	-	-	-	1	-	-	8
GROUP B	2	-	-	-	-	-	-	-	2
GROUP C	-	-	-	-	-	-	-	-	0
GROUP D	-	-	-	-	-	-	-	-	0

Figure 62. Correlation between paste type and forming technique in EH13.

PASTE / FORMING TECHNIQUE	P1	P2	P3	P4	P5	P6	P7	INDET.	TOTAL
GROUP A1	13	-	-	-	-	1	-	-	14
GROUP A2	10	2	-	1	5	1	1	6	26
GROUP B	4	-	-	-	-	-	-	-	4
GROUP C	-	-	-	-	-	-	-	-	0
GROUP D	-	-	-	-	-	-	-	-	0

Figure 63. Correlation between paste type and forming technique in ER1.

6.8
CONCLUSION

The Ekven ceramic, which is quite homogenous in terms of decoration and morphology, is however very varied in terms of technology. The variables observed in Ekven were also described in several sites in Alaska, in almost all Neoeskimo cultures. None of them can be clearly situated from a chrono-cultural point of view. In the available current data, the most informative trait is the curvilinear design which could enable us to assign the Ekven ceramics to a post-Old Bering Sea stage.

Apart from dating and chrono-cultural attribution issues (Bronshtein and Plumet 1995, Gerlach and Mason 1992), I was confronted in this study to the scarcity of the data available on Siberian and Alaskan ceramics. In spite of these problems, I am convinced that the technological variability observed in Ekven, over a large span of time, is an encouraging indication of the amount of information that Eskimo ceramics could yield, thus contributing greatly to the reconstruction of the chrono-cultural frame of the Bering Strait prehistory.

FIGURE 64. RADIOCARBON DATES FROM THE EKVEN EROSION FRONT
THE DATES ARRANGED BY HORIZONTAL LOCATION OF THE SAMPLES ALONG THE EROSION FRONT, FROM SW TO NE

EEF STRAT 1

FIELD NO.*	LAB. NO.	POSITION ALONG EROSION FRONT (M)	ALTITUDE (CM A.S.L.)	DESCRIPTION	14C YEARS (BP)	SIGMA	DELTA 13C °/00 PDB	CAL. AGE RANGES +/- 1 STDV (AND PROBABILITY) **	CAL. AGE RANGES +/- 2 STDV (AND PROBABILITY) ***	ASSOCIATED SEQUENCE AND FEATURE
D9	Ua-14896	50.30	550	Local wood: Salix sp.	850	75	-29.0	1040 (11.8%) 1090 1120 (6.3%) 1140 1150 (50.1%) 1270	1030 (95.4%) 1290	lower sequence feature B
D46	ETH-22035	48.28	612	Local wood: Salix sp.	260	50	-20.1	1520 (27.3%) 1590 1620 (29.3%) 1680 1770 (9.9%) 1800	1480 (73.9%) 1690 1730 (18.0%) 1810	upper sequence below feat. E
S4	B-7335	47.80	512	Mixed organic sediment	1220	30	-21.8	770 (65.6%) 890	690 (15.5%) 750 760 (79.9%) 900	lower sequence feature B
D6	Ua-14895	47.60	540	Local wood: Salix sp.	810	70	-27.1	1160 (68.2%) 1290	1030 (95.4%) 1300	lower sequence feature B
R2 / 98 : 252-62	IEMAE-1233	47.50	472-486	Local wood	2158	85	?	360BC (22.2%) 280BC 260BC (46.0%) 90BC	400BC (95.4%) 10	lower sequence feature B
D5	Ua-14894	47.20	500	Local wood: Salix sp.	1160	85	-27.2	770 (68.2%) 980	680 (95.4%) 1020	lower sequence feature B
S9	B-7333	46.65	515	Mixed organic sediment	1370	20	-21.7	648 (68.2%) 672	640 (95.4%) 688	lower sequence feature B
D10	Ua-14897	46.65	515	Local wood: Salix sp. + Betula sp.	765	70	-28.0	1190 (68.2%) 1300	1150 (82.4%) 1330 1340 (7.1%) 1400	lower sequence feature B
S10	B-7334	46.50	500	Mixed organic sediment	1130	30	-22.9	890 (11.5%) 905 910 (56.7%) 980	810 (93.4%) 990	lower sequence feature B
D12	B-7330	45.35	592	Driftwood charcoal	1000	20	-26.9	1000 (68.2%) 1033	990 (84.2%) 1040 1140 (7.2%) 1160	upper sequence feature F
S13	B-7336	44.85	582	Mixed organic sediment w. burnt bone	920	20	-23.2	1040 (46.9%) 1100 1110 (21.3%) 1160	1030 (95.4%) 1190	upper sequence feature F
D1	Ua-14893	44.40	472	Local wood: Salix sp.	745	85	-26.9	1180 (58.2%) 1310 1350 (10.0%) 1390	1150 (89.0%) 1410	lower sequence feature B
D2	B-7326	44.20	485	Local wood: Salix sp.	760	30	-29.0	1244 (68.2%) 1285	1220 (95.4%) 1295	lower sequence feature B
P4	B-7331	43.60	485	Mixed organic sediment with fur	1490	30	-17.5	540 (68.2%) 605	530 (93.9%) 650	lower sequence
D38	Ua-14902	37.85	557	Ericacea sp.	840	60	-25.9	1150 (62.4%) 1270	1030 (95.4%) 1290	upper sequence
D40	Ua-14903	35.60	420	Local wood: Salix sp.	985	60	-27.8	990 (36.7%) 1070 1080 (31.5%) 1160	960 (93.4%) 1220	lower sequence feature A
D13	Ua-14898	31.40	423	Local wood: Salix sp.	1035	55	-27.9	890 (9.7%) 920 950 (56.3%) 1040	880 (95.4%) 1160	lower sequence feature A, wall
D39	B-7339	30.90	415	Sod	1410	20	-26.5	622 (12.1%) 629 638 (56.1%) 658	605 (95.4%) 665	lower sequence feature A, wall
S18	B-7332	30.6	532	Mixed organic sediment	880	20	-25.2	1150 (59.3%) 1220	1040 (18.2%) 1090 1120 (11.7%) 1140 1150 (65.6%) 1220	upper sequence feature H
S21	B-7337	30.60	458	Peat/vegetal fiber	1290	20	-27.0	685 (38.0%) 720 745 (30.2%) 770	660 (95.4%) 780	

EEF STRAT 2

FIELD NO.*	LAB. NO.	POSITION ALONG EROSION FRONT (M)	ALTITUDE (CM A.S.L.)	DESCRIPTION	14C YEARS (BP)	SIGMA	DELTA 13C °/00 PDB	CAL. AGE RANGES +/- 1 STDV (AND PROBABILITY) **	CAL. AGE RANGES +/- 2 STDV (AND PROBABILITY) ***	ASSOCIATED SEQUENCE AND FEATURE
D16	Ua-14899	-20.80 -23.00	263	Local wood: Salix sp.	975	60	-27.1	1000 (33.2%) 1070 1080 (35.0%) 1160	970 (95.4%) 1220	sequence IV
D43	Ua-14904	-21.30	263	Local wood: Salix sp.	945	70	-26.7	1020 (68.2%) 1170	980 (95.4%) 1250	sequence IV
D45	Ua-14905	-23.00	335	Grass from boot insulation	490	75	-26.5	1320 (10.1%) 1350 1390 (58.1%) 1490	1300 (86.7%) 1530 1560 (8.7%) 1630	sequence VII feature 1
D23B	B-7329	-23.00	335	Local wood: Salix sp.	460	20	-26.7	1428 (68.2%) 1446	1410 (95.4%) 1475	sequence VII feature 1
D23A	Ua-14900	-23.00	335	Local wood: Salix sp.	300	65	-26.4	1490 (68.2%) 1660	1400 (88.6%) 1700	sequence VII feature 1
D26	B-7327	-30-31	300	Local wood: Salix sp.	500	20	-28.0	1416 (68.2%) 1434	1407 (95.4%) 1440	sequence VII feature 3
D25	Ua-14901	-30-31	300	Local wood: Salix sp.	320	65	-26.6	1490 (68.2%) 1650	1440 (93.4%) 1670	sequence VII feature 3

*   keyed to plates 2a (STRAT 1) and 4a (STRAT 2), except D16 and D43 outside STRAT 2
**   maximum cumulated probability at +/- 1 standard deviation: 68.2%; noted.
***   maximum cumulated probability at +/- 2 standard deviations: 95.4%; range probabilities lower than 6% have been omitted; dates are A.D. unless otherwise noted.

APPENDIX

YVON CSONKA

DATING THE EKVEN EROSION FRONT

All of the samples we collected to date the erosion front were chosen because of their association with archaeological contexts, such as occupation layers or, in a couple of cases, wall insulation (see plate 2a and 4a for the location of the samples in the profiles). Twenty-seven of these were sent for radiocarbon dating: thirteen were assayed by AMS in Uppsala, one by AMS in Zürich, and thirteen were submitted to high-precision conventional counting in Bern (in addition, our colleague Arkady Savinetsky from the Severtsov Institute of Ecology and Evolution in Moscow radiocarbon dated close to twenty samples from the erosion front, one of which is reproduced with his permission in the table below; see Khassanov and Savinetsky 2006). We strove to sample homogeneous material, preferring local wood twigs (Salix sp. and a few Betula). To sample such material in sufficient quantity was not always possible, however. Beside sixteen local wood samples, we thus have three samples of local vegetal material (grass, peat and sod), one charcoal from driftwood, and seven samples made up of occupation layer sediments containing local wood and plant fiber, but also animal hair and sometimes baleen.

The raw ages were calibrated using OxCal 3.5 with the intcal98 curve (Stuiver et al. 1998). No corrections for possible reservoir effect were introduced in the calibrations in table XX[1]. Some influence from a marine reservoir effect may be suspected for the "mixed organic sediment" samples, whose δ 13C values are comprised between -17.5 and -25.2‰ PDB. The Salix samples themselves may be suspected of contamination: even though they looked quite "dry", they may have been in contact with sea mammal fat, as almost everything in a Neoeskimo sea mammal hunter's house was (McGhee 2000:188; Morrison 1989:61). Their δ 13C values, all but one (the outlying ETH-22035 at −20.1) situated between -25.9 and 29.0‰ PDB, do not depart from the expected figures, however. The twigs have an average time width of about 10 years, with a maximum of

less than 30, so that age offset is not a problem. Some other potential biases related to Salix have been identified, but not solved (Morrison 1989: 60-61). Finally, a terrestrial reservoir associated with permafrost environments may also play a role; as it varies with time (between 50 and 200 years perhaps), it would affect not only the comparisons with dates obtained south of the permafrost zones, but also the relationships between the different dates within a single site (McGhee 2000: 188).

Whatever the case, the greatest potential for error in associating dates with assumed archaeological facts lies in the archaeological context itself. This potential appears to be well realized in some parts of the Ekven erosion front where, as in other Neoeskimo sites, one observes "the bewildering stratigraphic complexity created by successive house building episodes at one location" (Hall 1990:405; see also Morrison 1989:62).

---

[1] As of this writing, the discussion of the marine reservoir effect continues, also about the Bering Sea region. See, among others, recent publications by Blumer (2002), Dumond (1998: 111-118; 2002b: 347-350), Dumond and Griffin (2002), Khassanov and Savinetsky (2006).

THE EKVEN SETTLEMENT: ESKIMO BEGINNINGS ON THE ASIAN SHORE OF BERING STRAIT

REFERENCES

Aartolhati, T.
1987   Contorted structures in quaternary glacio-fluvial deposits in southern Finland. *Annales Academiae Scientiarum Fennicae*, series A, III, 143, pp. 1-51.

Ackerman, R.
1982   The Neolithic-Bronze age cultures of Asia and the Norton phase of Alaskan prehistory. *Arctic Anthropology* 19(2): 11-38.
1984   Prehistory of the Asian Eskimo Zone. In D. Damas, ed. *Handbook of North American 5*: Arctic. Washington: Smithsonian Institution, pp. 106-118.
1988   Settlements and sea mammal hunting in the Bering-Chukchi sea region. *Arctic Anthropology* 25(1): 52-79.
1998   Early maritime traditions in the Bering, Chukchi, and East Siberian Seas. *Arctic Anthropology* 35(1): 247-262.

Alekseev, V. P.
1972   Results of Historico-Ethnological and Anthropological Studies in the Eastern Chukchi Area. *Inter-Nord* 12: 234-244.
1979   The Genetic Structure of Asiatic Eskimos and Coastal Chukchis Compared to that of American Arctic Populations. *Arctic Anthropology* 16(1): 147-164.

Alekseeva, T., V. Alekseev, S. Arutiunov and D. Sergeev
1983   Nekotorye itogi istoriko-etnologicheskikh i populiatsionno-antropologicheskikh issledovanii na chukotskom poluostrove. In V. Alekseev et al.: *Na styke Chukotki i Aliaski*. Moscow: Nauka, pp. 3-64.

Anketell, J.M. and S. Dzulynski
1968   Patterns of density controlled convolutions involving statistically homogeneous and heterogeneous layers. *Annales de la Société géologique de Pologne*, 38 (4): 401-409.

Anketell, J.M., J. Cegla and S. Dzulynski
1970   On the deformational structures in systems with reversed density gradients. *Annales de la Société géologique de Pologne*, 40 (1): 3-29.

Arnold C. D. and C. Stimmell
1983   An analysis of Thule pottery. *Canadian Journal of Archaeology* 7(1): 1-21.

Arutiunov, S. A.
1979   Problems of Comparative Studies in Arctic Maritime Cultures Based on Archaeological Data. *Arctic Anthropology* 16 (1): 27-31.
1993   Geschichte der Erforschung der frühen Eskimo-Kulturen auf dem asiatischen Kontinent. In Aleksandr Leskov and Hansjürgen Müller-Beck, ed.: *Arktische Waljäger vor 3000 Jahren: unbekannte sibirische Kunst*. Mainz-Munchen: v. Hase & Koehler, pp. 53-63.

Arutiunov, S. A. and M. M. Bronshtein
1985   The Problem of Distinguishing between Old Bering Sea and Okvik Ornamental Styles. In R. Fellmann et al., ed.: *Jagen und Sammeln* (Festschrift for H.-G. Bandi). Berne: Stämpfli and Co., pp. 17-21.

Arutiunov, S. A. and W. Fitzhugh
1988   Prehistory of Siberia and the Bering Sea. In W. Fitzhugh and A. Cromwell, ed.: *Crossroads of Continents. Cultures of Siberia and Alaska*. Washington: Smithsonian Institution, pp. 117-129.

Arutiunov, S. A., I. Krupnik and M. Chlenov
1982   *Kitovaya Alleya: Drevnosti Ostrovov Proliva Seniavina* (Whale Alley: Antiquities of the Seniavin Strait Islands). Moscow: Nauka.

Arutiunov, S. A. and D. Sergeev
1969   *Drevnie Kultury Asiatskikh Eskimosov: Uelenskii Mogilnik* (Ancient Cultures of the Asian Eskimos: the Uelen Cemetery). Moscow: Nauka.
1975   *Problemy etnicheskoi istorii Beringomoria (Ekvenskii mogilnik)*. (Problems of the Ethnic History of the Bering Sea: the Ekven Cemetery). Moscow: Nauka.
1983   Nauchnie rezultaty rabot na Ekvenskom drevneesskimoskom mogilinike (1970-1974 gg.). In V. Alekseev et al.: *Na styke Chukotki i Aliaski*. Moscow: Nauka, pp. 200-29.
1990   Issues in the Ethnic History of the Bering Sea (Translation of Chapters 1 & 8 of Arutiunov and Sergeev 1975). *Soviet Anthropology & Archeology* 28(4): 50-77.

Balfet H., M. F. Fauvet Berthelot and S. Monzon
1989   Lexique et typologie des poteries. Pour la normalisation de la description des poteries. Paris: Presses du C.N.R.S.

Bandi, H.-G.
1993   Prähistorische Friedhöfe and der St. Lorenz Insel, Alaska. In A. Leskov and H. Müller-Beck, ed., 1993: *Arktische Waljäger vor 3000 Jahren: unbekannte sibirische Kunst.* Mainz-Munchen: v. Hase & Koehler, pp. 37-52.

Bandi, H.-G., ed. et al.
1984   *St. Lorenz Insel-Studien: Berner Beiträge zur archäologischen und ethnologischen Erforschung des Beringstrassengebietes, 1: Allgemeine Einführung und Gräberfunde bei Gambell am Nordwestkap der St. Lorenz Insel, Alaska.* Berne / Stuttgart: Haupt (Academica Helvetica; 5 / 1).

Bauch, H.A., T. Mueller-Lupp, E. Taldenkova, R.F. Spielhagen, H. Kassens, P.M. Grootes, J. Thiede, J. Heinemeier and V.V. Petrayashov
2001   Chronology of the Holocene transgression at the North Siberian margin. *Global and Planetary Change* 31: 125-139.

Beeching, A. and J. L. Brochier
2003   *Espace et temps de la préhistoire: biaisage et problèmes de représentation.* In: GASCO, J. & al. – Temps et espaces culturels du 6ème au 2ème millénaire en France du Sud. Actes des 4ème Rencontres de Préhistoire Méridionale, Nimes, 2001, Monographie d'Archéologie Méditerranéenne, 15, pp. 21-33.

Beregovaya, N.
1954   Arkheologicheskie nakhodki na ostrove Chetyrekhstolbovom (Medvezh'i ostrova k severu ot ust'ia r. Kolymy). *Sovietskaia Arkheologiia* 20: 288-312.

Blumer, R.
1996   Première expédition archéologique internationale en Tchoukotka, Sibérie nord-orientale: Rapport de la contribution suisse aux travaux de l'été 1995. In: *Annual Report*, 1995, pp. 110-150. Vaduz and Bern: Swiss-Liechtenstein Foundation for Archaeological Research Abroad.
1997a   Seconde expédition archéologique internationale en Tchoukotka, Sibérie nord-orientale: Rapport de la contribution Suisse à la campagne de 1996. In: *Annual Report*, 1996, pp. 57-78. Vaduz and Bern: Swiss-Liechtenstein Foundation for Archaeological Research Abroad.
1997b   Le matériel archéologique de Kitngipalak, Ile St-Laurent, Alaska, dans le contexte du Néoeskimo béringien. Master's thesis. Université de Genève, Département d'anthropologie et d'écologie.
2002   Radiochronological Assessment of Neo-Eskimo Occupations on St. Lawrence Island, Alaska. In D. E. Dumond and R. L. Bland, eds. *Archaeology in the Bering Strait Region: Research on Two Continents.* Anthropological Papers 59. Eugene: University of Oregon, pp. 61-106.

Blumer, R. and Y. Csonka
1998   Archaeology of the Asian Shore of Bering Strait: Swiss Contribution to the Third International Expedition. In: *Annual Report*, 1996. Vaduz and Zurich: Swiss-Liechtenstein Foundation for Archaeological Research Abroad, pp. 83-130.

Bogoslovskaya, L. S.
1993   Spisok poselenii chukotskovo poluostrova (2000 let do n.e. – 1994). *Beringiiskie zametki – Beringian notes* 2(2). Anchorage: National Park Service, pp. 2-11.

Bogoslovskaya, L., I. Krupnik and L. Votrogov
1982   The Bowhead Whale off Chukotka: Migrations and Aboriginal Whaling. *Report of the International Whaling Commission* 32: 391-399.

Bogoslovskaya, L., L. Votrogov, and T. Semenova
1981   Distribution and Feeding of Gray Whales in Chukotka in the Summer and Autumn of 1980. *Report of the International Whaling Commission* 31: 507-510.

Brigham-Grette, J., and D.M. Hopkins
1995   Emergent Marine Record and Paleoclimate of the Last Interglaciation along the Northwestern Alaskan Coast. *Quaternary Research* 43: 159-173.

Brigham-Grette, J., D. M. Hopkins, V. F. Ivanov, A. E. Basilyan, S. L. Benson, P. A. Heiser, and V. S. Pushkar
2001   Last Interglacial (Isotope Stage 5e) Glacial and Sea-Level History of Coastal Chukotka Peninsula and St. Lawrence Island, Western Beringia. *Quaternary Science Reviews* 20 (1-3): 419-436.

Brochier, J. L.
1984   *Travail de synthèse sur les stations de la baie d'Auvernier. L'habitat lacustre: les fumiers, couches archéologiques riches en matériel organique des stations littorales de la baie d'Auvernier, lac de Neuchâtel. Caractères sédimentologiques et processus de sédimentation.* Manuscript, Neuchâtel, Musée cantonal d'Archéologie, 34 p.
1986   Les sédiments, documents historiques: lecture de la stratigraphie d'un habitat médiéval. Lac de Charavines, Colletières (Isère). *Gallia* 44: 176-189.
1988   Les sédiments, documents archéologiques. *Nouvelles de l'Archéologie* 31: 15-17.
1994   Etude de la sédimentation anthropique sur le site néolithique de Kovacevo (Bulgarie). La stratégie des ethnofaciès sédimentaires en milieu de construction en terre. *Bulletin de Correspondance hellénique* 118(2): 619-645.
1999   Taphonomie des sites: fossilisation et conservation des espaces habités. *Actes des Premières Rencontres Méridionales de Préhistoire Récente*, Valence, juin 1994, pp. 19-28.

Bronshtein, M. M.
1993 Ekven – einzigartige archäologische Fundstelle in Nordostasien. In A. Leskov and H. Müller-Beck, ed. 1993: *Arktische Waljäger vor 3000 Jahren: unbekannte sibirische Kunst*. Mainz-Munchen: v. Hase & Koehler, pp. 73-83.

Bronshtein, M. M. and K. A. Dneprovsky
2008 L'art préhistorique esquimau d'Ekven. In Edmund Carpenter, ed.: Upside Down: *Les Arctiques* (catalogue d'exposition). Paris, Musée du Quai Branly, pp. 116-155.

Bronshtein, M. M., K. A. Dneprovskyi and H. Müller-Beck
2000 A Dwelling of Sea Hunters of Ancient Chukotka. Paper presented at the Alaska Anthropological Association's conference 2000, Anchorage.

Bronshtein, M. M., K. A. Dneprovsky and E.A. Sukhorukova, eds.
2007 *The World of Arctic Maritime Hunters: Steps into the Unknown*. Exhibition catalogue. Anadyr and Moscow: State Museum of Oriental Art.

Bronshtein, M. M. and P. Plumet
1995 Ekven: l'art préhistorique béringien et l'approche russe de l'origine de la tradition culturelle esquimaude. *Études/Inuit/Studies* 19(2): 5-59.

Butrym, J., J. Cegla, S. Dzulynski and S. Nakonieczny
1964 New interpretation of "periglacial structures." *Folia Quaternaria* 17: 1-34.

Butzer, K. W.
1982 *Archaeology as Human Ecology*. New York, Cambridge University Press.

Chichlo, B.
1981 Les Nevuqaghmiit ou la fin d'une ethnie. *Études/Inuit/Studies* 5(2): 29-47.

Chichlo, B., ed.
1993 *Sibérie III, Questions sibériennes: Les peuples du Kamtchatka et de la Tchoukotka*. Paris: Institut d'études slaves.

Coachman, L.K
1993 On the Flow Field in the Chirikov Basin. *Continental Shelf Research* 13(5/6): 481-508.

Collins, H. B.
1937 *Archaeology of St. Lawrence Island, Alaska*. Smithsonian Miscellaneous Collections 96(1). Smithsonian Institution, Washington.
1960 Comment, in Giddings 1960, pp. 131-136.
1964 The Arctic and Subarctic. In J.D. Jennings and E. Norbeck, ed. *Prehistoric Man in the New World*. Chicago: University of Chicago Press, pp. 85-114.

Courty, M.-A.
1982 *Etude géologique de sites archéologiques holocènes: définition des processus sédimentaires et post-sédimentaires, caractérisation de l'impact anthropique. Essai de méthodologie*. Thèse, Université de Bordeaux I.

Courty, M.-A. and J.-C. Miskovsky
1987 Introduction: place des sédiments archéologiques au sein des dépôts quaternaires et évolution des techniques. In Miskovsky, J.-C., ed. *Géologie de la préhistoire: méthodes, techniques, application*. Association pour l'Etude de l'Environnement Géologique de la Préhistoire. Paris: Géopré, pp. 385-388.

Crowell, A. L. and D. H. Mann.
1998 *Archaeology and coastal dynamics of Kenai Fjords National Park, Alaska*. Research/Resources Report ARRCR/CRR-98/34. Anchorage, National Park Service, 196 p.

Csonka, Y.
1986 Systèmes-experts et régularisation des raisonnements en sciences humaines: un exemple, l'origine des Inuit. *Bulletin de la Société suisse des américanistes* 50: 53-56.
1993 Possibilités de collaboration archéologique sur la rive asiatique du détroit de Béring: mission de reconnaissance. In H.-G. Bandi, ed. *Jahresbericht 1992*. Bern and Vaduz: Schweizerisch-Liechtensteinische Stiftung für archäologische Forschungen im Ausland, pp. 71-81.
1995 *Les Ahiarmiut: à l'écart des Inuit Caribous*. Neuchâtel: Victor Attinger.
1998a Tchoukotka: une illustration de la question autochtone en Russie. *Recherches amérindiennes au Québec* 28(1): 23-41.
1998b La nécessité d'une approche nuancée. In Debate: should ethnographic collections be returned? *Tsantsa* 3: 67-70.
2000 Archaeology of Bering Strait: Short Report on a Contribution to the Excavations in Wales, Alaska, in the summer of 1999. *Jahresbericht 1999*. Zurich and Vaduz: Swiss-Liechtenstein Foundation for Archaeological Research Abroad, pp. 59-66.
2003 Ekven, a Prehistoric Whale Hunters' Settlement on the Asian Shore of Bering Strait. In Allen P. McCartney, ed.: *Indigenous Ways to the Present: Native Whaling in the Western Arctic*. Edmonton: Canadian Circumpolar Institute, Studies in Whaling 6, Occasional publication No. 54/Salt Lake City: University of Utah Press, The Anthropology of Pacific North America. Pp. 109-136.
2006 L'origine des Inuit et la collaboration archéologique internationale au détroit de Béring. In B. Arnold, N. Bauermeister and D. Ramseyer, ed. *Archéologie plurielle: Mélanges offerts à Michel Egloff à l'occasion de son 65ᵉ anniversaire*. Archéologie neuchâteloise 34. Neuchâtel: Service et musée cantonal d'archéologie, pp. 157-167.
2007 The Yupik People and its Neighbors in Chukotka: Eight Decades of Rapid Changes. *Études/Inuit/Studies* 31(1-2): 23-37.

Csonka, Y., R. Blumer and B. Moulin
1999   Archaeology of the Asian Side of Bering Strait: Swiss Contribution to the Fourth International Fieldseason. In *Annual Report 1998*. Vaduz and Zurich: Swiss-Liechtenstein Foundation for Archaeological Research Abroad, pp. 83-130.

Dansgaard, W., S.J. Johnsen, N. Reeh, N. Gundestrup, H. B. Clausen, and C. U. Hammer
1975   Climatic Changes, Norsemen and Modern Man. *Nature* 255: 24-28.

Darby, D. A., J. F. Bischof and G. A. Jones
1994   Radiocarbon Chronology of Depositional Regimes in the Western Arctic Ocean. *Deep Sea Research* 44(8): 1745-1757.

Debets, G.
1975   Paleoantropologicheskie materialy iz drevneberingomorskikh mogilnikov Uelen i Ekven. In S. Arutiunov and Sergeev D.: *Problemy etnicheskoi istorii Beringomoria (Ekvenskii mogilnik)*. Moscow: Nauka, pp. 198-240.

Dikov, N. N.
1967   Uelenskii mogilnik po dannym raskopok b 1956, 1958 i 1963 godakh (The Uelen Cemetery according to Data from the Excavations in 1956, 58 and 63). In *Istoria i Kultura Narodov Severa Dalnego Vostoka*. Moscow: Nauka, pp. 45-79.
1972   Les pétroglyphes de Pegtymel' et leur appartenance ethnique. *Inter-Nord* 12: 245-261.
1974   *Chininski Mogilnik* (The Chini Cemetery). Novosibirsk: Nauka.
1977   *Arkheologicheskie pamiatniki Kamchatki, Chukotki i verknei Kolymi*. Moscow: Nauka.
1979   *Drevnie kultury severo-vostochnoi Azii*. Moscow: Nauka.
1988   The Earliest Sea Mammal Hunters of Wrangell Island. *Arctic Anthropology* 25(1): 80-93.
1997   *Asia at the Juncture with America in Antiquity: the Stone Age of the Chukchi Peninsula*. Translation by R. L. Bland. Anchorage: National Park Service [1st edition in Russian 1993, Nauka, St. Petersburg].

Dinesman L. G., N. K. Kiseleva, A. B. Savinetsky and B. F. Khassanov
1999   *Secular Dynamics of the Coastal Zone Ecosystems of the Northeastern Chukchi Peninsula*. Tübingen: Mo Vince Verlag [first edition in Russian, Moscow: Argus, 1996].

Dinesman, L. G. and A. B. Savinetsky
2003   Secular dynamics of the prehistoric catch and population size of baleen whales off the Chukchi Peninsula, Siberia. In Allen P. McCartney, ed.: *Indigenous Ways to the Present: Native Whaling in the Western Arctic*. Edmonton: Canadian Circumpolar Institute, Studies in Whaling 6, Occasional publication No. 54/Salt Lake City: University of Utah Press, The Anthropology of Pacific North America, pp. 137-166.

Dneprovsky, K. A.
2002   Ekven House H-18: A Birnirk- and early Punuk-period site in Chukotka. In Don Dumond and Richard Bland, eds.: *Archaeology in the Bering Strait Region: Research on Two Continents*. University of Oregon Anthropological Papers 59. Eugene: University of Oregon, pp. 167-206.

Dneprovsky, K. A.
2006   A Late Birnirk House at Paipelghak in Northern Chukotka: A Preliminary Report Based on the Excavations from 2002-2004. *Alaska Journal of Anthropology* 4(1-2): 34-53.

Douglas, B. C., M. S. Kearney, and S. P. Leatherman
2001   *Sea Level Rise: History and Consequences*. New York: Academic Press.

Dumond, D. E.
1984   Prehistory of the Bering Sea Region. In David Damas, ed.: *Handbook of North American 5: Arctic*. Washington: Smithsonian Institution, pp. 94-105.
1987   *The Eskimos and Aleuts*. Revised edition. Thames and Hudson, London.
1998   *The Hillside Site, St. Lawrence Island, Alaska*. Eugene: University of Oregon Anthropological Papers 55.
2000a   The Norton Tradition. *Arctic Anthropology* 37(2): 1-22.
2000b   *Henry B. Collins at Wales, Alaska, 1936: A Partial Description of Collections*. Eugene: University of Oregon Anthropological Papers 56.
2002a   The Legacy of Henry B. Collins. In D. E. Dumond and R. L. Bland, eds. *Archaeology in the Bering Strait Region: Research on Two Continents*. Anthropological Papers 59. Eugene: University of Oregon, pp. 9-24.
2002b   Words in closing. In D. E. Dumond and R. L. Bland, eds. *Archaeology in the Bering Strait Region: Research on Two Continents*. Anthropological Papers 59. Eugene: University of Oregon. Pp. 345-357.

Dumond, D. E. and R. L. Bland
1995   Holocene Prehistory of the Northernmost North Pacific. *Journal of World Prehistory* 9(4): 401-451.

Dumond, D. E. and D. G. Griffin
2002   Measurements of the Marine Reservoir Effect on Radiocarbon Ages in the Eastern Bering Sea. *Arctic* 55(1): 77-86.

Dyke, A.S., R. N. McNeely and J. Hooper.
1996   Marine Reservoir Corrections for Bowhead Whale Radiocarbon Age Determinations. *Canadian Journal of Earth Sciences* 33: 1628-1637.

Dzulynski, S.
1963   Directional structures in flysch. *Studia Geologica Polonica* 12: 1-136.
1966   Sedimentary structures resulting from convection-like pattern of motion. *Annales de la Société géologique de Pologne* 36(1): 3-21.

Ellis, J. M. and P. E. Calkin
1984   Chronology of Holocene Claciation, Central Brooks Range, Alaska. *Geological Society of America Bulletin* 95: 897-912.

Emery, K.O. and D. G. Audrey
1991   *Sea Level, Land Levels and Tide Gauges*. New York: Springer Verlag.

Fitzhugh, W. W., J, Hollowell and A. L. Crowell, eds.
2009   *Gifts from the Ancestors: Ancient Ivories of Bering Strait*. Exhibition catalogue, Princeton University Art Museum. New Haven, London: Yale University Press.

Ford, J. A.
1959   *Eskimo Prehistory in the Vicinity of Point Barrow, Alaska*. Anthropological Papers of the Museum for Natural History (New York), 47(1): 1-272.

Fortescue, M.
1998   *Language relations across Bering Strait: Reappraising the archaeological and linguistic evidence*. London/New York: Cassell.

Fujita, K., D. B. Cook, H. Hasegawa, D. Forsyth, and R. Wetmiller.
1990   Seismicity and Focal Mechanisms of the Arctic Region and the North American Plate Boundary in Asia. In The Arctic Ocean Region. In A. Grantz, L. Johnson, and J.F. Sweeney, eds. *The Geology of North America*, vol. L. Boulder: Geological Society of America, pp. 79-100.

Gasanov, S. S.
1982   Paleogeographic Environments in Eastern Chukchi during the Boreal Transgression. In A.I. Tolmachev, ed. *The Arctic Ocean and its Coast in the Cenozoic Era*. Order of Lenin Arctic and Anarctic Research Institute, Geographical Society of the USSR. New Delhi: Amerind Publishing Co., pp. 554-558 [Original Russian ed., 1970.].

Geist, O. and F. Rainey
1936   *Archaeological Excavations at Kukulik, St. Lawrence Island, Alaska*. Washington: U. of Alaska/US Government Printing Office.

Gelbert A.
1994   Tour et tournette en Espagne: recherche de macrotraces significatives des différentes techniques et méthodes de façonnage. In F. Audouze et D. Binder, ed. *Terre cuite et société. La céramique, document technique, économique, culturel*. Actes des XIVe Rencontres Internationales d'Archéologie et d'Histoire d'Antibes. Juan-les-Pins: Editions APDCA, pp. 59-74.
2000   *Etude ethnoarchéologique des phénomènes d'emprunts céramiques. Enquêtes dans les haute et moyenne vallées du fleuve Sénégal (Sénégal)*. Thèse de Doctorat de l'Université de Paris X-Nanterre.

Gelbert Miermon, A.
2006   Pottery from the Bluff of the Ekven Settlement. In Don E. Dumond and Richard L. Bland, eds. *Archaeology in Northeast Asia: On the Pathway to Bering Strait*. Anthropological Papers 65. Eugene: University of Oregon, pp. 159-189.

Gerlach C. and Mason O. K.
1992   Calibrated radiocarbon dates and cultural interaction in the western Arctic. *Arctic Anthropology* 29(1), pp. 54-81.

Giddings, J. L. and D. Anderson
1986   *Beach Ridge Archaeology of Cape Krusenstern*. Publications in Archaeology 20. Washington: National Park Service.

Gong, G. and S. Hameed
1991   The Variation of Moisture Conditions in China during the Last 2000 Years. *International Journal of Climatology* 11: 271-283.

Graumlich, L. and J. C. King
1998   Late Holocene Climatic Variation in Northwestern Alaska as Reconstructed from Tree Rings. Abstracts of the 25th Annual Meeting of the Alaska Anthropological Association, p. 12.

Gray, P.
2000   Chukotkan reindeer husbandry in the post-socialist transition. *Polar Research* 19(1): 31-8.

Grove, J. M. and R. Switsur
1994   Glacial Geological Evidence for the Medieval Warm Period. *Climatic Change* 26: 143-169.

Gulløv, H. C.
1996.   Ved porten til Den nye Verden: Nationalmuseet og de russiske udgravninger ved Bering Strædet. In: Nationalmuseets Arbejdsmark 1996. Copenhagen: National Museum, pp. 163-175.
2005   Arkæologiske udgravninger ved verdens ende. In Bent Nielsen, ed. *Tjukotka i fortid og nutid*. Københavns Universitet, Eskimologis Skrifter 18, pp. 13-38.

Gusev, S., A. Zagoroulko and A. Porotov.
1999   Sea mammal hunters of Chukotka, Bering Strait: Recent Archaeological Results and Problems. *World Archaeology*, Arctic Archaeology Issue 30(3): 354-369.

Hall, E.
1990   Post-depositional factors affecting the formation of the Utqiagvik site. In A. Dekin et al. *The 1981 Excavations at the Utqiagvik Archaeological Site, Barrow, Alaska*, vol. 1. Barrow: North Slope Borough Commision on Iñupiat History, Language and Culture, pp. 401-407.

Harritt, R.
1994   *Eskimo Prehistory on the Seward Peninsula, Alaska.* Anchorage: National Park Service, Alaska Regional Office.
1995   The Development and Spread of the Whale Hunting Complex in Bering Strait: Retrospective and Prospects. In Allen P. McCartney, ed. *Hunting the Largest Animals: Native Whaling in the Western Arctic and Subarctic.* Edmonton: University of Alberta, Canadian Circumpolar Institute, pp. 33-50.

Hassan, F. A.
1978   Sediments in archaeology: methods and implications for palaeoenvironmental and cultural analysis. *Journal of Field Archaeology* 5: 197-213.

Heiser, P. A. and J. J. Roush
2001   Pleistocene glaciations in Chukotka, Russia: moraine mapping using satellite synthetic aperture radar (SAR) imagery. *Quaternary Science Reviews* 20(1): 394-404.

Hoffmann-Wyss, A. B.
1987   *Prähistorische Eskimogräber an der Dovelavik Bay und bei Kitnepaluk im Westen der St. Lorenz Insel, Alaska.* H.-G. Bandi, ed.: St. Lorenz Insel Studien II (Academica Helvetica; 5/2). Bern/Stuttgart: Paul Haupt.

Hollowell, J.
2004   *"Old Things" on the Loose: The Legal Market for Archaeological Materials from Alaska's Bering Strait.* Ph.D. dissertation, Department of Anthropology, Indiana University.

Holzlehner, T.
1999.   *Artefakte auf Wanderschaft: Archäologie und Politik in Tschukotka.* Unpublished MA thesis, Department of Ethnology, University of Tübingen.

Hopkins, D. M.
1967   Quaternary Marine Transgressions in Alaska. In D.M. Hopkins, ed. *The Bering Land Bridge.* Menlo Park: Stanford University Press, pp. 47-90.

Huysecom E.
1994   Identification technique des céramiques africaines. In F. Audouze & D. Binder, eds. *Terre cuite et société. La céramique, document technique, économique, culturel,* Actes des XIVe Rencontres Internationales d'Archéologie et d'Histoire d'Antibes. Juan-les-Pins: Editions APDCA, pp. 31-45.

Ionin, A.S.
1961   Erosion by Aggradational Forms in the Bering Sea. *International Geological Review* 5(10): 1337-1346.

Ivanov, O.
1967   Novye nakhodki pamiatnikov drevneeskimoskoi kultury na zapadnom poberezhe beringova proliva (New discoveries of monuments of the ancient eskimo culture on the western shore of Bering Strait). In A. Krushanov, ed. *Istoria i kultura narodov severa dalnevo vostoka.* Moscow: Nauka, pp. 42-44.

Jacobson, S. A., ed.
2004   *Naukan Yupik Eskimo Dictionary.* Fairbanks: Alaska Native Language Center.

Jenness, D.
1928   Archaeological Investigations in Bering Strait, 1926. *Canada Department of Mines Bulletin 50, Annual Report for 1926.* National Museum of Canada, Ottawa.

Joos, M.
1976   Die sedimente der neolithischen Station Feldmeilen-Vorderfeld und einige Überlegungen zur Sedimentation im Uferbereich. In *Winiger J. Feldmeilen-Voderfeld. Die Ausgrabungen 1970/71.* Schweizerische Gesellschaft für Ür und Frühgeschichte, Basel, pp.106-142.

Joos, M.
1980   Die sedimentologische Analyse von Profil X/42 und ihr Beitrag zur Stratigraphie der Cortaillod-Siedlungen von Twann. In Ammann B., Joos M., Orcel A., Schoch W. & Schweingruber F. La colonne de sédiment X/42: Archéologie, botanique, palynologie, sédimentologie. *Die Neolithischen Ufersiedlungen von Twann,* vol.6. Bern: Staatlicher Lehrmittelverlag, pp. 69-118.

Jordan, J. W.
1990   Late Holocene Evolution of Barrier Islands in the Southern Chukchi Sea, Alaska. Unpublished master's thesis in Quaternary Sciences, University of Alaska, Fairbanks.

Jordan, J. W. and O. K. Mason
1999   A 5000 yr Record of Intertidal Peat Stratigraphy and Sea Level Rise from Northwest Alaska. *Quaternary International* 60: 37-47.

Khassanov, B. F. and A. B. Savinetsky
2006   On the Marine Reservoir Effect in the Northern Bering Sea. In Don E. Dumond and Richard L. Bland, eds. *Archaeology in Northeast Asia: On the Pathway to Bering Strait.* Anthropological Papers 65. Eugene: University of Oregon, pp. 193-202.

Knyazev, A. and A. B. Savinetsky.
1995   Drevneeskimoskii promysel kitov na poberezh'e Chukotskogo moria i Beringova proliva (Ancient Eskimo whaling on the coasts of the Chukchi Sea and the Bering Strait), *Bull. Moskovskogo obshchestva ispytatelei prirody,* 100(3): 22-33.

Krauss, M.
1994   Crossroads? A Twentieth-Century History of Contacts across the Bering Strait. In W. W. Fitzhugh and V. Chaussonnet, eds. *Anthropology of the North Pacific Rim.* Washington: Smithsonian Institution, pp. 365-79.

Krupnik, I. I.
1983a Drevnie i traditsionnie poseleniia eskimosov na iugo-vostoke chuktoskogo poluostrova. In V. Alekseev et al. *Na styke chukotki i Aliaski*. Moscow: Nauka, pp. 65-95.
1983b Early Settlements and the Demographic History of Asian Eskimos of Southeastern Chukotka (Including St. Lawrence Island). In H. N. Michael and J. Van Stone, ed. *Cultures of the Bering Sea Region: Papers from an International Symposium*. New York: International Research and Exchange Board, pp. 84-111.
1983c Gray Whales and the Aborigenes of the Pacific Northwest: The History of Aboriginal Whaling. In M. L. Jones, S. L. Swartz and S. Leatherwood, eds. *The Gray Whale: Eschrichtius robustus*. Orlando: Academic Press, pp. 103-120.
1984 Whale Alley: A site on the Chukchi Peninsula, Siberia. *Expedition* (U. of Pennsylvania Museum) 26(2): 6-15.
1987 The Bowhead vs. the Gray Whale in Chukotkan Aboriginal Whaling. *Arctic* 40(1): 16-32.
1988 Asiatic Eskimos and Marine Resources: A Case of Ecological Pulsations or Equilibrium? *Arctic Anthropology* 25(1): 94-106.
1993a Prehistoric Eskimo Whaling in the Arctic: Slaughter of Calves or Fortuitous Ecology? *Arctic Anthropology* 30(1): 1-12.
1993b *Arctic Adaptations: Native Whalers and Reindeer Herders of Northern Eurasia*. Hanover/London: University Press of New England [first edition in Russian, Moscow: Nauka, 1989].
1998 Jesup Genealogy: Intellectual Partnership and Russian-American Cooperation in Arctic/North Pacific Anthropology. Part I: From the Jesup Expedition to the Cold War, 1897-1948. *Arctic Anthropology* 35(2): 199-226.

Krupnik, I. I. and L. Bogoslovskaya
1999 Old record, new stories: ecosystem variability and subsistence hunting in the Bering Strait area. *Arctic Research of the United States* 13: 15-24.

Krupnik, I. I., L. Bogoslovskaya and L. Votrogov
1983 Gray Whaling off the Chukotka Peninsula: Past and Present Status. *Report of the International Whaling Commission* 33: 557-562.

Krupnik, I. I. and M. Chlenov. To be published. Yupik Transitions
1900-1960 Change and Survival at Bering Strait. Washington: Smithsonian Institution.

Lamblin, J.-M.
1993 Aperçu sur les problèmes d'alimentation en eau potable en Tchoukotka. In B. Chichlo, ed. *Sibérie III: questions sibériennes. Les peuples du Kamtchatka et de la Tchoukotka*. Paris: Institut d'études slaves, pp. 223-242.

Larsen, H.
1968 Near Ipiutak and Uwelen-Okvik. *Folk* 10: 81-90.

Larsen, H. and F. Rainey
1948 *Ipiutak and the Arctic Whale Hunting Culture*. Anthropological Papers of the American Museum of Natural History, New York, vol. 42.

Leont'ev, V. V. and K. A. Novikova
1989 *Toponimicheskii slovar severo-vostoka SSSR*. Magadan: Magadanskoe knizhnoe izdatel'stvo.

Leskov, A. and H. Müller-Beck, ed.
1993 *Arktische Waljäger vor 3000 Jahren: unbekannte sibirische Kunst*. Mainz-Munchen: v. Hase & Koehler Verlag.

Levin, M. G.
1963 *Ethnic Origins of the Peoples of Northeastern Asia*. Translations from Russian sources 3, Arctic Institute of North America, Toronto: University of Toronto Press.

Lucier, C. V. and J. W. VanStone
1992 Historic pottery of the Kotzbue Sound Iñupiat. *Anthropology* 18: 1-26.

Mason, O. K
1998 The Contest between the Ipiutak, Old Bering Sea, and Birnirk Polities and the Origin of Whaling during the First Millennium A.D. along Bering Strait. *Journal of Anthropological Archaeology* 17: 240-325.
1999 At the Tail of Asia: Heightened Storminess during Cold Climates in Late Holocene Northwest Alaska. In Proceedings of the First International Symposium on Biodiversity and Geomorphic Change, Y.A. Park, ed. *Korean Journal for Quaternary Research*, pp. 9-40.
2002 Paleoclimatic Records in the Ekven Site: Comparisons with Data from Alaska. In D. Dumond and R. Bland, eds. *Archaeology in the Bering Strait Region: Research on Two Continents*. University of Oregon Anthropological Papers 59. Eugene: U. of Oregon, pp. 261-272.

Mason, O. K., and Dupré, W. R.
1999 Was the Yukon delta Uninhabitable until 3000 Years Ago? The Interplay of Neoglacial Storms, Yukon River and Sea Level Changes. In: *Abstracts of the 26th Annual Meeting, Alaska Anthropological Association*. Fairbanks.

Mason, O. K., D. M. Hopkins and L. Plug
1997 Chronology and Paleoclimate of Storm-Induced Erosion and episodic Dune Growth across Cape Espenberg Spit, Alaska, U.S.A. *Journal of Coastal Research* 13(3): 770-797.

Mason, O. K. and C. Gerlach
1995a Chukchi Hot Spots, Paleo-Polynias, and Caribou Crashes: Climatic and Ecological Dimensions of North Alaska Prehistory. *Arctic Anthropology* 32(1): 101-130.
1995b The Archaeological Imagination, Zooarchaeological Data, the Origins of Whaling in the Western Arctic, and 'Old Whaling' and Choris Cultures. In A. P. McCartney, ed. *Hunting the Largest Animals: Native Whaling in the Western Arctic and Subarctic*. Edmonton: University of Alberta, Canadian Circumpolar Institute, pp. 1-31.

Mason, O. K. and Jordan, J. W.
1993   Heightened North Pacific Storminess and Synchronous Late Holocene Erosion of Northwest Alaska Beach Ridge Complexes. *Quaternary Research* 40 : 55-69.

Mason, O. K. and Jordan, J. W.
1997   Late Holocene Sea Level and Storm History of the Northern Seward Peninsula. Final Report to the National Park Service, Shared Beringian Heritage Project. Anchorage.

Mason, O. K. and Jordan, J. W.
2001   Minimal Late Holocene Sea Level Rise in the Chukchi Sea : Arctic Insensitivity to Global Change. *Global and Planetary Change* 32(1) : 13-23.

Mason, O. K., J. W. Jordan and L. Plug.
1995   Late Holocene Storm and Sea-Level History in the Chukchi Sea. *Journal of Coastal Research*, Spec. Issue 17 : 173-180.

Mason, O. K. and S. L. Ludwig
1990   Resurrecting Beach Ridge Archaeology : Parallel Depositional Histories from St. Lawrence Island and Cape Krusenstern, Alaska. *Geoarchaeology* 5 : 349-373.

Mason, O. K., D. K. Salmon and S. L. Ludwig
1996   The Periodicity of Storm Surges in the Bering Sea Region from 1898 to 1993, Based on Newspaper Accounts. *Climatic Change* 34 : 109-123.

Mazur, A. A. (no date)
        Geological Map of the Chukchi Peninsula. Lavrentiya, Museum.

McGhee, R.
2000   Radiocarbon Dating and the Timing of the Thule Migration. In M. Appelt, J. Berglund and H. C. Gulløv, ed. *Identities and Cultural Contacts in the Arctic. Proceedings from a Conference.* Copenhagen : Danish National Museum / Danish Polar Center, pp. 181-191.

Miskovsky, J.-C. and E. Debard
2002   Granulométrie des sédiments et étude de leur fraction grossière. In Miskovsky J.-C., ed. *Géologie de la préhistoire : méthodes, techniques, application.* Paris : Géopré. Association pour l'Etude de l'Environnement Géologique de la Préhistoire, pp. 479-501.

Morrisson, D.
1989   Radiocarbon Dating Thule Culture. *Arctic Anthropology* 26(2) : 48-77.

Moulin, B.
1991   *Hauterive-Champréveyres, 3. La dynamique sédimentaire et lacustre durant le Tardiglaciaire et le Postglaciaire.* Archéologie neuchâteloise 9. Saint-Blaise : Editions du Ruau.

Moulin, B. and Y. Csonka
2002   The Erosion Front at Ekven : A Stratigraphic and Geoarchaeological Approach. In R. L. Bland and D. E. Dumond, eds. *Archaeology in the Bering Strait Region : Research on Two Continents.* Eugene (Oregon) : University of Oregon Anthropological Papers No 59, pp. 227-259.

Munsell Color
1988   *Munsell Soil Color Charts.* Baltimore : Munsell Colors.

Naidu, A. S. and G. Gardner
1988   Marine geology. In M. J. Hameed and A. S. Naidu, eds. The Environment and Resources of the Southeastern Chukchi Sea. *Outer Continental Shelf, Mineral Management Study* 87-0113, pp. 11-28.

Niebauer, H.
1988   Effects of El Nino-Southern Oscillation and North Pacific Weather Patterns on Interannual Variability in the Subarctic Bering Sea. *Journal of Geophysical Research* 93 : 5051-5068.

O'Brien, S. R., P. A. Mayewski, L. D. Meeker, D. A. Meese, M. S. Twickler, and S. I. Whitlow
1995   Complexity of Holocene Climate as Reconstructed from a Greenland Ice Core. *Science* 270 : 1962-1964.

Okladnikov, A. P. and N. Beregovaya
1971   *Drevnie poselenia Baranova mysa* (Ancient settlements of Cape Baranov). Novosibirsk : Nauka.

Oswalt W.
1955   Alaskan pottery : a classification and historical reconstruction. *American Antiquity* 21 : 32-43.

Overland, J. and C. Pease
1982   Cyclone Climatology of the Bering Sea and Its Relation to Sea Ice Extent. *Monthly Weather Review* 110 : 5-13.

Pavlov, V. K. and P. V. Pavilov
1996   Oceanographic Description of the Bering Sea. In O. A. Mathisen and K. O. Coyle, eds. Ecology of the Bering Sea : A Review of the Russian literature. *Alaska Sea Grant Report* No. 96-01. Fairbanks : Alaska Sea Grant College Program, University of Alaska, pp. 1-96.

Plumet P.
1993   Le patrimoine archéologique au Kamchatka et en Tchoukotka. In B. Chichlo, ed. *Sibérie III, Questions sibériennes : Les peuples du Kamtchatka et de la Tchoukotka.* Paris : Institut d'études slaves, pp. 299-308.

1999   At a Crossroads : Archaeology and the First People in Canada (book review). *Recherches amérindiennes au Québec* 29(1) : 116-118.

Polyakova, Ye. I.
1990   Stratigraphy of Late Pleistocene / Holocene Sediments on the Bering shelf on the Basis of Diatom Complexes. *Polar Geology and Geography* 14(4) : 271-278.

Psuty, N. P.
1988 Sediment Budget and Dune/Beach Interaction. *Journal of Coastal Research* Special Issue 3: 1-4.

Rainey, F.
1941 *Eskimo Prehistory: The Okvik Site of the Punuk Islands.* American Museum of Natural History, New York.

Raushenbakh, V. M.
1969 *Novye nakhodki na Chetyrekhstolbovom ostrove.* (New finds on the Four Column Island). Moscow: Sovietskaïa Rossia.

Reanier, R. E., G. W. Sheehan, and A. M. Jensen
1998 Report of 1997 Field Discoveries, City of Deering Village Safe Water Cultural Resources Project. Unpublished Report, Ukpeagvik Inupiat Corporation (UIC) Real Estate, Science Division. Barrow.

Reuse, W. de
1994 *Siberian Yupik Eskimo: the language and its contacts with Chukchi.* Salt Lake City: U. of Utah Press.

Rice, P. M., ed.
1987 *Pottery analysis. A source book.* Chicago: The University of Chicago press.

Rudenko, S. I.
1961 *The Ancient Culture of the Bering Sea and the Eskimo Problem.* University of Toronto Press for the Arctic Institute of North America (Translations from Russian sources 1) [Original in Russian 1947].

Rye, O. S.
1981 *Pottery technology: Principles and reconstruction.* Washington, D.C.: Taraxacum.

Salmon, D. K.
1992 On Interannual Variability and Climate Change in the North Pacific. Unpublished Ph.D. dissertation, Institute of Marine Science, University of Alaska, Fairbanks.

Savinetsky, A. B.
2002 Mammals and Birds Harvested by Early Eskimos of Bering Strait. In D. E. Dumond and R. L. Bland, eds. *Archaeology in the Bering Strait Region: Research on Two Continents.* Anthropological Papers 59. Eugene: University of Oregon, pp. 274-305.

Schweitzer, P.
1990 *Kreuzungspunkt am Rande der Welt: Kontaktgeschichte und soziale Verhältnisse der sibirischen Eskimo zwischen 1650 und 1920.* Ph.D. dissertation, University of Vienna.

Schweitzer, P. and E. Golovko
1995 *Contacts across Bering Strait,* 1898-1948. U.S. National Park Service, Alaska Regional Office, unpublished report.

Selmer-Olsen, R.
1954 Om norske jordarters variasjon i korngradering og plastreitet. *Norges geol. Unders.* 186, 102 p.

Shcherbakov, F. A.
1969 Some Data on the Post-Glacial Transgression of the Bering Sea. In V.V. Longinov, ed. *Dynamics and Morphology of Sea Coasts.* Trans. by Israel Program for Scientific Translation, Jerusalem. [Pub. 1961 as *Dinamika i Morfologiya Morskikh beregov.* Moscow: Izadel'stvo Adkaemii Nauk SSSR.], pp. 124-131.

SLSA (Swiss-Liechtenstein Foundation for Archaeological Research Abroad)
1997 Principles for Partnership in Cross-Cultural Human Sciences Research with a Particular View to Archaeology. In B. Sitter-Liver and C. Uehlinger, eds. *Partnership in Archaeology: Perspectives of a Cross-Cultural Dialogue* (conference proceedings), Fribourg (Switzerland): Fribourg University Press, pp. 231-8.

Staley, D.P.
1994 *Archaeological Monitoring and Data Recovery for the 1993 Water and Sewer Project in Gambell, Alaska.* Albuquerque: Mariah Associates, Inc.

Stanford, D. J.
1976 *The Walapka Site, Alaska: its Place in the Birnirk and Thule Cultures.* Smithsonian Contributions to Anthropology 20, Washington.

Stein, J. K., and W. R. Farrand
1985 *Archaeological sediments in context. Peopling of the Americas.* Orono: Center of the Study of Early Man, University of Maine.

Stimmell C.
1994 Going to pot: a technological overview of North American Arctic ceramics. In D. Morisson and J.-L. Pilon, eds. *Threads of Arctic Prehistory: Papers in Honour of William E. Taylor, Jr.* Canadiam Museum of Civilization, Mercury Series 149, pp. 35-56.

Stuiver, M., P.J. Reimer, E. Bard, J.W. Beck, G. Burr, K.A.Hughen, B. Kromer, G. McCormac, J. Van Der Plicht and M. Spurk
1998 IntCal98 Radiocarbon Age Calibration, 24,000–0 cal bp. *Radiocarbon* 40(3): 1041-1084.

Svitoch, A. A.
1973 Structure and Age of Marine Terraces of the Lower Anadyr Depression. In V. L. Kontrimavichus, ed. *Beringia in the Cenozoic Era.* New Delhi: Amerind Publishing Co., pp. 83-95.

Tein, T.
1979 Arkheologicheskie issledovania na o. Vrangelia. In Valentina Skumina, ed. *Novye arkheologicheskie pamiatniki severa dalnego vostoka.* Magadan, pp. 53-63.
1985 Kultovye amulety c o. Ratmanova. In N. Dikova, ed.: *Novoe v arkheologii severa dalnego vostoka.* Magadan, pp. 109-115.
1990 Drevnie stoianki na mysakh Billingsa i Iakan (Shmidtovskii raion). In N. Dikova, ed. *Drevnie pamiatniki severa dalnego vostoka.* Magadan, pp. 112-122.

Thenhaus, P. C., J. I. Ziony, W. H. Diment, M. G. Hopper, D. M. Perkins, S. L. Hanson and S. T. Aigermissen
1982   Probabalistic Estimates of Maximum Seismic Horizontal Ground Motion on Rock in Alaska and the Adjacent Outer Continental Shelf. In U.S. Geological Survey in Alaska: Accomplishments during 1980, *U.S. Geological Survey Circular* 844, pp. 5-8.

Tissières, P.
1990   *Etude sédimentologique et géotechnique des dépôts deltaïques de Granges-près-Marnand.* Lausanne: Ecole Polytechnique Fédérale de Lausanne (thèse n° 818, 1989).

Vasil'evski, R.
1987   The Development of a Maritime System of Economy in the Northern Part of the Pacific Ocean Basin. *Études/Inuit/Studies* 11(2): 73-90.

Vesajoki, H.
1982   Deformation of soft sandy sediments during deglaciation and subsequent emergence of land areas; examples from northern Karelia, Finland. *Boreas* 11(1): 11-28.

Wang Y., and X. Ke
1989   Cheniers on the East Coastal Plain of China. *Marine Geology* 90: 321-335.

Water, M. R.
1992   *Principles of Geoarchaeology: a North American Perspective.* University of Arizona Press.

Wise, J. L., A. L. Comiskey and R. Becker.
1981   *Storm Surge Climatology and Forecasting in Alaska.* Anchorage: Arctic Environmental Information and Data Center.

Workman, W. and A. P. McCartney
1998   Coast to Coast: Maritime Cultures in the North Pacific. *Arctic Anthropology* 35(1): 361-370.

Zenkovich, V. P.
1967   *Processes of Coastal Development.* New York: Interscience Publishers, J. Wiley and Sons.

Zheleznov, N., N. Otke and I. Riga
1996   A u nas na dushe gorech'. *Krainyi Sever*, Anadyr, September 12, pp. 4-5.

www.ingramcontent.com/pod-product-compliance
Lightning Source LLC
Chambersburg PA
CBHW061002030426
42334CB00033B/3336

9781407312590